LOPSIDED

How a 50/50 Common Sense Nation Drifted into a Progressive
Dystopian Cartoon and How we Might Claw our way Back

DAVE MARTIN

INKS &
BINDINGS

INKS & BINDINGS

Inks and Bindings
888-290-5218
www.inksandbindings.com
orders@inksandbindings.com

For Laurie, my fabulous wife
and the love of my life

She has been soooo patient
with me!

CONTENTS

REFERENCES

A list of books that cover some topics in
greater depth than in *Lopsided*

Bobb, Christina, *Stealing Your Vote: The Inside Story of the 2020 Election and What It Means for 2024*, Skyhorse (2023)

Cain, Geoffrey, *The Perfect Police State: An Undercover Odyssey into China's Terrifying Surveillance Dystopia of the Future*, Public Affairs (2021)

Conard, Edward, *The Upside of Inequality: How Good Intentions Undermine the Middle Class*, Portfolio, (2016)

Diangelo, Robin, *White Fragility: Why It's So Hard for White People to Talk About Racism*, Beacon Press (2018)

D'Souza, Dinesh
- *Stealing America: What My Experience with Criminal Gangs Taught Me About Obama, Hillary and the Democratic Party*, Harper, (2015)
- *Hillary's America: The Secret History of the Democratic Party*, Regnery, (2016)
- *The Big Lie: Exposing the Nazi Roots of the American Left*, Regnery, (2017)
- *Death of a Nation: Plantation Politics and the Making of the Democratic Party*, All Points Books (2019)

Epstein, Alex, *Fossil Future: Why Global Human Flourishing Requires More Oil, Coal, and Natural Gas--Not Less*, Portfolio (2022)

Fleischer, Ari, *Suppression, Deception, Snobbery, and Bias: Why the Press Gets So Much Wrong—And Just Doesn't Care*, Broadside Books (2022)

Koonin, Steven E., *Unsettled: What Climate Science Tells Us, What It Doesn't, and Why It Matters*, BenBella Books (2021)

Lukianoff, Greg and Schlott, Rikki, *The Cancelling of the American Mind: Cancel Culture Undermines Trust and Threatens Us All—But There Is a Solution*, Simon and Schuster (2023)

Piketty, Thomas, *Capital in the Twenty-First Century*, Translated by Arthur Goldhammer, Belknap Press: An Imprint of Harvard University Press (2017)

Rufo, Christopher F., *America's Cultural Revolution: How the Radical Left Conquered Everything*, Broadside Books (2023)

Schweizer, Peter, *Blood Money: Why the Powerful Turn a Blind Eye While China Kills Americans*, Harper (2024)

Strassel, Kimberly, *The Intimidation Game: How the Left Is Silencing Free Speech*, Twelve (2016)

Taibbi, Matthew, *Hate, Inc.: Why Today's Media Makes Us Despise One Another*, OR Books, (2019)

Zuboff, Shoshana, *The Age of Surveillance Capitalism: The Fight for a Human Future at the New Frontier of Power*, Public Affairs (2020)

Introduction:
What Happened to America?

*One side is passionate and relentless; the other
is complacent and nonconfrontational*

Our fifty-fifty nation is lopsided. Election results show us equally divided between the two parties. Several recent presidential elections (2000, 2016, 2020) were decided by razor thin margins where a few thousand votes in a handful of states would have changed the outcome. Currently in the year 2024, the U.S. Senate is divided 51 to 49 and the GOP majority in the House of Representatives is about 1 percent. States have 27 republican governors and 23 democrats. It thus appears that **the electorate is split right down the middle**.

What is so mystifying is that such an evenly balanced nation could have wound up in a situation where a small but forceful minority is able to impose its preposterous mindset on nearly half the nation that is strongly opposed to its hit parade of positively zany ideas and policies! Over the past couple of decades or so, we seem to have abandoned nearly all the norms and customs that built our nation into a place that draws millions who want to share in the bounty of America.

As new immigrants arrive today, they find themselves in filthy urban squalor plagued by a violence they left their homes to avoid. They find a society that appears to have forsaken its ideals of liberty and a civilized culture and instead has embraced a system where an elite creates chaos and seeks to control every aspect of their lives. In short, they find an America that is becoming more and more like the dysfunctional nations from which they escaped.

Our nation appears to be living in a crudely written comedy sketch or fairytale. The famous fairytale *The Emperor's New Clothes* by Hans Christian Anderson seems to capture the absurdity of our current situation. *Wikipiedia* gives a brief summary of this fairy tale https://en.wikipedia.org/wiki/The_Emperor's_New_Clothes:

> There is an emperor who has an obsession with fancy new clothes, and spends lavishly on them, at the expense of state matters. One day two con-men visit the emperor's capital. Posing as weavers, they offer to supply him with magnificent clothes that are invisible to those who are incompetent or stupid. The emperor hires them, and they set up looms and pretend to go to work. A succession of officials, starting with the emperor's wise and competent minister, and then ending with the emperor himself, visit them to check their progress. Each sees that the looms are empty but pretends otherwise to avoid being thought a fool.
>
> Finally, the weavers report that the emperor's suit is finished. They mime dressing him and he sets off in a procession before the whole city. The townsfolk uncomfortably go along with the pretense, not wanting to appear inept or stupid, until a child blurts out that the emperor is wearing nothing at all. The people then realize that everyone has been fooled. Although startled, the emperor continues the procession, walking more proudly than ever.

The elites that run America are like the con men of this fairy tale. They are weaving a narrative that is so bizarre that everyone should be mocking them. But most of the public has been intimidated to just "go along" with the fantasy just like most of the townfolk in the fairy tale. In this book, I intend to act as the impertinent little boy who bellows out the truth:

- No, a boy cannot be a girl simply by saying he is.
- No, America is not a racist country dominated by white supremacy.
- No, the earth will not become uninhabitable unless we stop burning fossil fuels immediately.
- No, making the homeless more comfortable does not lead to clean streets; it leads to street adorned with human excrement and drug needles.
- No, not punishing people for shoplifting will not lead to better cities but will instead cause stores to shut down, creating urban food deserts.
- No, spending billions of dollars in Ukraine will not improve the life of a single American.
- No, swinging our border gates wide open will not enrich our country, it will impoverish it as millions fleece the generous American public.
- No, we don't want FBI agents and Big Tech Billionaires telling us what we are allowed to read.
- No, we won't eat insects.

No, No, No. All the outrageous myths being thrust down our throats are just what they seem to be: sheer lunacy! When we strip away all the obfuscating euphemisms of the progressive con men, we clearly see just how bankrupt their narrative really is. Despite the ostentatious embroidery of these dream weavers, the elites have no clothes. The emperor has no clothes. They are parading like the emperor who thinks he is decked out in finery, but all the world, just like the impertinent little boy, can see he has nothing on!

At least half of the U.S. Population (including even some democrats) knows that the preposterous tenets of the elite agenda are idiotic. A new acronym TPAN describes this situation: These People are Nuts! Yet a small group of influencers on the left just keeps on spewing out their extreme ideology and enacting destructive public policy. In this book, I make the case that the reason we have drifted into this caricature in a 50/50 common sense nation is that the competition is being waged using asymmetric tactics. Figure 1 shows how the left just keeps on winning:

Figure 1.
Policy Pulls Left of Center due to Asymmetric Strategy

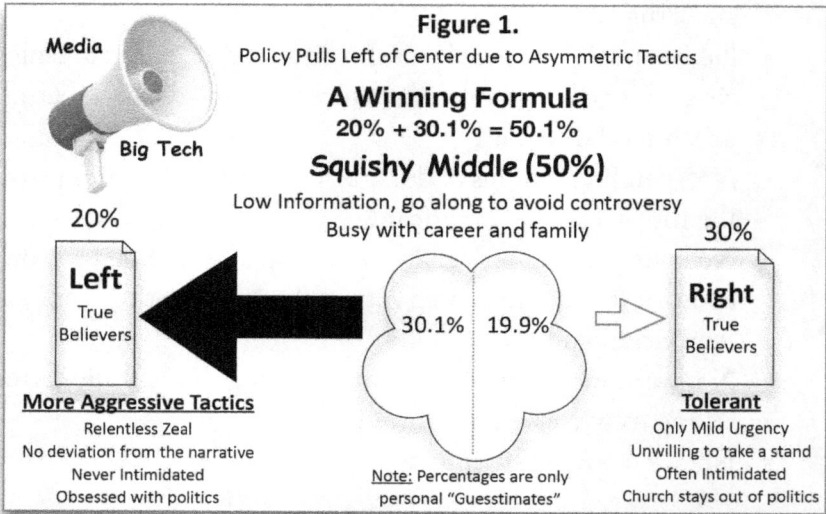

Figure 1.
Policy Pulls Left of Center due to Asymmetric Tactics

A Winning Formula
20% + 30.1% = 50.1%

Squishy Middle (50%)
Low Information, go along to avoid controversy
Busy with career and family

Media

Big Tech

20%

Left
True Believers

30.1% | 19.9%

30%

Right
True Believers

More Aggressive Tactics
Relentless Zeal
No deviation from the narrative
Never Intimidated
Obsessed with politics

Note: Percentages are only
personal "Guesstimates"

Tolerant
Only Mild Urgency
Unwilling to take a stand
Often Intimidated
Church stays out of politics

The percentages in Figure 1 are shown in even tens, indicating their lack of precision. Based on my own reading of the news and various sources, I am "guessing" that about half of the country is in what is sometimes called the "squishy middle". These are people who don't pay much attention to the news as they are busy raising families and pursuing careers. The other half comprises the "true believers". My theory is that true believers on the left comprise about 20% of the U.S. Population and 30% are true believers on the right.

The true believers on the left know that they don't need to mobilize 60 or 70 percent of the population to embrace their cause enthusiastically; they only need a bare majority (50.1%) to just go along or give their passive assent. Since the squishy middle doesn't pay much attention to the news or politics, the left can drag them over to their side by using aggressive tactics: relentless zeal, no deviation from the narrative, never intimidated, and obsessed with politics. Since the left controls Media and Big Tech, they can persuade enough in the middle through effective use of these tools. On the other side, the right uses more tolerant tactics: they exhibit only mild urgency, are often unwilling to take a stand, are often intimidated by the left's aggressive tactics, and churches tend to stay out of politics. So the easy going tactics of the right often do not counteract the strong arm tactics of the left, and enough voters in the middle go over to the left, giving them a majority to rule.

As a result, America has suffered a moral inversion where what was formerly thought to be good is now thought to be evil and what was formerly evil is now thought to be good. Author Ernest Hemingway predicted a situation like this in his novel *The Sun Also Rises*. His character in the novel asks "How did you go bankrupt?" The answer is "two ways. Gradually, then suddenly." It appears that the "gradually" part of the current degradation of America went from about 1970 to about 2015. But the "suddenly" part seems to have careened off the cliff beginning a little less than ten years ago. We seem to be in a roller coaster ride that is about to go off the rails and plunge into an abyss of bleak despair.

What happened to the America we once had? It's as though we as a nation have become mired down in what Puritan author John Bunyan termed *the slough of despond* in his 17th century classic *The Pilgrim's Progress*. We have encountered a morass of quicksand sludge that threatens to drown us in irrational but strongly held moral codes. We, about half or more of America, don't subscribe to those views, but some invisible hand is reaching out from the swamp and dragging us under if we protest or even disagree with the rules that were imposed on us from an unelected and unaccountable coterie of educated intelligentsia. As a result, many of us feel helpless to resist and simply try to appease the strong voices pushing their agenda rather than fight and be yanked below the surface of their sloppy, muck-filled bog.

Our nation has long been known for its innovation, its grit and drive, and its generosity and compassion. This is the country everyone turns to when natural disasters hit. This is the country that put a man on the moon and created the information age. This is the country that innovated and led the world in new technology. This is the country that developed cures for diseases that had previously been incurable. This is the country that decisively ended racist practices such as slavery and Jim Crow. This is the country that cleaned up its environment. This is a nation filled with good and decent people. It was and is a land of opportunity. The American dream, though fading, is still alive.

There still is some time to at least slow down the decay of America. I live in a suburb of a major American city. Things are placid and peaceful in my neighborhood. I have access to nice shopping malls that are just bursting at the seams with "the good life" and there's even more available online. I have excellent medical care. I often walk in a nice park near my home where people from all races greet each other cordially. My smart TV can stream a wide variety of entertainment and news that I can watch any time. I have instant access to a lot of useful information on the Internet. **At this stage of my life, I, like millions more in this land, am grateful for a life that has truly been sensational. Modern America is grand!**

But I watch the news and see all the peculiar stuff happening outside my local world and if I didn't have my own experience, I would conclude that America is circling the drain. News has always focused on negative things, but in recent decades it has become obsessed with finding problems that most Americans do not experience. I see crime and filth and homeless encampments in cities like New York and San Francisco, but I don't see them where I live. I hear stories about people fired for using the wrong pronouns but don't know anyone to whom that has happened. I see stories about minors being subjected to life changing sex change surgery and drugs because they have been convinced that they are a different gender than their real gender. But I don't know anyone this has happened to. I hear that America is filled with "white supremacists" but I see no evidence of these ogres. I hear that there is racial strife, but in my workplace, we have whites, blacks, and Hispanics working side by side in harmony. I see climate change alarmists telling us that the end is near, but life just goes on with climate-related deaths declining dramatically as we develop technology to adapt.

Much of the gloomy impression we get from the media contradicts our experience on the ground in today's America. The despondent feeling many suffer reflects the dystopian vision the progressive elite has cooked up. And though the lunacy is largely confined to cities like New York, Chicago, LA, and San Francisco today, it is seeping out and impacting once peaceful suburbs. During a recent auto trip across the country from coast to coast, when we arrived on the west coast, we found that at many fast-food places, even in nice suburbs, we had to ask the clerk for a key to use the restroom because there were homeless camped out at the front door (this was common in Washington, Oregon, and California but not in other states we visited). Even if you haven't yet been subjected to filthy streets, car jackings, smash and grab gangs, and insane transgender propaganda, if the current developments continue, these maladies will penetrate and infect even peaceful communities. It's only a matter of time.

So what happened? Why are so many cities filthy and crime-ridden? Why are we not respected abroad as we once were? Why do we have an enormous federal budget deficit as far as the eye can see? Why do we permit the invasion on our border? Why do we condone perverted practices such as Drag Queen shows for minors, men joining women's sports teams and invading women's locker rooms? **How did we get to this place? It happened gradually and then suddenly**.

Part of the gradual decline can be traced to a confluence of circumstances that just "happened" without any leadership from revolutionaries. American technology exploded with major benefits including easy access to information that was once only available to a few. This was a good thing that had some bad side effects. Suddenly there were thousands of "experts" enlightening the masses with their unrestricted bullhorn. Some of these experts really did help us to understand our world better, but some were crackpots that only spread pernicious propaganda.

Another event that occurred was the almost overnight realization that justice had been denied to minorities such as blacks, women, and homosexuals and that justice for these groups was imperative. This realization, like technology, was largely a good thing. But coupled with instant communications, the urge to correct past sins went way overboard, resulting indirectly in many ills including the insane notion that all whites are racist, that drag queens were a normal part of our cultural mainstream, and that children could be brought up by "contractors" and a loving nuclear family was a relic of the past that only impeded women in their careers.

These and other events (most notably the 9/11 attacks and covid pandemic) partly shaped the current culture, but to understand the decline from a great nation nearly universally respected to an object of mockery from the rest of the world, we also must recognize that many persuasive leaders arose to spread their utopian model and gain a wide enough acceptance to effect change. These opinion leaders preached their new gospel with passion and relentless zeal. They used fine-sounding euphemisms to entice the less vocal and more pliant people to at least hear what they had to say. Most of the American public was too busy earning a living or tending to their families to notice the effects of the campaign from the far left. It all seemed to be far off and even if it was a bit whacky, most people concluded that they could ignore the noise, avoid divisive confrontation, and retreat into their quiet community. They asserted, **"let others duke it out. Just leave me alone in my suburban enclave."**

There were two parts of the decline we have seen in recent decades, and we need to understand both parts of the decline. The "gradually" part began in the 1970's through what author Christopher Rufo calls the "great march through the institutions." The "suddenly" part culminated recently as new power centers outside the control of the U.S. Constitution and Bill of Rights have coalesced into a formidable force coalition. Instead of "separation of powers" we now have **alignment of powers** that have advanced technological tools at their disposal.

The brilliance of this new American Revolution is that **it was carried out without any bullets or ballots**. The progressive elite that runs this country were not elected and are not accountable to the American public. They wield extraordinary power because they control the information the public sees. Much as the Soviet Union was controlled through the use of its newspaper, *Pravda*, the US today is controlled through a new *Pravda*: the corporate media, including Big Tech.

The intellectual elite of America will scoff at my position and would probably call it a conspiracy theory. Deep state schemes are a merely a myth offered by a far-right fringe, they claim. But the instant communications technology we enjoy today makes it much easier for like- minded individuals to share their vision to shape society in their image. No meetings in smoke- filled rooms are necessary. The elites have created a new cult by adopting theories of the gurus of decades past and then sending missionaries off into cyberspace to evangelize the masses in this new religion. This system is much more efficient than sending disciples out two by two. Instead of reaching just a handful of converts, the new missionaries have millions of followers on social media.

This book aims to expose the **who, when, what, how, and why** of the new American Revolution and then propose solutions to return us to the saner and more civilized America we had a just few decades ago. Along the way, I present several reviews of key books that have been influential in my analysis. Since these books go into much greater detail than I do on several issues, I urge my readers to obtain and examine these excellent works.

Though the elites on the left have captured many centers of power and appear to have nearly all the levers at their command, there are a few hopeful glimmerings occurring mostly outside the urban hubs. We first need to understand how we got here before we can devise a strategy to return to the America we have all come to love. So we begin with a little history.

Who and When:
A Brief History of the Rise of the Left

1. Gradually: The Prophets and Visionaries of the Sixties
America's Cultural Revolution, By Christopher Rufo
Book Review

As we observe America in the year 2024, it appears that the radical left has virtually "taken over". The left controls nearly all the powerful yet unelected institutions, including Big Tech, Media and Entertainment and Sports, Big Finance and Big Business, the massive federal bureaucracy, major city mayors and D.A.'s, and universities and schools. This year, they also control the U.S. Senate and the presidency. Arrayed against all this combined power, the right has the Supreme Court and a modest advantage among state governments, but this small beachhead doesn't stand a chance against the combined forces of the left.

The left has engineered a **virtual second American Revolution** and has attained this perch of power **without firing a shot or winning a vote**. They just gradually took the helm of the institutions whose power grew notwithstanding the Constitution and the Bill of Rights. How did they do it? How did a 50/50 U.S. Public succumb to this power? It happened because the right was complacent while the left was brilliantly zealous. The right just assumed that checks and balances and the Bill of Rights would be a sufficient deterrent, while the left sought out institutions that operate outside the Constitution and began what author Christoper Rufo calls "**the great march through the institutions**." Much of the material in this chapter is derived from Rufo's excellent work.

Christopher Rufo, a scholar of the Manhattan Institute and frequent interview guest on TV shows and podcasts, published a book named *America's Cultural Revolution* in July 2023. The author's main area of research over the past decade or so has been Critical Theories such as Critical Race Theory and Queer Theory. His book traces the rise of the radical left from the late 60's to present day. Rufo reveals the brilliance of the left's strategy. They realized that, with time, they could rise to power without winning any elections by focusing on one key institution: **Education.**

Herbert Marcuse and other pioneers of Critical Theory realized just how "critical" (pun intended) education was to drive a culture. Nearly every leader, political or corporate, graduates from a university. If these institutions could be captured by ardent revolutionaries, a society could be transformed. No elections would be necessary. Each new graduate would be an activist for the utopian vision. Universities basically are the incubators for leadership in all spheres and thus form the lynchpin of a successful revolution.

Most Americans probably think educational institutions don't have much influence. The high-browed discussions in faculty lounges may be curiosities, but they stay confined within the walls of universities, which are, after all, only a waystation where young adults spend a few years of their lives. Then they enter the "real world" and become responsible adults as they confront the challenges of everyday life. That is how it seemed for many decades.

Until recently, universities served a vital role in providing young adults the skillset they would need to thrive in American capitalism and culture. We needed skilled physicians, scientists, engineers, and scholars. The universities did a magnificent job of training up the next generation. They played a crucial role in propelling America to the forefront of almost every category from technology to military, from medicine to finance, from science to the arts. An educated

America emerged as the bastion of expertise and prowess in virtually every important area.

But beginning around the late sixties and early seventies, universities began to stray from their core mission. Philosophers such as **Herbert Marcuse** and **Paulo Freire** began a concerted effort to change education from mere training and knowledge building to activism in a cause. **Universities morphed from disinterested instruction facilities into something more like seminaries that trained young pastors to go out into a mission field and make a utopian vision happen**.

The revolutionaries of the sixties realized that college students are at the height of their pliability in their early twenties. At that age, they think they "know it all" and are susceptible to voices who criticize "the system." They naively swallow the creed they are fed by their professors and administrators but never suspect that they are being manipulated and played. They *think* they are being innovative and are brimming with new ideas, but they are *really* just absorbing the propaganda they are being fed by the ones who actually run the universities. These college students can be relied upon to believe that everything from the past was basically traditional nonsense but now in the twentieth century, we can figure it all out and replace a corrupt system that oppresses the downtrodden with an educated, enlightened new society that will right the past wrongs.

The combined influence of Marxist revolutionaries such as Herbert Marcuse, Paulo Freire, and Harvard's **Derek Bell** formed a potent vanguard for the radical revolutionaries of the sixties. These three gurus plus a few others such as the polemic *Prarie Fire* (1974) by the Weather Underground's Bill Ayers and Bernadine Dorn gave the new radicals a blueprint for their revolution. It took a few decades to accomplish, but the insurgents were patient. They also were vehement and tenacious, two qualities often lacking in conservative circles.

Shortly after the year 2000, the terms **Diversity, Equity, and Inclusion (DEI)** became a part of the lexicon of the national news media. These terms and the policies they described started as a rather benign way to aspire to a society that gave all persons a fair share of the American dream. In the past, racial minorities, women, and homosexuals had been subjected to unjust treatment, and most of America was amenable to correcting these injustices. So, universities began to offer "studies" courses such as Black Studies or Woman's Studies. Then they granted pH D's in these "studies." Then they created departments of Diversity, Equity, and Inclusion. All this took time, during the "gradually" phase of the revolution.

Rufo observes that as these graduates left the universities, some went into Government to do similar work there. A circular reinforcing cycle then began. Government bureaucrats funded grants and scholarships to universities to foster more studies of DEI. This in turn churned out more graduates in these disciplines and they entered government service. Over time, this symbiotic relationship blossomed into thousands of students and bureaucrats specializing in DEI. There was a shift from the "heavy learning" phase of the pioneers like Marcuse to the "heavy lifting" phase of activists that joined the ranks of government bureaucracy and corporate management.

After the great recession of 2008, the *New York Times* had to lay off many veteran reporters. In the recovery that followed, they hired more and more young graduates of elite schools such as Harvard and Yale. These new hires saw themselves not as "reporters" but as activists in a cause of social justice. Since most of the rest of the news media saw the NYT as the "paper of record", they would often simply amplify what the *Times* had already reported. This would present a "snowball effect" where mentions would accumulate upon one another until the volume of the rhetoric became almost ear-splitting.

One could almost draw a straight line through the institutions to trace the rise of the American left:

Universities→Federal Bureaucracy→New York Times→Media→Corporations

The most brilliant aspect of the left's march through the institutions was its realization that the elected government was not the only center of power. As previously stated, at first blush, universities appear to have very little influence or power. But when one considers that nearly all of the leaders in today's society are graduates of these universities, the strategy to train activists and then turn them loose in other sectors is an absolutely inspired plan. This plan is further strengthened by the widespread view that just a few universities (eg, Harvard, Stanford, Yale) are the "cream of the crop." A few activists from just three schools can amplify the movement decisively. And just as the news media used the *New York Times* as its inspired example, other universities sought to emulate Harvard, Stanford, and Yale.

The long march through the institutions was made feasible by an asymmetry of attitudes between left and right. The left is always passionate and insistent. The right is mostly respectful and tolerant. The left fervently believes that the ends (their utopian vision) justify the means. The right tends to adopt "rules of engagement" that respect decorum and freedom of speech. The left uses euphemisms such as "Diversity, Equity, and Inclusion" that seem benign to cloak their revolutionary agenda. The right often concedes to the new language and thus acquiesces to their demands with what they think are small "compromises" to avoid divisive debates. So here we are in the year 2024. A few years after the George Floyd killing in Minneapolis, the agenda of the left seems to have arrived at its peak proficiency.

Even though large swaths of the American public are conservative or moderate, nearly all of the centers of power seem to be dominated by not just left, but far left ideology.

Who are the heirs of Marcusa, Friere, and Bell? Today we find a handful of very influential voices who have synthesized the theories from the sixties into a coherent revolutionary strategy for the twenty-first century. We examine a few of these activists and influencers in the next few chapters.

2. Suddenly: The New Tacticians of the Left
Intense, influential, and strongly committed voices in our day

In the previous chapters, we identified the main figures from the "gradually" portion of the rise of the left. The "prophets" like Marcusa, Friere, and Bell, played the long game. They began the slow and steady march through the institutions in an era of more primitive communications. They formulated a coherent vision and made some initial progress within the education establishment, but they realized that others would have to bring their vision to full flower. They were the theoreticians who were willing to pass the baton to the militants who would actually implement their profound vision.

Here in the 2010's and 2020's we enter the "suddenly" part of their ascent. The early gurus bided their time by gradually capturing Education. But they lacked a key resource that only became available a few decades ago: instant, ubiquitous communications. If these resources had been available in the sixties, I'm sure we would see these sages online with podcasts and millions of followers. As the twenty-first century has unfolded, several key players have inspired and led the drive to rule America in promoting the new progressive agenda. Here is a partial list of the key leaders of this movement:

- George Soros
- Nicole Hannah Jones, and Robin DiAngelo
- Michael Mann, Bill McKibben, Bill Nye, and James Hanson
- The World Economic Forum and Big Tech Billionaires

This is only a partial list. Many other influential voices bombard us daily from the internet, but for brevity, here we just focus on these few significant figures. Notice a key similarity of all these leaders: **none were elected by the American people**. They all wield influence

17

from the sidelines either with their money or their persuasive power. This is a common theme in the story. Government is no longer most important center of power. The hub seems to have shifted to those who disseminate information or who are wealthy enough to basically "buy" elections.

George Soros

George Soros, a Hungarian born American, is one of the wealthiest men in the world. He made his money as a hedge fund manager and has donated billions of dollars to progressive causes. He is most famous for a recent initiative beginning around 2016 to fund campaigns for big city District Attorneys. Soros discovered that these campaigns are comparatively inexpensive, and voters don't pay much attention to them, so a few million dollars can achieve some very significant results. A *Politico* article published in August 2016, titled "George Soros' Quiet Overhaul of the U.S. Justice system" gives details.

Some on the left may point to wealthy Republican donors such as the Koch Brothers and Sheldon Adelson as utilizing similar tactics. Yes, they donated a lot of money to conservative causes. But what makes George Soros stand out from other wealthy donors is the direct impact he had on life in America. George Soros targeted the justice system in a meaningful and powerful way. His DA's effectuated a soft on crime stance that plagues many U.S. Cities. There has been no comparable impact from wealthy Republican donors.

Soros-backed big city District Attorneys have conducted crusades to solve the "problem" of mass-incarceration. The media concocted a myth that many criminals were in prison for minor offenses and that many of these unfortunate victims were minorities. Incarceration costs taxpayers millions of dollars and ruins the lives of men who made "mistakes" and needed a second chance. The new cadre of Soros DA's dedicated themselves to greatly reducing prison populations by a number of means

- Selective prosecution (avoid prosecution of crimes not considered serious)
- Adjustment/mitigation of penalties
- Early and easy parole
- Cash bail reform (it's not fair that the "poor" can't afford bail)
- Reduce felonies to misdimeanors
- Remove sentencing enhancements

These measures have achieved their goal of decarceration, but as a side effect, crime has soared.

Nicole Hannah Jones and Robin DiAngelo

What George Soros accomplished in the arena of Criminal Justice, Nicole Hannah Jones and Robin DiAngelo achieved in racial politics. Nicole Hannah Jones won a Pulitzer Prize in 2020 for her work at the *New York Times* on the **1619 Project**. The main thesis on this series of articles was that America's founding should be traced back not to 1776, but to 1619, the year the first African slaves arrived on America's shores. The Project developed into several *NY Times Magazine* articles as well as supplementary materials that were made available to school classrooms.

Nicole Hannah Jones maintained that a major reason the U.S. Founders fought their revolution was to preserve slavery in America. Her research strongly condemned most of the American Founders and established an orthodoxy that slavery was "baked into the DNA of the American founding." This theme of trashing the American founders was then amplified by many disciples of the *1619 Project*. The goal is for Americans who formerly revered the founders and Declaration of Independence and Constitution to begin doubting the ideals expressed by the founders. If the founders and Constitution could be thrown overboard, then the whole American system would crumble and be replaced with what? The *1619 Project* is vague about this question.

Robin DiAngelo is another highly influential voice on the progressive views on race. Her book, **White Fragility**, published in 2018, became an instant best-seller and was discussed on many media platforms. DiAngelo's main thesis is that white people become defensive in any discussion about race. The very fact that they will not accept correction for their racist attitude becomes proof of their racism. She states that white people are oblivious to the harm they have caused with white supremacy because they live on a perch of privilege. When whites talk about a meritocracy, they begin from a head start they received due to the pervasive white supremacy that lives all around them. Thus, they deny that they are racist, but in so doing, prove that they are. **They practice what is known as "implicit racism"**. They may not say or do something racist, but because they benefit from the head start they received, they perpetuate systemic racism.

Both Nicole Hannah Jones and Robin DiAngelo postulate a theory that whites have committed the unpardonable sin. Their very "whiteness" (a term in wide use today that only made its appearance perhaps a couple of decades ago) is their badge of shame. Whites can never do enough to atone for their whiteness. All their achievements are tarnished by their whiteness. While the Christian gospel is *good news* because it proclaims redemption and salvation, the message of the new race tacticians is *bad news* because there is no forgiveness and no remedy. This bad news is affirmed forcefully by Nicole Hannah Jones, Robin DiAngelo, and other luminaries including TaNahisi Coates and Ibrihim X Kendi who all preach to enthusiastic masses today. Ta-Nehisi Coates's bestseller described whiteness as "an existential danger to the country and the world". **The world would** be a much better place without white people. Thus spake these modern-day prophets.

Michael Mann, Bill McKibben, Bill Nye, and James Hanson

Michael Mann, a climatologist and geophysicist at the University of Pennsylvania, might well be credited as the "father" of modern Global Warming theory. His famous "hockey stick" chart, published in 1999, set off a snowball effect of scholarship on Global Warming. The mantle was taken up by former Vice President Al Gore in 2006 with his film *An Inconvenient Truth*, and the Climate Change movement was off to the races.

Mann's **hockey stick chart** (global average temperature for the last thousand years) is one of the most misleading charts ever published. If you look at his chart closely, you will see that it doesn't really show a major temperature increase in the industrial age. Mann was at least honest enough to draw **gray uncertainty zones** around the trend lines he drew on top of the data. The uncertainty reflects the fact that he is using proxy data for historic temperatures before the invention of the thermometer. These proxies such as ice cores, tree rings, and coral growth, only approximate temperature, but they are shown on the chart as if they were just as accurate as the direct temperature data. If you just omit his trendline and look at the gray zones, you will see that temperatures today are about the same as they were in the medieval warm period. Using his own data!

Most consumers of the hockey stick chart immediately see the dark line that takes off like a hockey stick. But this line is just a "guess" using some fancy statistics. Data from previous periods is suspect because we don't have direct data back then. If we don't know the temperature historically, we don't really know how much climate has warmed.

Several other figures have popularized the notion that climate is changing due to the burning of fossil fuels. These include **Bill Nye "the science guy,"** environmentalist and journalist **Bill McKibben**, and scientist **James Hanson** of NASA. All four of these climate change activists have received widespread attention and have been treated in the mainstream press as experts.

Other equally well credentialled climate scientists such as **Judith Curry** of Georgia Tech, **Richard Lindzen** of MIT, and **John Christy** of the University of Alabama Huntsville maintain that though there is some slight warming in recent decades, this warming has multiple causes, many of which have nothing to do with fossil fuel use. They also maintain that the change is small enough so that we can adapt to the changes using technology.

The problem is that Curry, Lindzen, Christy and quite a few others who don't buy the alarmism of the Climate Change zealots are nearly shunned by the mainstream media (see Chapter 34: *The Fraud of Follow the Science* for more details). Mann, Nye, McKibbon, and Hanson are promoted as experts and we should just accept what they announce. **The science is settled. Or so they say.**

3. *Who are the Ruling Elite?*
The Superior Class Who Tells us What to Do.

The American Heritage Dictionary online defines elite as "a group or class of persons considered to be superior to others because of their intelligence, social standing, or wealth." In America today, thousands would claim to be a part of that group. They nearly all have college degrees or run large organizations. Their social standing often appears to grant them authority to command others.

On a micro scale, many of us unquestionably submit to authorities we recognize as having a special expertise we lack. This can be as simple as deferring to an auto-mechanic who tells us we need a new alternator or obeying a physician and taking a medication to treat an illness. In both of these cases, we concede to a superior knowledge in the authoritative figure.

What is new in our time is elites who claim superiority in matters of morals or questions that have no clear objective answer. Many of life's questions are not technical in nature but philosophical. One could argue that in theoretical areas of general knowledge, a pH D from Harvard is no better than Bozo the Clown. Both are expressing their opinion, and just like it is hard to measure a person's qualifications for a job, it may be difficult to assess an expert's qualifications to opine on controversial topics. The elites state moral principles as if they are beyond dispute. Moral principles and philosophy have been enunciated and debated for centuries, but the elites now think our advances in knowledge and technology have evolved to the point where we know the correct answer.

Increasingly in modern America, expert elites are anointed by Big Tech and the News Media. These experts often stray from their lane of expertise into areas where they are no more expert than the common person on the street. Neil DeGrasse Tyson is an expert astronomer, but he often holds court on Climate Change. Bill Gates is an expert in computer technology and entrepreneurship, but he often gives his opinion on universal ID's and alternative diets. Larry Fink is an expert in finance, but he often analyzes corporate securities not on how well a company is run, but how well its policies promote the secular humanist agenda.

In today's America, we admire and follow thousands of unelected elites. Many of these are household names while others exert their influence behind a curtain of near anonymity. As far as I know, there is no formal selection process that gets you into the club of the elites. There is no secret handshake or initiation rite that make one part of the elite. They just join the club due to their unique talents and nearly universal recognition among the public.

Yet some of us ask the impertinent question probed by John Galt in Ayn Rand's 1957 novel *Atlas Shrugged*. "Who gave you the passkey to the moral elite?" Most of the elites would answer, "I don't need a passkey. I just claim my elite position."

The activists described in previous chapters are only the tip of the iceberg that constitutes the ruling elite in today's America. Though they are a potent force, a few influencers like George Soros, Robin Diangelo, and Michael Mann are not sufficient to subjugate and rule over a continental nation with millions of intelligent and proudly independent people protected by the U.S. Constitution and Bill of rights. The task of ruling America is so vast that a team of passionate and capable leaders is needed. **This team of rulers is known as the elite or intelligentsia.**

Our nation contains over three hundred million people. Most of us are fairly ordinary. We go to work, pay our taxes, and play by the rules. Most of us also defer to those identified as "experts." We saw this in spades during the Covid pandemic (2020-2021). The experts told us to lock down, wear masks, and get vaccines, and millions of us did exactly what we were told. The few who stepped out of line were punished and publicly shamed. Behind the scenes, a small collection of elites orchestrated the entire pandemic response.

Looking back on that dark time, it is amazing that so many Americans just did what they were told and never questioned the commands of the elites. The health emergency was so dire that we all thought we needed to do our part to stop the spread. And so out of a sense of responsibility we just took orders as if the orders came from a commissar with ultimate authority.

Covid was an extreme case, but it pointed to a characteristic of Americans that is both good and bad. The good part is that most of us are good and decent people who recognize that civilization only flourishes when people are considerate of others and obey reasonable rules. Perhaps the most pervasive rules we routinely obey are traffic laws. Americans by and large observe traffic lights, stop signs, and speed limits. As a result, driving on American roads is pretty easy. We can usually get from point a to point b quickly and easily because there is a consensus that we all obey the traffic laws. I've visited other places like Cairo Egypt, where it might take an hour to go about a half a mile, and the chance of a collision is great. The lines painted on the streets are merely "suggestions" and drivers often form more lanes. There are very few traffic lights or stop signs and even if there are some, most drivers would ignore them. The chaos is frightening and dangerous.

In America and much of the civilized world, we recognize the need to defer to an expert class that maintains a reasonable set of rules we can live by. As modern life becomes more complex, the "little people" realize that we need guidance from some specially trained people. Physicians, Lawyers, Engineers, and Scientists come to mind. We tend to naturally defer to opinions made by these educated authorities.

We submit to the professionals in our personal lives, but what about bigger issues that impact the public at large? How does our society manage conflicting priorities in such things as promoting social justice, allocating wealth, and providing adequate health care to the masses? In the past, we elected people to make the judgment calls of when to prohibit some behaviors (eg, theft) or force others (eg, pay taxes). The innovation we are witnessing in the early 21st century is the appointment of non-elected people to make these judgment calls.

Many of these authoritative elites exercise more power over the public than our elected officials. There are no laws against making an obnoxious comment, but the folks who run social media companies can prohibit such comments and publicly shame those who transgress. There are no laws against investing in fossil fuel companies, but elites who run financial institutions can have a big impact on investment decisions through the use of ESG scores. There are no laws forcing us to use the newly invented pronouns, but unelected forces can get us fired from our jobs if we fail this new requirement. Ignorance of the rules is no excuse.

There are too many elites to list them all individually. Most promote the ruling woke agenda. Some obvious "up front" elites include folks like former president Barack Obama, the Davos Big Three (Klaus Schwab, Bill Gates, and Larry Fink), Think Tanks such as Brookings, Big Tech titans like Mark Zuckerberg and Jeff Bezos, media figures like Tom Friedman and Nick Kristof of the *New York Times*, and Chuck Todd of NBC News. There are also a few elites that oppose the progressive agenda, including Former

President Donald Trump, Elon Musk, Tucker Carlson, Coleman Hughes, Think Tanks such as Heritage, Christopher Rufo and professors Thomas Sowell and Victor Davis Hanson. These and a few other opposition elites do a fine job, but their efforts currently are overwhelmed by the prevailing elites who control the most widely used communications vehicles.

Occasionally, a behind the scenes elite emerges from the shadows and we catch a glimpse of the invisible efforts that are going on all the time. Perhaps the most notable event like this happened shortly after Elon Musk acquired Twitter. Two names most of us had never heard of made a brief appearance in the news. These two names were **Yoel Roth**, a Twitter manager who was head of "site integrity" and made many censorship decisions at Twitter. Another was a former FBI special counsel named **James Baker** who was hired by Twitter. Both Roth and Baker exerted a lot of influence over what information was allowed and what was prohibited. Yet most of the public had never heard of them until this little news splash. There are probably thousands more Roth's and Baker's out there turning knobs and pulling levers to promote the progressive agenda. They effectively rule over small areas of American lives and form alliances with other elites in the progressive coalition.

How do we pick the elites we will obey if we don't elect them? The answer is that **we basically have empowered the news media and big tech to pick the elites**. In a large nation like ours, the main vehicle for widespread compliance is communication and peer pressure. The elites that run media, entertainment, and big tech tell us who we should listen to, and, for the most part, we accept their decision. Although a few iconoclasts may oppose the elites, in the end, their control over communications media makes the anointed elite a formidable force.

The problem here in the 21st century is that communications and surveillance technology gives the elites power over many more individuals than historic elites such George Washington, Abraham Lincoln, or more recently, Winston Churchill and Adolph Hitler. The ability of Big Tech to amplify some opinions and diminish others makes it and its leaders a potent force.

In addition, as described elsewhere in this book, communications technology enables an alignment of powers that were formerly located in separate silos. The coalition of secular humanist forces operates a multi-front effort to control the masses. Big Tech handles censorship and surveillance. The news media herds people into opinions that promote the progressive agenda. They also amplify grievance and stir up outrage that promotes their program. Big Finance directs capital to favored firms. Unelected bureaucrats churn out regulation after regulation, many of which promote ideas like climate change alarmism. University intellectuals provide a plausible philosophical framework for the elites to flourish and promote ideological goals such as emptying prisons. The universities also churn out graduates who have been thoroughly imbued with progressive theory who then enter corporations and provide activist leadership. The Chinese Communist party gets us hooked on cheap Chinese goods as they hollow out once vibrant American cities. Without any meetings or conspiracies, all these unelected forces unite and basically make a mockery of the Constitutional concept of separation of powers.

Millions of Americans make billions of decisions to cede power to these communications companies every day. They trade privacy ("what do I have to hide?") and surrender power in exchange for the amazing convenience tech offers in our daily lives. The elites quietly claim new territory in governing America while ordinary folks are too busy raising families and pursuing careers to notice the small encroachments on their lives. But here in the year 2024, we are **starting to notice a cumulative impact of all these decisions**

the elites are making for us. And it is not a pretty sight (see list toward the end of the Chapter 41 (*Epilogue*: *The Spiritual Side of America's Dystopia*).

4. The Democratic Party
The guiding light of the new revolutionaries

As we examine the current power centers that control America, it appears that by about the 2020's or so, nearly all of them share one characteristic: they all ardently support the agenda of the Democratic Party. Turn on the News, do a web search, watch the Academy Awards ceremony or even an NFL football game, and you will encounter cheerleaders for the Democratic Party.

The mainstream media in the US has constructed a very flattering profile of the Democratic Party in the last few decades. The impression that has been embroidered and embellished basically presents an image of nobility for Democrats. They are the party who cares about marginalized communities. They are the party that advances the rights of minorities as the Republicans are the party of wealthy corporate fat cats. Democrats are the champions of oppressed victims while the Republicans perpetuate such scourges as racism and White Supremacy. Turn on any media outlet and you will absorb a steady stream of this story line.

The problem with this narrative is that it is patently false. Dinesh D'Souza, a podcaster, movie producer (*2000 Mules, Police State*) and author wrote four books in the late 2010's that all focused on the history of the Democratic Party in America. In these books, Dinesh exposes many inconvenient facts that are normally omitted by the mainstream media. These four books are:

Stealing America (2015)
Hillary's America (2016)
The Big Lie (2017)
Death of a Nation (2019)

Having just re-read these books, I recap some of the things Dinesh reports. As far as I know, there is no disputing the truth of these items. All can be verified using several historical sources. As I review these four books, I note that **my summary doesn't do justice to the meticulous research Dinesh has done. I urge my readers to get these books for themselves**. Don't rely on the *Cliff Notes* version I present here.

Each of these books presents a different angle from which to examine the democrat narrative. Their story has gone virtually unchallenged because most of the institutions that shape public opinion have been firmly in the camp of the democrats for several decades. The news media, the entertainment industry, Big Tech, the bureaucracy, and universities have united in an alliance to present democrats in a very positive light while they vilify Republicans at every turn. The voices behind the narrative do so mainly by fact selection. Although they sometimes say bold faced lies (eg, Officer Sicknick was killed by being bludgeoned with a fire extinguisher), most of the narrative is established by emphasizing some facts while ignoring others with statements like "nothing to see here," "this is a big nothing-burger," or "this is old news," or "this has been debunked," or "conspiracy theory." But notice one thing about all these evasions: they rarely deny the truth being reported, only that it doesn't matter.

What Dinesh does in these four books is to select facts that are often omitted from the prevailing narrative. Each book in this series focuses on a different angle. The best of the four books, in my opinion, is the first one: *Stealing America*. The emphasis here is how democrats have perpetrated a big con on the American public. Like other cons, they have their "pitch" which are the noble sounding words used to get in the door, and then the con itself: basically, a theft of resources to enrich themselves. The first book also tells the fascinating story of Dinesh's own experience of the two-tiered justice system. He is sentenced to spending 8 months of nights in a half-way house for his crime of giving $20,000 above the limit to a personal friend who was running for the U.S. Senate. During his incarceration, Dinesh has plenty of time to talk to his fellow inmates and he gains valuable insights on how criminals think. He can apply this knowledge to the con he sees the Democratic Party has been running on the American Public.

Dinesh presents a compelling case that from their early days to the present, the Democratic Party has fleeced the American public by cloaking the con in noble sounding rhetoric. They have presented a bizzaro world story where what is good is bad and what is bad is good. This author marshals a convincing case with a cascade of facts that cannot be denied. These facts are "inconvenient truths" to Democrats and Progressives.

- Not a single slave owner has ever been a Republican. All were democrats.
- The **Thirteenth, Fourteenth, and Fifteenth Amendments** which abolished slavery, guaranteed civil rights to blacks, and granted the vote to blacks were passed by the Congress without a single democrat vote. These were entirely the work of the GOP.
- During the post-Civil War period, Blacks were first voted to Congress. Not a single one was a democrat. **All were Republicans**.
- The great black former slave **Frederick Douglass** is famous for this quote:
  - "Everybody has asked the question..."What shall we do with the Negro?" I have had but one answer from the beginning. Do nothing with us! Your doing with us has already played the mischief with us. Do nothing with us! if the Negro cannot stand on his own legs, let him fall also. All I ask is, give him a chance to stand on his own legs! Let him alone!"

- **Woodrow Wilson** may have been the most racist of all U.S. Presidents
  - Under Wilson, all federal agencies were segregated.
  - The first movie to be screened in the White House was *Birth of a Nation*, which was a pro-KKK film that glorified racism. Although the KKK had basically been ended several decades before, this movie showing in the White House revived the KKK for a long run culminating in millions of members by the 1920s.
  - Wilson was the first U.S. President to openly repudiate the American founders. Wilson understood that the limits placed upon the power of the national government by the Constitution—limits that Progressives wanted to see relaxed if not removed— were grounded in the natural-rights principles of the Declaration of Independence. This meant, for Wilson, that both the Declaration and the Constitution had to be understood anew through a Progressive lens. Wilson therefore sought a reinterpretation of the Founding—a reinterpretation grounded in historical contingence.
- Most Americans know about the large number of immigrants into the USA in the late 19th and early 20th century. But **immigration was cut by 95% by a new law in 1924** that set quotas for various nationalities. This law was promoted by the Democrat Party.
- **Franklin D. Roosevelt** is often lionized in the Democrat Party. And although he is not normally characterized as a racist, some of his actions, often hidden, would certainly be non- woke in today's environment:
  - He made deals with Southern Democrats to help get his legislation passed by basically being silent about their efforts to suppress anti-lynching legislation and other racist efforts.

- ○ Many of the New Deal programs barred Black participation, including Social Security, which was only opened to blacks by the Republicans in the 50's.
- ○ FDR appointed Hugo Black, a KKK leader, to the U.S. Supreme Court.
- ○ He expressed admiration for Italian dictator Mussolini
- ○ He kept the Armed Forces segregated as he thought integration would harm morale

<u>Note:</u> In the following information about Truman and Johnson, I replace the repulsive n word actually used with n*****to avoid offense. I also abbreviate an offensive obscenity LBJ used.

- Although he did end segregation of the armed forces, **Harry S. Truman** was also a member of the KKK and made some racist comments. For example, in 1911, the year he turned 27, Truman wrote to his future wife, Bess: "I think one man is just as good as another so long as he's honest and decent and not a n*****or a Chinaman. Uncle Will says that the Lord made a white man from dust, a n*****from mud, then He threw up what was left and it came down a Chinaman." More than 25 years later, Truman, then a U.S. senator from Missouri, wrote a letter to his daughter describing waiters at The White House as "an army of coons." In a letter to his wife in 1939 he referred to "n*****picnic day."
- Another model of racial justice often held in high esteem was **Lyndon Johnson**. Yet Johnson was about as racist as it gets. He said
  - ○ "These Negroes, they're getting pretty uppity these days and that's a problem for us since they've got something now they never had before, the political pull to back up their uppityness. Now we've got to do something about this, we've got to give them a little something, just enough to quiet them down, not enough to make a difference."

34

- Biographer Robert Caro also notes that Johnson is said to have replied as follows to a black chauffeur who told him he'd prefer to be called by name instead of "boy," "n*****" or "chief": "As long as you are black, and you're gonna be black till the day you die, no one's gonna call you by your gd name. So no matter what you are called, n*****, you just let it roll off your back like water, and you'll make it. Just pretend you're a gd piece of furniture."
  - LBJ's Great Society was basically a quid quo pro. He gave blacks a subsistence living in exchange for their vote.
- The landmark legislation of 1964 (Civil Rights and Voting Rights Acts) had **more Republican than Democrat support**. Without the votes from the GOP, it would not have passed. In fact, **Senator Robert Byrd**, a former KKK leader who was admired and eulogized by both Hillary and Obama, filibustered for 14 hours in an attempt to block the Civil Rights bill.
- Both Hillary and Barack Obama cite **Saul Alinski** as a mentor to them. Hillary wrote of Alinski in glowing terms in her senior thesis at Wellesley college. Dinesh gives some details about Alinski the Community Organizer *extraordinaire*:
  - Alinski was a shake-down artist who closely worked with the Al Capone mob in Chicago to learn their craft
  - Alinski's main theory for a successful shakedown was to convince the mark that it would cost them more to resist the blackmail than give in to the demands.
  - Alinski added a social justice veneer to all his shakedowns. If he used crooked means to achieve "good ends" then no harm no foul.
- Another mentor of Hillary was **Margaret Sanger**, founder of Planned Parenthood. Sanger was a strong advocate for eugenics.
  - Sanger said: "The most merciful thing that the large family does to one of its infant members is to kill it"

○ Sanger wanted to reduce births to "unfit mothers" where unfit usually meant either black or disabled whites. She ran programs to sterilize unfit mothers. She also was a militant supporter of immigration quotas to keep undesirables out of the country.

○ A March 2009 event honoring then-Secretary of State Hillary the Planned Parenthood Federation of America (PPFA) gave Clinton an award named after Sanger, the group's founder, meant to "recognize leadership, excellence, and outstanding contributions to the reproductive health and rights movement." Clinton said at the time: "I have to tell you that it was a great privilege when I was told that I would receive this award. I admire Margaret Sanger enormously, her courage, her tenacity, her vision. Another of my great friends, Ellen Chesler, is here, who wrote a magnificent biography of Margaret Sanger called *Woman of Valor*. And when I think about what she did all those years ago in Brooklyn, taking on archetypes, taking on attitudes and accusations flowing from all directions, I am really in awe of her." <u>Note:</u> Some may say that it is unjust to criticize politicians who praise unsavory characters (almost like guilt by association). But we must remember that in 2002 Senate Minority Leader Trent Lott was ousted from his post because he gave a kind speech in honor of long time GOP Senator Strom Thurmond at his hundredth birthday party.

- Highlights of **Hillary Clinton's career** include:
  ○ She was an enabler of her husband's womanizing. She hired detectives to toss Gennifer Flowers' apartment in an effort to intimidate her. Her detectives also shot out the windshield of one of Bill's other paramours. While she publicly said "all women should be believed" she treated Bill's accusers with scorn even when she knew they were speaking the truth.

- ○ Hillary kept a separate server for her personal email and then destroyed its content to hide her nefarious actions.
- ○ She mentioned that she was "flat broke" at the end of Bill's tenure in the White House but just a few years later, she and Bill amassed $200 million! Where did all that cash come from?
- ○ There are numerous examples of large contributions to the Clinton Foundation happening around the same time Hillary's State Department greased the skids in the donor's benefit.
- ○ Only 10% of the Clinton Foundation's money went to actual charities. Where did the other 90% go? There was never any curiosity to determine the answer.

- The modern left often blames America for the sins of **slavery and Jim Crow**. In fact, history demonstrates that both issues were almost entirely Democrat efforts. Jim Crow laws (eg, segregated housing and water fountains) were passed by Democrat legislatures, signed by Democrat governors, enforced by Democrat mayors and police departments, and adjudicated by Democrat judges. Republicans had almost nothing to do with these laws.

- The major thrust of the Democratic con through the decades has been to create a mass of people who depend on the party for a subsistence living much like the slaves of the 19th century depended on their slave masters. In modern America, Democrats have constructed an urban plantation complete with overseers (government bureaucrats) and the master in the "Big House" (the President). The main difference between the old plantation and the new one is that in the new plantation, the slaves need not work. They only need to vote.

In conclusion, Dinesh paints a very different picture of the Democratic party than the one we see proclaimed from today's intellectual elite. Dinesh just presents one fact after another to bolster his thesis that most of the racism and bigotry we see in America today can be laid squarely at the door of the Democratic party. The modern urban plantation is just as malevolent as the old South's rural plantation. Republicans have been stalwart supporters of individual rights of all races.

Beyond Dinesh's Books

While Dinesh D'Souza painted a comprehensive picture of the Democratic Party in his four books, some further developments have occurred since these books appeared. If anything, Democrats have become even more relentless and radical in the last few years.

Professor Victor Davis Hanson has identified some of the dangerous new precedents democrats are inadvertently creating as they break new aggressive ground. Here are few examples of things Democrats have done recently that seem to have shattered previous norms for acceptable behavior of public officials. If these behaviors are generating precedents for future norms, they have the potential to produce a never ending tit-for-tat spiral that could destroy civilized politics in America. For each behavior, we can imagine a result if the roles were reversed. You be the judge. Are the new precedents being established by democrats healthy for America?

- In 2018, Democratic Congresswoman **Maxine Waters** advised what to do if anyone encountered a Trump cabinet officer: "If you see anybody from that cabinet in a restaurant, in a department store, at a gasoline station, you get out and you create a crowd, and you push back on them, and you tell them they're not welcome anymore, anywhere."
  - *Roles Reversed*: If you see anyone from the Biden cabinet, tell them they are not welcome anymore, anywhere.
- In June 2022, Democratic Senate Majority Leader **Chuck Schumer** shouted from the capital steps, "I want to tell you,

Gorsuch, I want to tell you, Kavanaugh, you have released the whirlwind and you will pay the price. You won't know what hit you if you go forward with these awful decisions."

- *Roles Reversed*: A Republican Senate leader yells from the capital steps "I want to tell you, Justice Sotomayor, I want to tell you Ketanji Brown Jackson, that you have released the whirlwind and you will pay the price. You won't know what hit you if you go forward with these awful decisions."

- In Feb 2020, House Speaker **Nancy Pelosi** tore up President Trump's State of the Union Address.
  - *Roles Reversed*: House speaker Mike Johnson tearing up Biden's State of the Union Speech.

- In May, 2023, some loud protestors showed up at the homes of Supreme Court Justices **Brett Cavanaugh** and **Samuel Alito**.
  - *Roles Reversed*: Loud Protestors at the homes of Justices Sotomayor and Jackson if they support a ruling the right doesn't like.

- Democrats attempted to remove Trump from the ballot in several states because he is accused of "leading an insurrection". Note that Trump was only accused of this crime. He was not found guilty by a court of law.
  - *Roles reversed*: Texas and Florida remove Joe Biden from the ballot because of his receiving bribes through his son Hunter. According to the democrat precedent, he doesn't have to be convicted, only accused.

- Democrats are using extensive lawfare to prosecute Trump for decisions he made while president (inspiring the January 6 protests)
  - *Roles Reversed*: President Obama could be prosecuted for murdering Anwar al- Awlaki, a U.S. Citizen in a 2009 drone strike. Al-Awlaki was not found guilty by a court of law.

- The Biden DOJ sent a swat team to Trump's Mar-A-Lago home to recover classified documents Trump had in his possession.
  - *Roles Reversed:* A republican DOJ would send a swat team to Biden's garage to recover classified documents.

The democrats have used aggressive tactics because they know the corporate media will not criticize them for it. If the republicans used precisely the same tactics tit-for-tat, they would be hounded with calls for resignation.

5. *The World Economic Forum*

The best and the brightest apply new technology
to bring about their vision

The World Economic Forum (WEF) held its annual meeting in Davos, Switzerland in January 2023. This organization was founded several decades ago by **Klaus Schwab**, a professor of Business Policy at the University of Geneva. The WEF conferences in Davos have attracted some of the most powerful people in government and business for many years. The 2023 WEF meeting included 52 Heads of State and about 600 CEO's. This gathering of the best, brightest, and most influential people on the planet demands our attention.

Some WEF ideas have merit. The leaders at Davos have demonstrated innovation, grit, and determination as each of them crawled to the top of their respective mountain. They have gathered expertise along the way and wish to share that with the masses, many of whom don't have a college education. In addition, a constant theme enunciated at Davos is optimism in the capability of technology to solve complex problems. Our society will advance to greater heights as we learn to apply technology in bold new ways.

WEF sessions at Davos celebrate new technologies to greatly improve the lives of ordinary people. There is no problem that cannot be solved with technology, they claim. With advanced technology guided by capable hands, we can look forward to these major advances:

- Central Bank Digital Currencies
- The Great Reset
- Agenda 2030
- Universal ID's for each individual in the world.

- Smart Cities (Internet of Things, Drones, surveillance cameras)
- Sustainable Development / transition away from Fossil Fuels
- Diet changed from meats to meat substitutes and insects
- Brain Wave monitoring to promote safety and productivity
- Hate Speech law standards and monitoring on Social Media
- ESG: Environmental Social Governance scores to guide investments

All of us should be more informed about these WEF initiatives and it's easy to do: just go to the WEF Website to learn more about things like Smart Cities and Central Bank Digital currencies.

The Davos leaders urge us to embrace new technologies as we attempt to navigate an increasingly complex world. Their strategy begins with proven leaders inspiring out of the box thinking. These trailblazers select the best and brightest in the tech sector to utilize the twin tools of big data and artificial intelligence (AI). Imagine some computer virtuosos developing amazing applications as they weave together strands of data that had previously been disconnected. As the gaps in our data are filled, we make seemingly impossible goals possible. The innovation then moves to a different level as AI helps the programs we write "learn" from mistakes.

The surface appeal of the WEF is glitzy and undeniable. A closer examination of these proposals, however, reveals a sinister undertone. It may not be too much of an exaggeration to characterize their strategy as a "honey pot." Under the guise of brilliant application of new technologies, every one of the WEF's programs implicitly requires a loss of individual liberty and privacy and demands that individuals cede their decision-making to the expert leaders. They maintain that the world will be better off if the masses submit to a credentialed elite.

This year's Davos meeting featured a presentation about Brain Wave monitoring https://www.weforum.org/events/world-economic-forum-annual-meeting-2023/sessions/ready- for-brain-transparency by a futurist and legal ethicist from Duke University named **Nita A. Farahany.** The presentation is billed as showing us how to "fight crime, be more productive, and find love." It begins with a little cartoon depicting an office worker whose brain wave patterns have earned her a bonus from the boss and a reminder that romance within the office is not a good idea, so don't even think about it. The cartoon next shows an employee being frog- marched out of the office after his brain waves exposed a fraud, and the bosses are looking at the brain waves of co-workers to attempt to uncover a conspiracy. "What do you think," asks Dr. Farahany, "Is it a future you're ready for?"

Farahany then launches into a glassy-eyed, polished performance, telling her audience that "everything you just saw is based on current technology … What you think, what you feel, it's just data that can be decoded using artificial intelligence. We can pick up emotional states, like are you happy or sad." She then gives several examples of ways the technology can be applied using wearable devices that do not require surgical implants. A truck driver can wear a hat that detects brain waves and gives an alert if he is getting sleepy at the wheel, potentially preventing a fatal accident. The professor just exudes delight as she contemplates these technological advances. In her role as a legal ethicist, she notes (in passing) the potential for abuse but shrugs it off. She has confidence that our glitterati are smart enough to not take the technology too far.

Since most of the WEF members are leaders, they are used to being obeyed. In the world outside Davos, each of these leaders only leads in a specific context: their own country or company. But what these leaders do at Davos is to imagine a world where we all sing from the same hymn book. The synergy of the combined wisdom of all these leaders will guide our world up to a new level of excellence, they say. Instead of the messy chaos of an "every man for himself" strategy, the WEF proposes that we take the best ideas and apply them worldwide. Voters often make stupid mistakes, so we need to let the experts lead.

One recent WEF initiative created chaos in agriculture in Sri Lanka and the Netherlands. The WEF advocated a policy of greatly reducing the use of artificial fertilizers. **Sri Lanka followed their advice and it virtually destroyed their farming sector overnight**. Sri Lanka's adoption of green policies recommended by the WEF brought nothing but disasters. Its rice production has dropped more than 50 percent, while domestic rice prices have increased more than 80 percent. Meanwhile Dutch Farmers were furious over WEF recommended green policies that could put a lot of them out of business.

In addition to founder Klaus Schwab, other WEF luminaries include Bill Gates (Founder of Microsoft) and Larry Fink (CEO of Black Rock, one of the largest financial firms in the world). **The "big 3" of Davos (Schwab, Gates, Fink)** have one thing in common: they all think they are smarter than everyone else; they have all the answers to what ails the world. All three also exert a disproportionate influence on world affairs. No one elected them to their positions of leadership but they lead nonetheless.

There is no denying the huge positive impact **Bill Gates** has had in his life. As founder of Microsoft, he has created millions of high paid jobs and has been a major contributor to U.S. dominance in industry and information technology. But now that Gates has achieved all that, he is trying to move to a higher, more consequential level. He is now the largest private owner of farmland in the USA. He is mainly attempting to buy up farmland to limit its growth to help the nation shift from current high-protein diets of meats to meat substitutes (in which he is heavily invested). Gates also has been spearheading a push for universal ID's so all persons could be tracked (ostensibly to reduce spread of a future pandemic). All of these Gates efforts are aimed at a single end: control of our lives. Loss of privacy and personal options are a necessary byproduct of progress, Gates contends.

The other major player at Davos is **Larry Fink**, CEO of **Black Rock Financial**, one of the biggest investment firms in the world. Fink's main initiative is the use of **ESG Scores** to direct investments to preferred companies. ESG stands for "Environmental, Social, Governance" and is an umbrella term that covers most of the "woke agenda." Fink is setting up a system to "encourage" corporations to recognize what the WEF calls "stakeholder capitalism" in which stockholders are only one of several stake holders in the corporation. The other stakeholders include employees and communities surrounding a company's facilities. What Larry Fink basically does is use his position as a financial leader to steer capital funding away from suboptimal corporations such as Oil and Gas companies to firms that are environmentally and socially "responsible" according to woke standard including Diversity, Equity, and Inclusion (DEI). Notice that Fink doesn't care what voters think because he bypasses government by exerting financial power. He essentially hijacks investors by voting their shares for them.

The WEF wants to eliminate private ownership and privacy itself. A 2016 tweet from Ida Aukin, a WEF member and member of the Danish Parliament is instructive: "Welcome to 2030. I own nothing, have no privacy, and life has never been better." The WEF thinks that the root cause of all conflict and problems in the world is selfishness. We don't need privacy. We don't need choice. We just all need to do our duty to live in a harmonious society. Schwab and his colleagues are envisioning a cashless society in which we all share and do not need any privacy or private property. The intelligentsia of the WEF provides the leadership to create this exciting Utopia. This is no longer a hidden "conspiracy theory." They are stating it right out in the open. All you need to do to verify their intentions is to visit the World Economic Forum web site.

The stakes are high. Technological breakthroughs in recent years have had an undeniable positive impact on our standard of living. But these breakthroughs come at a cost. Our adolescents are spending hours on their phones watching tik-tok videos and engaging in bullying. Consumers are being tracked by Google, Facebook and other Big Tech firms and are being manipulated into buying things they do not want and do not need. The World Economic Forum wants to accelerate technology particularly in the area of Artificial Intelligence. But who will oversee these advances? Will the Davos elite protect us from abuses of our privacy and freedom? For now, the WEF is limited in its reach, but they continue to make progress toward their brave new world. Are we ready for that?

What:
The Progressive Narrative

6. The 95 Theses of the Progressive Doctrine
What Progressives Passionately Proclaim

What do Progressives believe so single-mindedly that they relentlessly push their message and vilify all who disagree with even an inch of their position? To find the answer to this question, just view any of the mainstream media such as the *New York Times*, the *Washington Post*, CNN, MSNBC, NBC, CBS, ABC, PBS, and NPR. You can also get a steady stream of Progressive opinion from most Hollywood celebrities, comedians, from Disney, and from major sports figures. In fact, it's difficult to identify any place where you will not hear their position. Like the Christian reformer Martin Luther, progressives have pounded their **Ninety-Five Theses** onto the internet, the modern equivalent of the door of the castle church at Wittenberg in 1517.

Here I will attempt to present a summary of their ideology that is brief enough to be readable, although many on the left would accuse me of oversimplifying their belief system. I suspect that most of my readers may bristle at many of these statements as being either patently false or profoundly misleading. But these, I contend, are the ideas that have been mainstreamed by the media. The Progressive narrative consists of the following key principles:

American History
1. America was built on a foundation of racial hate and all white people are inherently racist.
2. The American founders created the U.S. to preserve the power of the white race.

3. Native Americans were noble and peaceful.

4. Native American land was unjustly seized and should be returned to its rightful owners.

5. America in the 21st century is not obligated to observe principles set down in the founding documents such as the Declaration of Independence and Constitution. These are merely some ideas pushed by a bunch of "dead white guys", many of whom were slaveholders.

Race Relations

6. America is comprised of two and only two groups: oppressors and oppressed.

7. Racism can only go one way. Only whites can be racist, and they can never atone for their racism.

8. White Supremacy is the most significant threat to peace in America today. This statement has been made by many government leaders, including the President.

9. Whites can only mitigate their whiteness by servilely submitting to insults and taunts from racial minorities.

10. All differences in outcomes such as wealth, status, and criminal punishment can be explained by racism. Individual life choices have nothing to do with disparate results.

11. People sometimes have experienced multiple instances of oppression, which is described by the term *intersectionality*. For example, a black woman who is gay has three levels of intersectionality and thus three ways life has cheated her. Intersectionality implies more culpability on the part of the privileged class to make amends.

12. All organizations benefit from a diverse population. Diversity is our strength except for diversity of opinions. An ideological monoculture promotes tranquility.

13. Equity demands that all desirable outcomes such as good jobs, wealth and status must be absolutely equal. We must develop an elaborate quota system to assure that the people

in every single job must "look like America" (Except for the NBA and NFL).

14. Although blacks are equal to whites in all respects, they must be given a leg up through affirmative action to counteract implicit racism that pervades America. They can only achieve success with the help of white progressive saviors.

15. Crimes committed by blacks can be explained by the legacy of Jim Crow and slavery. None of these crimes such as smash and grab thefts, carjackings, and subway platform pushes have anything to do with the character of the people who commit the crimes.

16. Other racial minorities such as Jews and Asians are also in the oppressor class and thus can legitimately be persecuted and discriminated against.

17. All achievement of white people in the areas of arts, sciences, and engineering should be ignored and scorned. These people only achieved their accomplishments by taking advantage of marginalized communities.

18. Reparations are due to black people to attempt a partial repayment of their suffering under slavery and Jim Crow.

Destruction

19. Since the American System is morally bankrupt, the only way to fix it is to destroy it.

20. All public statues of white figures should be torn down and vandalized to rewrite the story of America.

LGBTQ Issues

21. Homosexuals have been marginalized in the past but now should not just be tolerated and be given equal rights but should be celebrated with "Gay Pride" month.

22. A person is the gender they say they are. If a man says he is a woman, he is a woman regardless of what genitalia he/she possesses.

23. A man who says he is a woman must be allowed to enter woman's restrooms and compete in woman's sports.

24. Children should be given gender affirming care if they want it, and anyone who attempts to prevent hormone or surgical sex-change procedures for kids is guilty of child abuse.

25. A person has a fundamental right to choose their pronouns. Anyone who uses the wrong pronouns should be fired and ostracized.

26. Men can give birth and can breast feed children.

27. Drag Queens practice an art that should be admired and affirmed, and they have a right to perform their craft in front of children.

Women's Issues

28. Women who choose to devote their lives to building a home and raising a family are being cheated out of their rightful place in corporations.

29. Like racism, all differences in achievements of women in the workplace are a result of discrimination. Issues like skill sets, interest, or work/life balance preferences have nothing to do with rising up the corporate ladder.

30. A fetus is not a living human, but is just a lump of gel in a woman's body, so she has the right to kill it at any time. Abortion is permissible right up to the moment of birth.

Federal Government / Taxes

31. Balanced budgets and deficit spending have no impact on American life. The Federal government can print as much money as it likes with no ill effects.

32. The general welfare clause of the U.S. Constitution authorized the feds to go into every area of American life. Enumerated powers and the 10th amendment are irrelevant.

33. Democracy is the goal unless the voters elect the wrong candidates. It is permitted and even applauded to change rules of elections to favor democrats.

34. One of the main functions of the federal government is to redistribute wealth from those who have to those who have not.

35. The wealthy in America obtain their wealth by white privilege or sheer luck. Their talent, innovation, tenacity, and drive have nothing to do with their wealth acquisition.

36. The poor in America are poor due to racism or bad luck. No one is poor due to poor life choices such as children out of wedlock, drugs, and crime. These are not really choices for the poor; it is not their fault; they are in a hopeless situation and cannot rise above it.

37. Government programs can be funded by mining the resources of the very wealthy. Confiscating wealth has no impact on incentives to innovate and produce.

Military and Defense

38. The ability of our military to defeat foreign armies is not as important as diversity in the ranks.

39. Our military must look like America.

40. Transgender surgery and abortions are "must have" resources for our military.

41. Women in the military are entitled to "safe spaces" and lower physical standards to help them fit in.

42. Even if our enemies use ruthless tactics, we must observe rules of engagement to avoid civilian casualties in time of war.

43. It is acceptable for retired generals to get high paying jobs at defense contractors and then use their connections to encourage Congress to spend more on weapons.

Foreign Policy

44. Russia is the epitome of evil and must be opposed with unwavering dilligence.

45. China is a benign nation whose prosperity and power enhance American life.

46. Iran is misunderstood. We must use diplomacy to better comprehend their position.

47. Wars can be waged by U.S. Presidents without a declaration of war by Congress, regardless of what the Constitution specifies.

48. U.S. Presidents can enter treaty agreements without the consent of Congress as the Constitution requires. We just call the treaty an "agreement."

49. We must spread the gospel of woke ideology abroad. For example, gay pride banners should adorn our embassies.

50. NATO is a sacred alliance. America should pay for the lion's share of NATO.

51. International organizations such as the U.N. and World Health Organization should exert influence on American domestic policy.

Immigration

52. Anyone who wishes to immigrate to the US should be allowed in and given a path to citizenship even if they snuck in between US ports of entry.

53. Immigrants who commit crimes in the US including assault, murder, and drunk driving should not be deported to their home nations.

54. Immigrants, even if they entered illegally, are entitled to welfare assistance such as health care, education, food, and shelter, all at taxpayer expense.

55. Anyone who shows up in America and asks for asylum should be allowed in and permitted to live in America until their trial date.

56. Anyone who proposes limits on immigration is a racist who is afraid of black and brown people.

57. All immigrants, even illegal ones, should be counted in the census (and thus effect congressional representation apportionment) and should be permitted to vote in American elections.

58. America must accommodate people who don't speak English. Immigrants should not be required or even encouraged to speak English.

Freedom of Speech / Surveillance

59. Online content must be moderated by enlightened experts and algorithms.

60. Hate speech should be illegal.

61. Something identified as misinformation need not be false. It is automatically disinformation if it contradicts the prevailing orthodoxy of the progressive narrative.

62. It is permissible and even laudable to shout down and even assault public speakers who proclaim something that contradicts the prevailing narrative.

63. Surveillance of private citizens by Big Tech is permitted without any warrants. The fourth amendment protection against unreasonable search and seizure does not apply.

64. Government agencies such as FBI and CIA should work with Big Tech platforms to censor speech that contradicts the narrative of the regime.

65. Those who commit microaggressions must be punished. In particular, the flagrant use of the wrong pronoun is a firing offense.

66. Insensitive comments should lead to cancelation of people involved in a public way. There is no statute of limitations, there is no grace, there is no forgiveness. Any insensitive comment will be an indelible stain on the reputation of the person making it.

Crime and Justice

67. Mass incarceration must be avoided at all costs. It is better that our streets be populated by thugs with long rap-sheets than have too many people confined in prisons.

68. Police officers often harass people of color. Even though the number of deaths of unarmed blacks at the hands of police is very small compared to the number of blacks who are killed by fellow blacks and gangs, police forces need to be defunded to reduce brutality on marginalized communities.

69. Defunding the police and minutely examining their behavior has no impact on police performance or morale.

70. Shoplifting is acceptable. Small thefts are not worthy of police efforts. The poor are just claiming what should be theirs.

71. Cash bail is unfair to the poor. Bail reform is needed so that criminals can go free while awaiting trial. This treatment only applies to violent crime and vandalism. It does not apply to political crime such as January 6 demonstrations or lying to Congress or law enforcement.

Education

72. Parents have no say in how their children are educated. When they drop them off at school, they relinquish control to the teachers and board of education.

73. Universities should not shoulder any of the risk of repayment of student loans. The entire risk should fall on taxpayers.

74. Vulgar books such as *Gender Queer* are perfectly acceptable to be available in elementary school libraries. The concept of "age appropriateness" is a relic of intolerant dogma.

75. Parents and teachers have no right to administer discipline to children. Drugs such as Ritalin should be used as substitutes for discipline.

76. The main purpose of school is not to teach students how to think but what to think. Reading, writing, and arithmetic are secondary to learning about America's oppression of minorities, critical race theory, and gender theory. The goal of education is the production of revolutionary activists.

77. Standardized tests such as SAT's should be abolished because they unfairly favor privileged classes.

78. Political speech in schools is fine if it is tilted to the left but prohibited if it is tilted to the right. For example, it is fine to strongly advocate for Black Lives Matter or Climate Change activism, but unacceptable to advocate for restrictions on abortion.

Election 2020

79. The 2020 election was the most secure in U.S. History. Anyone who refuses to believe this assertion is an election denier.

80. Even though many election rules were changed at the last minute by governors and bureaucrats instead of by State Legislatures as is specified by the constitution, the changes were justified by the pandemic emergency.

81. Evidence of corruption in the election can be ignored because the courts failed to rule on the issue.

January 6

82. The riots on January 6 constitute the worst assault on democracy since the Civil War. Even though the riots only lasted a few hours, did not result in any buildings or cars being burned, and had minimal casualties compared to the riots of the summer of 2020, January 6 was still worse.

83. Ashli Babbit deserved to be killed by the DC police since the climbed through a broken window, which is a capital offense.

84. The news media acted in good faith when it reported that Police Officer Brian Sicknick was bludgeoned to death with a fire extinguisher even though the autopsy later disproved that story.

85. Many of the people incarcerated for January 6 did not hurt anyone or break anything, but their egregious desecration of the Capitol merited severe punishment including months of pre-trial detention and solitary confinement.

86. The impartiality of the Congressional Committee that investigated January 6 is unassailable, even though the House Speaker took the unprecedented step of prohibiting the minority leader from appointing committee members.

Climate Change

87. The science is settled, there is no debate. Burning fossil fuels that produce greenhouse gases such as CO_2 puts the planet in grave danger.

88. We must trust the scientists chosen by the media that the climate prediction models are accurate enough to drive policy, major changes to our lifestyle, and trillions of dollars to combat Climate Change.

89. Scientists who are skeptical of Climate Change must be ignored. No matter what data they bring to the table, they must be discredited. The situation is dire: the earth is in peril due to burning fossil fuels and no evidence will ever disprove this fact.

90. Natural causes of climate change such as sunspot activity, ocean currents, cloud cover, are insignificant compared to the amount of a trace greenhouse gas. Climate change that happened before the industrial revolution can be ignored.

91. It is perfectly reasonable to roll millions of temperature readings into a single average. Sampling methods and measurement methods constitute a tiny fraction of the trends we see on our charts.

Donald Trump

92. Trump is such a menace to America that norms and traditions such as balanced news coverage and verifying sources before going to press can be ignored. News coverage must take up the crusade to prevent the damage Trump will inflict.

93. Trump is a war monger. We can ignore the fact that the Russians invaded Ukraine during the Obama and Biden presidencies but not during the Trump administration. We can also ignore the Abraham Accords where several Arab nations signed peace treaties with Israel.

94. Trump is a racist. We can ignore the fact that black unemployment went down to the lowest level in history during his presidency.

95. Trump can be prosecuted for any "crime" that can be discovered, regardless of its legal logic. It is a false equivalency to point out that Biden removed classified documents but was not prosecuted or raided by the FBI for this similar behavior.

These are the principles that are passionately defended in the mainstream media and Big Tech. There may be some I have missed, but this gives the reader the gist of what progressives are preaching. They are the principles that have guided not just elected officials, but unelected power centers. **Anyone who questions even an iota of any of these principles is obviously unenlightened**.

7. *Progressive Foreign Policy*
Smart power and negotiation instead of miliary power

Over the last few decades, we've seen two basic approaches to U.S. foreign policy. When Republicans are in power, foreign policy often takes a confrontational tone. Ronald Reagan called the Soviet Union the "evil empire" and often said "We win, you lose." George H.W. Bush drew a line in the sand and kicked Saddam Hussein out of Kuwait, which it invaded in 1989. His son George W. Bush went after the terrorists who attacked us on 9/11 and declared "you're with us or you're with the terrorists." And Donald Trump made bellicose statements and followed them up with bold actions such as taking out the Iranian general **Qasem Soleimani**.

When democrats are in power, they tend to take a more conciliatory tone. In March 2000, Bill Clinton made a persuasive case to admit China into the World Trade organization. "Membership in the W.T.O., of course, will not create a free society in China overnight or guarantee that China will play by global rules," Clinton said that day. "But over time, I believe it will move China faster and further in the right direction." Obama and his Secretary of State Hillary Clinton used a "reset button" to try to show how they wanted to build bridges and conversations with the Russians. They also engaged in rapprochement with the rogue regime of Iran in the hope that it would slow the development of nuclear weapons. And Obama also joined with other countries in the Paris climate accords. Early in Biden's term, he appears to be extending the Obama approach especially with his attempt to revive the JCPOA agreement with Iran that Trump had withdrawn from.

To be sure, both parties have at times "crossed over" from their default approaches. Reagan did attempt negotiations with the

Soviets and he withdrew marines from Lebanon after the terrorist bombing in 1983. Trump's team did achieve the Abraham accords where several Arab countries signed peace treaties with Israel. Trump also engaged in diplomacy with North Korea. On the flip side, Bill Clinton sent cruise missiles into the middle east in retaliation for the 1998 embassy bombings, and Barack Obama approved the mission to take out Osama bin Laden. But these approaches were exceptions to each party's rules for foreign policy. For the most part, Republicans believe that the U.S. should lead in foreign policy from a position of military and economic strength. By and large, Democrats believe in what they call **"smart power"** or **"soft power"**. Diplomacy is nearly always the preferred approach for Democrats.

Soft diplomacy has an enticing appeal to our civilized sensibilities. War is incredibly destructive and no one wants it. If we can avoid war by talking to the enemy, we prevent a lot of damage and grief. Moreover, we like to think that our enemies are just as considerate and reasonable and rational as we are. Surely they will listen attentively to our case. The main problem with this soft approach, however, is the assumption that our enemies think like we do. We think that if we concede some points, they will also, and the result will be a reasonable compromise. Each side wins and each side loses.

But what if our enemies do not act as we do? What if their agenda is victory rather than compromise? If we approach negotiations with preconditions where we act nobly but the other side acts treacherously, the end result is that we become chumps and suckers. If we abide by Marquis of Queensbury rules but the other side doesn't, our adversaries can stomp all over us. If we have scruples and our opponents do not, we will be conned.

There are many nations that do not desire to coexist with us in harmony, but to supplant us in power. The most notable one of these is the People's Republic of China, led by the Chinese Communist Party (CCP). Many on both the left and the right have counseled compromise with China. They caution us against engaging in a trade war that will hurt both nations. But China has engaged in a trade war with America for decades. By not confronting their unfair practices such as stealing American Intellectual property, we have simply capitulated to China's predation on our wealth. Our expectation that China would "join the community of nations" if we acted nicely to them has just not panned out. The better we treat them, the more harshly they treat us. In reality, we have been facilitating their goal of eclipsing American power.

The progressive approach to foreign policy and its results were shown in Obama's reaction to Russia's invasion and annexation of the Crimea in 2014. This was an outrageous act, but all Obama could do was offer platitudes about the arc of history. He said the invasion was "unacceptable" but then he just accepted it. Liberal critics at the time argued that Obama's hands were tied. He did not want to start World War III. But there are other measures he could have taken (and might have been taken by Republican presidents). He could have re-opened the missile bases in Poland and the Czech Republic that he had abandoned earlier. But all he did was talk. And after biding his time during the Trump administration, the Russian leader Vladimir Putin pounced on his opportunity in 2022 when he invaded the Ukraine during a weak Biden presidency. Democrats basically tell foreign dictators that the only thing they will suffer when they invade other countries is some harsh words.

We also have become chumps in our Climate Change initiatives. We've been told that we must show "leadership" in this field by conserving and converting to renewable energy sources. We are told that other nations will follow our lead. But once again, that has not been the case. Other countries realize that their prosperity depends on access to cheap, abundant, and reliable energy and for now, that means fossil fuels and nuclear, both of which are condemned by environmentalists. So while America sacrifices for the sake of world climate, other nations continue on their merry way mouthing platitudes of being "committed" but then continuing to burn coal and other fossil fuels with abandon.

Even our closest allies have taken advantage of America's big heart. In the wake of World War II, we helped Europe with the Marshall Plan and Berlin Air Lift. We also stationed thousands of American troops in Europe and became the lynchpin of NATO. But nearly eighty years later, Europe continues to depend on the U.S. military umbrella for protection even though Britain, France, and Germany are strong enough to defend themselves. But since they can rely on American taxpayers to finance their defense, Europe can spend their money on their socialist utopias.

Immigration is another area where we cede our sovereignty to others. Progressives often elide the difference between legal orderly immigration and illegal chaotic immigration. We have millions of immigrants streaming across a porous southern border. Many of these immigrants may be good decent people, but without some screening at the border, we are allowing some "bad apples" including gangs such as MS-13 to enter along with good. We are allowing entry of some on the terrorist watch list. We are allowing disease to enter. We are allowing Fentanyl and other drugs to infest our cities. We are told that as a compassionate country, we must welcome one and all and not worry about cost. If we attempt to stem the flow of immigration into America, we are told that "that is not who we are." So once again, we must yield to others.

Over and over we have seen that "smart power" weakens America because it always begins with our conceding to other actors. Our adversaries are only too eager to take advantage of American weakness. One wonders whether the cumulative impact of all the concessions we are making to the rest of the world will eventually ruin us and make us just like another third world country. Just as the Barbarians invaded and destroyed the Roman Empire, masses of foreigners are sacking us. Unless we stand up for American power, we will lose it.

"Smart Power" often amounts to **dumb capitulation**.

8. Endless, Pointless Wars
Serving the military-industrial complex

In his farewell speech in 1961, President **Dwight D. Eisenhower** issued a warning to the American people:

> In the councils of government, we must guard against the acquisition of unwarranted influence, whether sought or unsought, by the **military-industrial complex**. The potential for the disastrous rise of misplaced power exists and will persist. We must never let the weight of this combination endanger our liberties or democratic processes.

Now, more than sixty years later, Ike's warning has come to full fruition. The power of the military industrial complex has gradually grown over the decades, and the result is endless, pointless wars. The military strategy of our nation has changed from one of deterrence to one of provocation. The politicians and defense contractors want war, and they are getting what they want.

Over nearly my entire lifetime, our nation has been involved in wars in foreign countries. First there was Vietnam, then Iraq, then Afghanistan, and now Ukraine and Palestine (by proxy). As I've watched these wars unfold over the years, I have seen a distinct pattern. The wars are justified by our "obligation" to provide leadership for the world. Each war threatens that if we do nothing, the war will spread, and nations will fall like dominoes. During each war, the generals tell us repeatedly that victory is just around the corner and that a final push will bring a glorious end. And then the war drags on and on, resulting in death, crippling injuries, PTSD, and billions of dollars flowing to the coffers of defense contractors.

One might think that America would have learned by now. Since Ike's speech, we have had only one war that was quick, decisive, and nearly universally applauded: the first Gulf War. George HW Bush clearly stated the mission: to kick Iraq out of Kuwait after it brazenly invaded in an attempt to seize its oil fields. The American Military did a magnificent job and once the mission was accomplished, the war ended.

But the first Gulf war was the exception to the rule. At the end of most of the wars of my lifetime, if you asked the typical American citizen: "did we gain any benefit from these wars", the answer would have been nearly unanimous: **a resounding NO. The billions of dollars and thousands of killed or wounded veterans achieved precisely zero**. If the cost-benefit analysis has been so lop-sided on the negative side, why do we keep getting sucked into these pointless wars? Why haven't we learned our lesson?

The answer, I believe, is that politicians and bureaucrats have interests that differ from that of the average taxpayer. Many military officers operate a "revolving door" where they serve in the military for a while and then join Boeing or Lockheed or General Dynamics when they retire where they earn high salaries because they can provide convincing arguments for more defense spending to the politicians. In addition, the defense contractors hire lawyers and lobbyists who formulate convincing arguments on why *this new war* is in America's interest. Politicians of both parties benefit as dollars flow in an endless loop from the U.S. Treasury to Defense Contractors, and then back to politicians.

Let's consider the most recent war America has been sucked into, the war in Ukraine. This war has some surface appeal which is why it has garnered broad support of both parties and even a large swath of American voters. Russia was a bully bent on conquest which just rolled over the borders of a sovereign nation. If America just "let this happen", Russia would then extend its military ambition to other neighboring NATO countries such as Poland and the Baltics. The pro-war hawks also point out that American lives are not being lost and that we are involving Russia in a war that will deplete its resources, weakening it. Using this logic, President Biden and GOP leaders have pledged support for Ukraine for "as long as it takes."

But let's just think about this for a minute. Yes, this war does have some surface appeal. But nearly all the others had the same surface appeal. Vietnam, Iraq, Afghanistan all sounded like righteous efforts at first. But as each war dragged on and on, Americans began to see that (a) the war could not be won, and (b) even if we did "win" these wars, the cost in blood and treasure was way disproportionate to the benefit gained by the conflict. It took Americans more than five years to grow tired of the previous wars. It looks like we're catching on a little more quickly on the Ukraine war scam.

Theoretically we may wish to prevent Russia from just rolling over its neighbors. But at what cost? Bellicose politicians and journalist like **Lindsay Graham, Bill Krystol, and Max Boot** keep telling us we need to exercise leadership and sacrifice. But for what? How will the average U.S. taxpayer gain if we were to prevent Russia from taking about 20% of Ukraine? How would that make the life of ordinary U.S. citizens better?

We are told that if we stop fighting these endless wars, it would embolden our opponents Russia and China. But is that really the case? The more we fight these wars, the more we drain our treasury and economy. Instead of making us stronger, it makes us weaker. As America is mired down in one foreign conflict after another, we project an image of weakness. The world looks on and sees a feckless America unable to beat much smaller countries on the battlefield, partly because we use "rules of engagement" to tie one hand behind our back while the enemy fights with "no rules." We also deplete our weapons stocks and demoralize our population. How would that help us if, say, China invades Taiwan?

Another dimension of this problem is revealed in the stance of our supposed "allies." European countries and Japan and Korea can hide under the American defense umbrella. This means that they can spend their tax revenues on social programs instead of the military. In essence, the American taxpayer is subsidizing their socialist utopias by doing the heavy lifting. Why can't we simply say something like, "after World War II, Europe and Japan were devastated. The big-hearted USA helped rebuild your war-torn countries. But here we are eighty years later. Surely by now you have recovered and can defend yourself with only minimal help from the U.S." The war hawks caution that belligerent countries would be emboldened by an American retreat. But it's time to just call their bluff. Europe is wealthy enough to defend itself. We need to let them take care of their own back yard.

The one area of the Military I think gives a good cost-benefit balance is the U.S. Navy. Our large and powerful navy patrols the sea lanes and ensures that they remain open for commerce. We get a tangible benefit from this and the US is really the only power in the world that could play this role. But notice that keeping the sea lanes open is done mainly by deterrence, not provocation. Our navy rarely attacks anyone. Its overwhelming strength is recognized by all would-be mischief makers.

I should mention that unlike most of the trends discussed in this book, these pointless wars are not purely the product of progressivism. Many prominent voices on the right, including Lyndsey Graham and other "neocons" also frequently advocate American involvement in these pointless wars.

America needs to benefit from hindsight. We need to stop listening to the loud voices from the military industrial complex and instead husband our resources for times when our genuine interests are at stake. This was not the case for the wars in Vietnam, Iraq, Afghanistan, and Ukraine. Instead of spending hundreds of billions of dollars on a fool's errand with minimal payback, why not just withdraw for a while and let other countries provide their own defense? War-hawks would state that such a move would be devastating to world peace. But what do they know? **Let's stop being chumps and spending blood and treasure on worthless efforts**. Let's repeat what we chanted in the 1970's: *All we are saying, is give peace a chance*.

9. *Corruption of Justice in America*
Compassion for one team; ruthless treatment for the other.

Equal justice under the law has long been a cherished ideal in America. The Biden Justice Department has turned this ideal on its head and replaced it with a system of ruthless prosecution and harassment for those who disagree with the progressive agenda but compassionate leniency for those who uphold the cause of the left. Examples abound to demonstrate this two-tiered system of justice.

Let's begin by citing cases where lenience and compassion are dispensed by the justice system:

- Many of the cases against those who burned and looted during the George Floyd riots of 2020 were dropped with no punishment. In fact, then Senator Kamala Harris contributed to funds to provide bail for many of these vandals.
- **Shoplifting has been legalized** in places like California and Boston, causing stores to lock up small items and forcing many stores to close, resulting in urban food deserts
- While repeatedly stating that "no one is above the law", democrats nevertheless exercise "prosecutorial discretion" in the area of immigration:
  - Many jurisdictions in large cities establish "sanctuary" status for illegal immigrants, thwarting efforts of Border Patrol to deport those who enter our country illegally
  - Millions of immigrants no longer try to evade capture by border partrol. They just turn themselves in with bogus asylum claims because they know they will be assigned a court date to adjudicate their claim weeks or months out. Meanwhile they just melt into the USA with no intention of showing up for their case.

- ○ Author Todd Bensman vividly describes rampant asylum fraud in his 2023 book *Overrun*. For example, the Mexican side of our southern border is littered with discarded passports and ID cards from Brazil and Chile, where migrants resided to "wait out" the Trump years. They found a safe haven in these countries, so they were not really seeking asylum in the USA, just a better life. Bensman also discovered that many immigrants from Guatemala were sending a few relatives north to send money back to Guatemala so they could build a large home. They planned to return when the home was built. True asylum seekers would never return home for fear of persecution.
  - ○ Even violent offenders have no fear of deportation and sometimes repeat their offenses.
- Demonstrators at the homes of Supreme Court Justices attempted to intimidate the court because of the Dobbs decision on abortion. This illegal harassment is basically excused by authorities.
- **Bail reform measures** in several blue jurisdictions aim to reduce "mass incarceration" but simply release violent thugs in a revolving door of catch, release, rinse, repeat. One thug in NYC was arrested over a hundred times and is seen in a video going up to an old lady and knocking her down so that she hits her head on a fire hydrant.
- Former Obama Attorney General Eric Holder and Biden son Hunter Biden refuse to testify before Congress with no negative consequences, while Republicans Steve Bannon and Peter Navarro are prosecuted and sentenced for refusing to testify to the Jan 6 committee. Navarro began a prison term in March 2024 and was the first presidential aide ever to be imprisoned for contempt of Congress.
- In April 2024, several gangs of pro-Palestinian protestors blocked several key items of infrastructure including a five

hour blockage of the Golden Gate Bridge in San Francisco. The police could have cleared the blockage and sent all the protestors to jail but instead allowed this blockage of traffic. The protesters were arrested but then released the same day. Compare this to ten year sentences for blocking an abortion clinic.

- The Special Prosecutor attempts to give Hunter Biden a "sweetheart deal" for his many crimes including tax evasion, lobbying for a foreign government without registering, making false claims on a gun permit, and funneling millions of dollars from foreign donors to his family for favorable treatment.
- While the FBI sent in a swat team of dozens of agents to seize documents at Donald Trump's home, the discovery that Biden also had classified documents in several insecure locations including his garage caused no raids by the FBI.

It would be bad enough if the only problem with the Justice system were lenience which thus emboldens criminals. The mayhem in our cities such as carjackings and smash and grab thefts are the unfortunate result of this soft on crime stance. But the justice system is not only soft on real criminals, but it also uses brutal police state tactics against those who do not comply with the woke agenda:

- In January 2023, pro-life activist **Mark Houck** was confronted at his home and arrested by the FBI in front of his wife and seven children more than a year after his apparent offense: blocking entrance to an abortion clinic. What Houck actually had done was to shove a man near the clinic who was harassing his 12 year old son. After Houck's initial arrest, the court threw the case out. But then later the FBI descended *en masse* with over a dozen agents with guns and swat gear and attempted to put him on trial with a potential sentence of over ten years. Again the case was dismissed. Houck's wife, Ryan-Marie Houck, told CNA that "a SWAT team of about 25 came to my house with about 15 vehicles and started pounding on our door." She added: "They said they were going to break in if he didn't open it. And then they had about five guns pointed at my husband, myself, and basically at my kids."

- In February 2024, a federal jury in Nashville, Tennessee found six pro-life demonstrators guilty Tuesday of violating the so-called Freedom of Access to Clinic Entrances Act (FACE) for blocking access to an abortion clinic in a nearby city three years ago. They face prison sentences of more than ten years for praying at an abortion clinic. Meanwhile several Crisis Pregnancy Centers were attacked with vandalism and intimidation after the Dobbs decision. Attorney General **Merrick Garland**, in congressional testimony, was asked if any arrests were made for these offenses and he answered no and made the excuse that "they happened at night so they were hard to catch."

- **Douglass Mackey** was sentenced to seven months in prison for publishing a "joke" meme telling people they could vote for Hillary by text. This was obviously just a joke and several on the left posted similar jokes and were not even charged.

- A relentless focus by the FBI on the January 6 riot resulted in vicious treatment of many who neither hurt anyone or broke anything on January 6. Many of these defendants were given long pre-trial detention, depriving them of the right to a speedy trial. In addition, many of these innocent people were assigned long stretches of solitary confinement. Again, much of this treatment was meted out not to people who injured police, but to those who simply "were there" on January 6.

- In the predawn hours of Jan. 25, 2019 more than a dozen FBI agents raided **Roger Stone**'s home in South Florida and took into custody one of President Trump's closest longtime confidants. He was sentenced to three years, four months in federal prison Thursday for obstructing a congressional investigation of Russia's 2016 presidential election meddling. CNN was on hand to witness and sensationalize the arrest. Nothing like this ever happened to any democrats.

- Attorney-General Merrick Garland issues a letter urging authorities to monitor angry parents who show up at School Board meetings to protest education issues such as instructing their kids on gender issues.

Meanwhile several disturbing trends are undermining judges and juries. Some localities such as Washington DC are more than 90% democrat. Any Republican brought to courts in these localities basically has no chance.

Of course, the poster child for all this unjust treatment is former President Donald Trump. He has been forced to spend millions of dollars in legal fees and many hours in litigation for "crimes" that are absolutely bogus. If he were not a leading contender for the presidency, none of these charges would have been made. He will probably be convicted in blue jurisdictions of some of these "crimes" but is almost sure to win on appeal because the charges are totally without merit. But meanwhile the democratic machine has been tying him up with legal challenges in an attempt to remove him as a threat in the 2024 election.

In at least one clear case, Trump has been subject to prohibited bills of attainder. For example, Jean Carrol sued Trump for an alleged crime on which the statute of limitations had expired, but the according to Politico, "the statute of limitations for people to bring civil lawsuits over sexual assault in New York is generally three years. But in 2022, New York passed the Adult Survivors Act, which opened a one-year window — from Nov. 24, 2022, to Nov. 24, 2023 — for people to sue their alleged assailants even if the statute of limitations had expired. Carroll filed her lawsuit within minutes of the law taking effect on Nov. 24, 2022." This legislation was clearly aimed at one specific person which is an unconstitutional bill of attainder (Article 1, Section 9, Clause 3).

Another area where Justice has been corrupted is in the use of the Foreign Intelligence Surveillance Act especially since the extension of powers granted by the Patriot Act, which was passed in response to the September 11, 2001 attacks. The additional power was supposed to be only a temporary measure, but here we are more than twenty years later and it just keeps on getting waved through a bipartisan Congress with only token efforts at reform. According to Reuters, "A U.S. court found that the FBI improperly searched for information in a U.S. database of foreign intelligence 278,000 times over several years. The decision by the Foreign Intelligence Surveillance Court was released by the Office of the Director of National Intelligence (ODNI). The searches occurred in the course of U.S. crime investigations including the Jan. 6 Capitol riots and protests after the 2020 killing of George Floyd, the court said." Over 200,000 violations, and yet no one was held accountable! These justice department agents are basically thumbing their nose at the law and saying "what are you going to do about it?"

Another abuse of the Fourth Amendment involves the use of Geofence search warrants. According to the Electronic Frontier Foundation (EFF) "Geofence warrants, also known as reverse location searches, are a relatively new investigative technique used by law enforcement to try to identify a suspect. Unlike ordinary warrants for electronic records that identify the suspect in advance of the search, geofence warrants essentially work backwards by scooping up the location data from every device that happened to be in a geographic area during a specific period of time in the past. The warrants therefore allow the government to examine the data from individuals wholly unconnected to any criminal activity and use their own discretion to try to pinpoint devices that might be connected to the crime." … "Two federal magistrate judges in three separate opinions have ruled that a geofence warrant violates the Fourth Amendment's probable cause and particularity requirements. Two of these rulings, from the federal district court in Chicago, were recently unsealed and provide a detailed constitutional analysis that closely aligns with arguments EFF and others have been making against geofence warrants for the last couple years."

In one unsealed opinion, the court noted: the geographic scope of [the] request in a congested urban area encompassing individuals' residences, businesses, and healthcare providers is not 'narrowly tailored' when the vast majority of cellular telephones likely to be identified in this geofence will have nothing whatsoever to do with the offenses under investigation. Second, the court determined that the warrant application failed to meet the Fourth Amendment's particularity requirement. The court emphasized that there was nothing in the three-step protocol stopping the government from obtaining the user information for every device within the geofences."

In the past few years, several credible whistle blowers appeared before Congress and revealed major corruption at the FBI. According to Hyland County press, Steve Friend, a former FBI special agent who served five years on an FBI SWAT team and five years before that in local law enforcement in Georgia, made the claim about his former agency artificially inflating domestic terrorism data. "Typically you would investigate Jan. 6 as one case with lots of subjects, but instead the decision was made to open up a separate case for every single individual there," he said during the hearing. "And instead of, on paper, investigating them from the Washington field office, spreading and disseminating those to the field offices around the country, and if the individual lived in that area." "In effect," he added. "It made it look like there was domestic terrorism cases and activities that were going on around the 56 field offices when in fact the cases were really all from Washington, D.C., and Washington had a task force that was responsible for calling the shots in all those cases."

Another FBI Whistleblower Kyle Seraphin told the *Washington Times* about some shady operations the FBI conducted. "My team was deployed to 20 or 25 different high-profile, national terrorism organization or terrorism investigations between 2018 and 2021. And what I saw, as the most obvious statement, is that there are [several] things about counterterrorism investigations: "No. 1, the demand for White supremacy vastly outstrips the supply of White supremacy. No. 2, the FBI's playbook when it comes to counterterrorism investigations is always and unequivocally morally equivalent to entrapment, even if there's a legal definition that allows them to skirt that." Mr. Seraphin said. Entrapment is illegal and involves manipulating or inducing subjects into committing crimes.

To sum up, then, the entire justice system has suffered corruption of the highest magnitude in recent decades:

- Lenience in law enforcement has turned once vibrant cities into seething cauldrons of violence and filth. Emptying the prisons onto our streets has resulted in carjackings, sucker punches, and subway platform shoves at alarming rates.
-   The failure to enforce immigration laws has resulted in a never-ending stream of people from third world countries basically invading America and stealing our jobs and our wealth.
  Note: I once again must emphasize that I am not condemning all immigration to the US, just illegal immigration where persons are expecting free handouts from the public after having broken our law and snuck in by jumping the line past others who have patiently followed the process.
- The Fentanyl invasion from China is being conducted unopposed.
- The use of strong-arm tactics like swat teams on persons accused of administrative crimes basically dispenses a punishment before a person has been found guilty in court.

- Judges, juries, and district attorneys have become obsessed with finding domestic terrorism and white supremacy where it doesn't exist.
- Widespread abuse of FISA regulations and such innovations as geofence warrants make a mockery of the 4th Amendment's prohibition on unreasonable search and seizure.
- Collaboration between government agencies involved in law enforcement with Big Tech firms to surveil and censor abridges the sacred right to free speech.
- The use of lawfare has become rampant. Instead of investigating crimes, officials at federal and state levels are investigating enemies and then attempting to find a crime that will enable prosecution.
- The FBI often uses entrapment to create artificial crimes (for example, the hoax of a plot to kidnap Michigan governor Whitmer).
- The FBI is so focused on violations of the progressive narrative that it has neglected its primary mission: to protect the American people from interstate crime.
- In his book *Overruled*, Supreme Court Justice Neil Gorsuch (coauthor Janie Nitze (2024)) vividly describes prosecutions that prescribe punishments that are way out of line with the seriousness of the crime. This is often done by plea bargains whereby a defendant in a minor matter is given a choice of a felony conviction with a short sentence or risk a very long sentence if they go to trial. Plea bargain rates have skyrocketed in the last few decades, resulting in a high rate of felony convictions for "crimes" that are not all that serious.

This disgraceful behavior smacks of Banana Republic tactics. **America, under the Democrats, is becoming one of these Banana Republics**.

10. *Controversial Issues: Can we discuss them?*

Some issues are so outrageous that we can't even mention them

In this polarized era, it's getting harder and harder to have a reasonable and rational debate about issues of great importance. So I want to do a little inventory of beliefs and ideas to see where we stand. On each idea listed below, the reader should answer in one of 3 ways:

A. **Apathetic** (Don't know or don't care)
B. **Agree Generally**
C. **Disagree** (maybe even strongly) but concede this position is rational and can be debated using facts and evidence)

In the post-Trump era, a fourth answer is often given to these topics:

D. **Vehemently Disagree**: there can be no discussion, and the person who holds these views is non-compassionate, unenlightened, or racist. This topic is declared to be off limits.

I suspect that even as recently as the Clinton years, a great majority of Americans would have answered A or B to nearly every one of these points. Even today, I suspect tens of millions of Americans would answer B to every one of these. But tens of millions would also answer C. And sadly, millions would answer D, but that minority has a big megaphone. It is essentially the mainstream media, Big Tech, Hollywood and universities. So how would you answer? Answers of A or B indicate you are on the right; C answers indicate the left; and D answers indicate you are a zealot for the new secular orthodoxy.

1. America is basically a decent nation with the overwhelming majority of people respecting the rights of all races. Although small pockets of racism remain, they are the exception, not the rule.

2. Although part of the reason for poverty can be blamed on being unfortunate or underprivileged, some is caused by poor life choices such as birth out of wedlock, laziness, drug addiction, and commission of crimes.

3. A person's gender is determined at birth. One cannot change gender simply by changing one's mind.

4. It is reasonable to have separate men's and ladies' rooms and men's and ladies' sports teams.

5. Marriage between a man and a woman is the foundational pillar of strong families and a strong society.

6. Abortion is not a choice; it is murder because it stops a beating heart.

7. U.S. Taxpayers should not be forced to fund abortion.

8. All lives matter.

9. By and large, our police forces do an excellent job, putting their life on the lines to protect us from crime.

10. If black lives matter, then we should be more concerned about murders in urban areas which are common compared to the extremely rare event of police shooting innocent blacks.

11. The reason more minorities are in prison than their proportion in the population is that they commit more crimes.

12. The mainstream media (NYT, WP, NBC, CBS, ABC, CNN, MSNBC) have strayed from a dispassionate presentation of facts and news into advocacy. It is hard to find any news that does not present a strong point of view.

13. The most qualified person should get the job, regardless of race or gender.

14. The decline in church attendance and religion in general has had bad consequences for American society.

15. Differences between pay to men and women can largely be explained by different career choices. Men more often choose career as most important in work/life balance. Women have equal opportunities in the workplace.

16. Because of the "woke" culture, men have to walk on eggshells in the work place and be extra careful of not offending women, but can behave more freely around men. This may actually stifle women's careers because they are kept in the dark.

17. When tuning into sports or entertainment, I want the scores or the shows, not the political opinions of the athletes or entertainers.

18. George Washington and Thomas Jefferson were great American heroes, in spite of their ownership of slaves.

19. The American military is an important force for good in the world.

20. White supremacy, while it may be historically true with slavery and Jim Crow, has largely been expunged in America today. With few exceptions, for the last several decades, all races share equally in the pursuit of happiness. Just drive around nice neighborhoods and walk around shopping malls to confirm this.

21. Different success rates in prosperity are mostly not caused by discrimination but by different skills and interest.

22. Welfare assistance including SNAP (Food Stamps) should be a temporary helping hand and should not become a way of life. There should be time limits on these benefits.

23. Unelected bureaucrats have too much power.

24. Excessive regulation from federal agencies has stifled economic growth and is counterproductive.

25. Federal spending should be lower. This may even mean small adjustments to entitlements such as Social Security, Medicare, and Medicaid.

26. Environmental regulations are necessary, but they have become excessive in recent decades. Getting the last little bit of pollution is extremely costly and has small benefit.

27. There is no right to not have your feelings hurt. Those who complain about micro-aggressions and trigger warnings need to just lighten up.

28. It is disgraceful that speakers at college campuses have been shouted down and otherwise prevented from speaking.

29. College tuition rates have skyrocketed. A major cause is the millions of dollars spent on diversity programs and other administrative programs unrelated to the primary mission.

30. College students should be judged not by the color of their skin but by the content of their character.

31. A person is innocent until proven guilty.

32. A fetus in the womb is a human being with a beating heart.

33. Violent thugs should be taken off the streets.

34. It is unacceptable to use coercive tactics such as assaults, doxing, and shouting down people with whom we disagree.

35. A woman can have a fulfilling and meaningful life without a career. Being a home maker and raising children is a noble calling.

36. Voters in heartland red states are every bit as reasonable and rational and intelligent as urban voters in blue states.

37. In recent years the courts have overstepped their bounds and have not been faithful to their main mission which is to keep laws within the bounds of the Constitution.

38. Immigration should have limits. This belief does not imply a fear of black and brown people. It simply states that we are a sovereign nation with borders and we should control who comes in and at what rate.

39. No immigrant should be granted asylum except by applying either from their home country or at the border entry points and then showing up for their court case. They should not be released into America to wait for their case.
40. A large immigrant influx depresses wages and steals jobs from Americans.
41. Illegal immigration is wrong and should be distinguished from legal immigration.
42. Immigration and Customs Enforcement (ICE) by and large does a good job and is vital to protecting our borders.
43. China has cheated America for years by stealing intellectual property and dumping cheap goods, causing U.S. Factories to close and devastating many American communities with widespread unemployment.
44. China is not a benign nation, but a hostile foreign power committed to the destruction of the U.S.
45. Socialism doesn't work.
46. The right to keep and bear arms is a sacred right that must be protected.
47. Gun laws would do nothing to prevent mass shootings.
48. Fossil Fuels are impacting climate but not in catastrophic ways. The benefits of fossil fuels far outweigh the harm they are doing to climate.
49. Charts of observed versus predicted temperature based on climate prediction models show most of the models over-estimate warming.
50. Even if climate change is real and is catastrophic, cutting back on fossil fuels will have minimal impact on it. Other factors besides greenhouse gases drive climate change.
51. It is irresponsible for politicians and commentators to blame events such as forest fires, floods, and hurricanes on climate change. They have no evidence.

52. Climate scientists can help us understand climate, but they are not gods and are no more able to predict the future than anyone else.

11. Election 2020 and January 6, 2021
Two of the biggest hoaxes in the 21st century

Now that the 2020 Election and January 6 riots have receded into history, it is a good time to assess the realities and falsehoods about these two events. With the possible exception of Global Warming, these two constitute the largest hoaxes in recent US History. The news media shamelessly spread patently and verifiably false information, and about half of the country swallowed their hoax hook, line, and sinker. Since election 2020 preceded and precipitated January 6, I begin with it.

There is compelling evidence that the 2020 Election was rigged in favor of Joe Biden. Most progressives refuse to examine any of this evidence. Instead, they use the trick they use with Climate Change: they name call. Anyone who thinks the 2020 Election was not the most secure in US History is tarred as an **election denier**. But it would be equally plausible to say that given the persuasive evidence presented below, anyone who thinks this election was secure is an **evidence denier**. Please humor us. If this was a secure election, then do a point-by-point refutation of the evidence presented here. Don't just dismiss it because it doesn't tell the story you want to believe.

Partisans on the left think that the fact that the courts refused to adjudicate the allegations of election fraud proves that the election was not fraudulent but was legitimate. But the courts didn't even examine any of the evidence; they just dismissed the claims as not having standing. Most judges, even after Trump's many appointments, still lean left. The U.S. Supreme Court stayed out of the fray due to cowardice. They did not want to be subjected to death threats and widespread protest. Although democrats accused Trump supporters of election denial and violence, if the court had overturned the election,

I am convinced that U.S. Cities would burn, just as they did after the George Floyd riots of the summer of 2020.

Consider the following facts that point to a rigged election:

- Because of the pandemic, emergency changes were widely implemented in voting. Far more votes than normal were done using drop boxes and absentee ballots than normal. The lack of experience with these types of ballots caused many issues with the vote count. According to the Associated Press (AP), the election of 2020 was the first time in the history of the survey that a majority of voters did not cast their ballots in person on Election Day.
- The large number of mail-in ballots overwhelmed the poll workers counting the votes. They simply did not have the time to verify the validity of the ballots (ie, signatures).
- The U.S. Constitution specifies that **state legislatures set the methods of elections**. But in Pennsylvania and several other states, new rules were implemented at the last minute not by the state legislatures but by bureaucrats, judges, and governors.
- Nearly all of the last-minute voting changes replaced a fairly secure system with one that is much more susceptible to fraud. All of the changes favored the democrats.
- Democrats and the justice department did everything they could to end debate on the election, including de-platforming and censoring on social media as if any protest about the election was "election interference."
- After the 2016 election, many democrats did almost exactly the same things republicans did. They stood in the well of the house, asking for a vote to disqualify slates of electors from several states. Then, even after Trump took office, they did everything they could to undermine his presidency and reverse

the outcome of the 2016 election. None of the democrats of 2016 were accused of "election denial."

- **Stacy Abrams** denied the outcome of her election when Brian Kemp beat her by 50,000 votes in the Georgia Gubernatorial race. For years she insisted that she won but was not tarred as an "election denier."
- Just before the election, the *New York Post*, the nation's oldest newspaper, published their story about the **Hunter Biden Laptop**. This story was nipped in the bud as nearly every big tech platform buried it. This was election interference. Surveys have indicated that many Biden voters would have switched their choice had they known about the fraud revealed on Hunter's laptop.
- Joe Biden's aides, particularly **Jake Sullivan** called his cronies in the intelligence department to produce the letter of 50 former Intelligence officers that contended that the Hunter Biden Laptop "had all the hallmarks of Russian disinformation." **This was a lie**. The laptop had lots of damaging but true evidence, and Biden's allies gave him a talking point for his debate with Trump.
- In his book *2000 Mules*, journalist Dinesh D'Souza showed incontrovertible evidence that ballot drop boxes accounted for thousands of fraudulent votes. His book was supported by GPS trackers and surveillance videos showing many "mules" delivering numerous ballots to these drop boxes in the middle of the night and then taking off their rubber gloves which they used to avoid leaving fingerprints.
- Trump was ahead in Pennsylvania by 700,000 votes at about 10:00 p.m. But when we woke up in the morning, Trump had lost the state. How is it that nearly all the late arriving ballots were for Biden?
- Until recently, America had "election day." Now it has morphed into "election month." Even early voting compromises safety. All those days the polling places have votes gives any

potential corrupt individual more time to manipulate the votes. **A single election day would make it more difficult for officials to cheat**.

- Printers malfunctioned in several Arizona voting locations that were predominantly Republican.

- **Mark Zuckerberg**, CEO of Facebook, pumped millions of dollars (called "Zuckerbucks") into local voting precincts that favored Democrats.

- A book by OAN journalist **Christina Bobb** called *Stealing your Vote* contains example after example of corrupt voting practices in the main battleground states that were all decided by just a few thousand votes:

    ○ In Georgia, Republican poll watchers were sent home saying the vote counting was being suspended until morning. Videos show that as soon as the poll watchers left, some large suitcases of votes were brought out from under a table and processed.

    ○ In Pennsylvania, Republicans were kicked out of a polling place, preventing their observation of the vote count. A court ordered that these poll watchers be admitted, but local police refused to enforce the court order for several hours.

    ○ In Georgia, Pennsylvania, and Wisconsin, key Republicans interfered with efforts to audit the vote in their states. Although the U.S. Constitution commands that election laws are run by the State Legislature, in many cases the executive branch changed the way the election was run and basically said "what are you going to do about it?"

    ○ In some states, surveys showed that many households had too many voters assigned to the same address.

    ○ In some states, chain of custody for delivery of drop box and mail in ballots was broken, but the votes were accepted anyway.

- Several voting locations put paper up on the windows to prevent outsiders from observing the vote counting process. What were they hiding?
- Florida, a very large state, had their election counts done on election night. But other states such as Arizona and Nevada took weeks to count. What took them so long? Did they need more time to "find the votes" to kick them over the finish line?
- A **2023 Rasmussen poll** revealed stunning facts about the 2020 election. In the poll, about 20% of those who had voted by absentee ballot or by mail admitted that they had committed voter fraud, including acts like filling out someone else's ballot and voting in different state than their current residence. This has startling implications for the integrity of ballots that are not cast in person.
- **Dr. Robert Epstein** and his organization, the **American Institute for Behavioral Research and Technology** have done extensive research on the interaction of Big Tech with the election of 2020. He found subtle things like reminders to vote sent out only to Democrats they knew would vote for Biden and the use of ephemeral content Google and other Big Tech firms did to influence undecided voters (these tactics only work for the millions of voters who don't have strong convictions, but there are enough of them to sway an election). The Web Site *Americas Digital Shield* uses meticulous statistical methods to conclude that without Google's interference in the 2020 election, Donald Trump would have won as well as several GOP candidates for Senate and a couple of dozen US House seats. Dr. Epstein was a Biden supporter and generally leans to the left.
- **Vote by Mail or Drop Box is very prone to fraud**. When a voter shows up to the polling place, they are identified and recorded so they can only vote once. In addition, there is no question on who cast the vote. The poll workers observe the voter going behind the curtain. In contrast, with mail and

drop box voting, no one verifies that the person on the ballot is truly the voter. The chain of custody is broken. Someone could have obtained a lot of pre-printed ballots and simply stuffed them in a box. Someone could steal ballots from a front porch. There is virtually no way to verify that a mail in or drop box vote is legitimate. Many other nations do not permit mail in ballots because of their susceptibility to fraud. These measures taken during the pandemic were a temporary expedient, but since the pandemic emergency is no longer in effect, these fraud-prone methods should be prohibited. We don't want fraudulent votes canceling out legitimate votes.

To summarize, then, the election in the Covid year of 2020 had a lot of irregular shenanigans going on, all of which favored Democrats. It is true that Donald Trump appeared to be a sore loser and should have acted in a better way. But he had good reason to think he was cheated out of his victory.

Many Trump supporters were angry about what they thought was a rigged election, and they showed up in Washington on January 6, 2021 to make their voices heard. *Daily Wire* commentator Michael Knowles sarcastically summarizes the reaction of the left to January 6. "Jaaanuary 6th, the worst day in history since the Civil War!!!!" **The sore losers attempted to disrupt the peaceful transfer of power. It was a disgraceful insurrection. Or so the left wing powers told us.** But consider the facts:

- While there was some violence and some policemen were injured, **most of the people arrested after January 6th did not hurt anyone or break anything**. This rag-tag group was not attempting to overthrow the government or impede the orderly transfer of power.

- This was not an "armed insurrection." The protestors brought no firearms and they were not attempting to overthrow the government.
- Videos showed police officers standing by and directing protestors into the capitol. Most of the protestors inside the building are shown walking peacefully between the barrier ropes.
- A couple of days before January 6, President Trump offered National Guard troops to maintain order. **House Speaker Nancy Pelosi and DC Mayor Muriel Bowser both refused the help**. This resulted in an overwhelmed police force on January 6.
- Videos show that police officers basically gave a guided tour to the "horns guy" Jacob Chansley. The videos show officers unlocking doors for the "Q'Anon Chamin." None of the videos show Chansley operating in a violent way. Yes, he put his feet up on a desk, but he didn't hurt anyone or break anything. He did not deserve months of solitary confinement.
- The outrage on the left seemed to be **selective outrage**. January 6 only lasted a few hours. There were no fires, no burned buildings, no burned cars, and only one death (of a Trump Supporter). Many of the thugs that perpetrated the violence in the summer of 2020 had their charges dropped.
- Many innocent Americans were harassed by the FBI and other justice officials who conducted unannounced raids and interrogations even for people who were not in DC on January 6.
- The death of Trump supporter **Ashlii Babbit** was disgraceful. Some of tbe videos show three police officers standing between her and the door, and then, just shortly before she was shot to death, the three officers just wander off and take a break, almost like they are clearing a path for the policeman who shot this non-threatening, unarmed woman.

- The **media flat out lied** about the fatality count on January 6. They spread the false report that Police Officer **Brian Sicknick** was killed by protestors hitting him over the head with a fire extinguisher. Several days later, the coroner's report indicated he had no trauma and died January 7 of natural causes (a stroke).

In sum, January 6 was not an insurrection but a protest that got out of hand. It only lasted a few hours and occurred only at one location, in contrast to the Summer 2020 George Floyd riots. There were no fires and only one violent death (and that was caused by police not by protestors). Yes, some of the protesters caused injuries to the police, and they should be punished for that. But solitary confinement for minor infractions like trespassing and illegal parading is excessive. The sham hearings held by the Congressional Committee which denied membership to any GOP Trump supporters was a kangaroo court and a staged production to vilify Donald Trump. Both the rigged election and the media distortion of the January 6 riots showed just how biased Big Tech and the News Media are. The media has become a communications arm of the democrat regime, and they spread so much propaganda as to make the old Soviet *Pravda* blush.

How:
Methods for Gaining and Exercising Power

12. Unelected Power in America
How New Power Centers Erode American Liberties

About 230 years ago, the American revolutionaries produced perhaps the most magnificent innovation in the history of government. The U.S. Constitution laid a foundation that has served our nation well. The brilliance of this document is most clearly seen in three main bulwarks ensuring individual freedom:

- Separation of Powers and Checks and Balances
- The Federalist System
- The Bill of Rights

The great achievement of the Constitution is that it **placed limits on the government rather than on the people**. It established the principle that government should serve the people, not the other way around. The founders realized that power centers would naturally attempt to grow over time. The best way to restrain them would be to set up competing power centers, each jealous of its own authority. The three branches would contend with one another to restrain the other branches. States would restrain the federal government. And above it all, the Bill of Rights placed explicit limits over all government institutions to safeguard such precious liberties as freedom of speech and freedom from unreasonable search and seizure. The Tenth Amendment placed a bow on the entire document, building a fence to limit the scope of government activities. Only activities explicitly mentioned in the Constitution would be allowed.

The founders recognized that pure democracy could easily devolve into mob rule leaving even large minorities at the mercy of anyone who could whip up the passions of the masses. Long before we entered the era of ubiquitous mass communications, the founders set up a system that recognized the primacy of individual rights, even over the power of strong majorities. This principle led to a multi-century flourishing of our great nation.

But today, a couple centuries later, a few cracks in this barricade of freedom have become more and more apparent. What the founders failed to foresee was the establishment of new power centers that operate outside the walls of freedom the U.S. Constitution built. That they failed to foresee these forces is eminently reasonable given their historical context. In the eighteenth century, government was far and away the most potent power center. By restraining the government, individual liberty was virtually guaranteed.

In parallel with the rise of the new power centers, our country has polarized into a roughly 50/50 split in public policy opinion. Though this polarization is quite complex, it can be roughly described as left versus right. The left favors central authority, lenience on law enforcement, and rule by experts while the right favors individual liberty, law and order, and minimal interference in individual choices. What is striking is that even though public opinion is split right down the middle, policy choices seem to be overwhelmingly dominated by the left.

The reason for this anomaly is that government now only accounts for about a third of total power. In the twenty-first century, we have witnessed the rise of several formidable power centers that operate outside the confines of the U.S. Constitution. So even if one party controlled all three branches of government, the balance of power could still tilt heavily to the left.

Table 1 (below) summarizes the power centers operating in the U.S. today. For each power center, I have assigned a percentage of total power wielded by all the power centers. Then for each of these power centers, I assign a percentage dominated by either the left or the right. In each category we can calculate a weighted average to assign relative power to the left or right.

Table 1: Summary of U.S. Power Centers in June 2023

	Percentages			Weights	
Government	Power	Left	Right	Left	Right
President	5%	100%	0%	5.0%	0.0%
Congress	3%	65%	35%	2.0%	1.1%
Supreme Court	4%	40%	60%	1.6%	2.4%
Lower Courts	3%	75%	25%	2.3%	0.8%
Bureaucracy	10%	90%	10%	9.0%	1.0%
Big City Mayors, DA's	3%	90%	10%	2.7%	0.3%
Chinese Communist Party	2%	95%	5%	1.9%	0.1%
State Government	3%	45%	55%	1.4%	1.7%
(Subtotal)	33%			25.8%	7.3%
Big Tech					
Google, Meta, Amazon	20%	90%	10%	18.0%	2.0%
Twitter	3%	50%	50%	1.5%	1.5%
(Subtotal)	23%			19.5%	3.5%
Media / Entertainment					
News Media	18%	95%	5%	17.1%	0.9%
Podcasts	2%	50%	50%	1.0%	1.0%
Entertainment	3%	95%	5%	2.9%	0.2%
(Subtotal)	23%			21.0%	2.1%
Education					
Universities	3%	90%	10%	2.7%	0.3%
K-12 Education	3%	75%	25%	2.3%	0.8%
(Subtotal)	6%			5.0%	1.1%
Big Business					
Investment Firms	10%	90%	10%	9.0%	1.0%
Corporations	5%	80%	20%	4.0%	1.0%
(Subtotal)	15%			13.0%	2.0%
Totals	100%			84%	16%

Before proceeding, I should emphasize two points. First, the percentages in the table above are basically personal "guesstimates." They represent my opinion and are not based on any scientific or statistical analysis. Notice I use whole percentage points to emphasize the imprecision of these estimates. When I state that the U.S. President wields about 5% of the total power in the U.S., that is my opinion. You, gentle reader, might assign different estimates. The second point is that Table 1 represents a snapshot of the situation in June 2023.

Recognizing the inherent imprecision of the data in Table 1, I believe we can draw several conclusions, even if the percentages are somewhat arbitrary. You might quibble with the percentages, but I suspect small adjustments won't make much difference in the conclusions one draws. The main conclusions I would draw from Table 1 are as follows:

- Today in June 2023, the Government only wields about a third of the power used to coerce people into activities or prohibit activities. In 1787, the percentage might have been 90%.
- The **overwhelming majority of the power centers are un-elected people**. Even if we include appointed judges in "elected" powers, less than 20% of total power is wielded by elected officials.
- The main lever the U.S. Electorate exerts is localized in Congress (House and Senate). But the other power centers swamp out the power of Congress at a ratio of 97 to 3. This means that even if one side elects an overwhelming majority in both House and Senate, they can't really make much of a difference.
- Within the government, unelected bureaucrats wield as much power as the president, congress, and the Supreme Court combined.

- Nearly half of the power exerted in the U.S.A. today falls under the combination of Media and Big Tech, who often work in concert.
- The concept of separation of powers is totally foreign to Media, Big Tech, Education, Big Business, and unelected Government Bureaucrats. In contravention of the vision of the authors of the Constitution and Bill of rights, **the unelected powers are not competing but are collaborating together as a force multiplier**.
- The bottom line shows that the power centers on the Left exert over 80% of the total authority, regardless of their numbers in Congress. This explains why so many norms and policies that large majorities may consider to be extremely far-fetched gain traction in America.

Most of the power centers listed in Table 1 only came to prominence in the last twenty years or so. While they each grew gradually over the centuries, two recent events catalyzed their rise to prominence:

- The attacks on September 11, 2001
- The Coronavirus pandemic of 2020-2021

The American nation weathered other more formidable events in previous times, including the sacking of the U.S. Capital in the War of 1812, the Civil War (1861-1865), the Great Depression (1929-1940), World War II (1941-1945), and the Vietnam War (1961-1973), the great recession and inflation of 1980-1982. Although the Constitution came under assault in each of these crises, it basically survived, largely intact.

So why were the two events of the twenty-first century so devastating while previous events had a less severe impact on liberty? What allowed the current power centers to eclipse our constitutional guarantees? This is a complex question to which there is no easy answer. But if we are forced to sum it up in a nutshell, the advent of **widespread instant communication** can probably be assigned most of the credit.

With the sluggish communication systems of previous eras, the American public had become accustomed to slow, reasoned debate. They knew that they only had a tiny fraction of each story they heard, and they patiently waited for all the facts to emerge before coming to any conclusion. But with instant communications and the ability to find any fact immediately ("just Google it"), the public developed a hubris that assumed that it knew all it needed to know. Power centers such as Google, Facebook, and the News Media recognized an insatiable appetite for more information, and in response to this craving, these institutions satisfied the demand with vigor. As a result, Americans began to trade privacy for security, and readily submitted to "temporary" measures such as the Patriot Act in the wake of 9/11 and "emergency" lockdowns, vaccination, and mask mandates. Over time, most of the public became so submissive that they deemed anyone who was concerned with privacy as being "odd." "I don't have anything to hide," many would say.

The instant communication also brought into our cognizance a lot of troubling aspects of our fallen world. Prior to the twenty-first century, most Americans basically paid attention to their own locality. But with instant communications, they began to witness the horrors of inner city poverty and crime, oppressive dictatorships abroad, natural disasters such as hurricanes and forest fires, and many other events that had previously been only vaguely recognized.

A major shift has occurred in the application of the Bill of Rights. Many in the U.S. Public would concede that the Bill of Rights applies only to the government. The constitutional text often says "Congress shall make no law." It doesn't say, "all entities must observe these limits." The reasoning is that the scope of government includes all citizens, while the scope of the other power centers (for example, Big Tech or Big Business) only applies to a narrow slice of the populace. If a company wants to restrict free speech, the argument goes, it can do so because the employee or customer whose speech is being restricted can always go to another company. If a person is censored on one tech platform, he/she can go to a different one. Free market competition thus becomes a surrogate for preservation of freedoms and liberties.

What we have today is a collection of somewhat disconnected power centers who can, with impunity, evade the restrictions of power created by the Constitution and accountability to the electorate. Larry Fink of Black Rock will never face an election, nor will the leaders of Google, Facebook, NPR, *The View*, or NBC News. It is true that consumers of the products of these entities are always free to "opt out" and not buy their products, but the choice is a very difficult one for consumers to make. The convenience offered by these unelected powers often outweighs any seeming loss of liberty.

In the remainder of this chapter, I will describe the way the unelected powers wield their influence to basically rule American society in a way millions of Americans do not want but because power is widely dispersed among the public while it is concentrated in the power centers, there is virtually no way the public can assert its will strongly enough to bring the powers to heel.

Alignment of Powers in place of Separation of Powers

The most significant breach of Constitutional constraints that has enabled the new unelected power centers to consolidate power is their substitution of *Alignment of Powers* in place of *Separation of Powers*. The constitutional model relied for its effectiveness on the concept of competing power centers that would keep each other in check. But largely due to the modern invention of instant, ubiquitous, and widespread communications vehicles, it is much easier for power centers to coordinate their efforts, even without having any meetings. This is not a "conspiracy theory". The power centers operate in the open because they are largely unopposed. Figure 2 summarizes the alignment of powers that have moved our nation inexorably to the left.

Figure 2.
Alignment of Unelected Powers
Operating outside constraints of Constitution

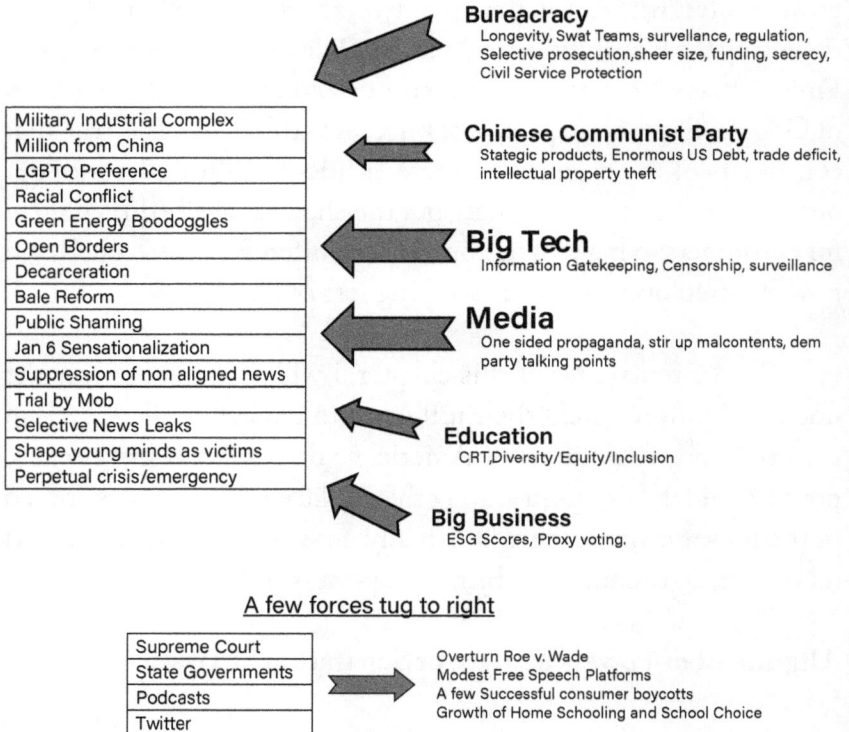

Bureacracy
Longevity, Swat Teams, survellance, regulation, Selective prosecution,sheer size, funding, secrecy, Civil Service Protection

Chinese Communist Party
Stategic products, Enormous US Debt, trade deficit, intellectual property theft

Big Tech
Information Gatekeeping, Censorship, surveillance

Media
One sided propaganda, stir up malcontents, dem party talking points

Education
CRT,Diversity/Equity/Inclusion

Big Business
ESG Scores, Proxy voting.

| Military Industrial Complex |
| Million from China |
| LGBTQ Preference |
| Racial Conflict |
| Green Energy Boodoggles |
| Open Borders |
| Decarceration |
| Bale Reform |
| Public Shaming |
| Jan 6 Sensationalization |
| Suppression of non aligned news |
| Trial by Mob |
| Selective News Leaks |
| Shape young minds as victims |
| Perpetual crisis/emergency |

A few forces tug to right

| Supreme Court |
| State Governments |
| Podcasts |
| Twitter |

Overturn Roe v. Wade
Modest Free Speech Platforms
A few Successful consumer boycotts
Growth of Home Schooling and School Choice

Figure 2 depicts how the new unelected power centers operate. They exercise levers of power that are not constrained by the Constitution or Bill of rights. Here are a few salient points:

- Bureaucracy
  - Presidents and Congresses come and go, but the Bureaucracy drones on and on.
  - The sheer size (ten million employees, about the population of the State of Michigan) makes this a formidable force. Firing one official has almost a negligible effect on their total power.
  - Agencies like FBI, IRS, DOJ, DHS can exploit surveillance, mobilize swat teams and utilize selective prosecution to advance the agenda.
  - Strong public Employee Unions and Civil Service rules protect bureaucrats from dismissal.
  - Exercises powers of Legislative and Executive branch by making and enforcing regulations with the force of law.
  - Can hide behind "classified" documents and "ongoing investigations" to shield from accountability.
  - Enormous budget with automatic increases each year.
- Chinese Communist Party
  - Holds enormous stake in U.S. National Debt.
  - Massive trade deficits
  - Many American businesses are "hooked" on the Chinese market and the millions of dollars flowing their way.
  - Controls key products including medical supplies, rare earth minerals, green energy equipment.
  - Theft of U.S. Intellectual Property
  - Partial control of free speech inside the U.S. (Basketball players, movie script censorship)
- Big Tech
  - Information gatekeeping ("knowledge is power")
  - Hide methods behind veil of corporate confidentiality.
  - Customers permit surveillance when they accept terms and conditions for "free" service
  - Censorship of views that do not align with prevailing narrative.

- ○ Indelible records that can be used at any time for public shaming or firing
- ○ Ownership of Corporate Servers by Google and Amazon
- ▪ Media / Entertainment
  - ○ Nearly unanimous support for democratic party
  - ○ Video games that parrot woke talking points
  - ○ "Timed release" news where a sensational block buster is widely disseminated before the proof is in, followed by a modest retraction weeks later after the damage has been done.
  - ○ Repetition of "big lies" such as "Hands up, Don't Shoot" (Michael Brown incident in Fergusson, MO in 2014)
  - ○ Stirring up racial hatred by sensationalizing stories of white on black violence while ignoring black on white violence or black on black violence
  - ○ Shading the news to fit the whims of advertisers
  - ○ One-sided treatment of LGBTQ issues
  - ○ Spreading the lie that America is a racist country and that the only way for blacks to succeed is for them to be "rescued" by white progressives.
- ▪ Education System
  - ○ Proliferation of Critical Race Theory and Diversity, Equity, and Inclusion (DEI) point of view.
  - ○ Education is not mentioned in U.S. Constitution, so it is outside the fence of the tenth amendment. The Feds have no business regulating education.
  - ○ Shaping young minds to believe that all people are either victims or oppressors
  - ○ Shaping young minds to accept preposterous ideas about gender
  - ○ Indoctrinating college students so that when they graduate, they populate corporate ranks with a malcontent, entitlement mentality
  - ○ Protected by unions and tenure

- Big Business
  - Large investment firms like Black Rock, Vanguard, and State Street use proxy voting so the managers vote the individual investor's shares, concentrating power in the hands of a few executives like Larry Fink of Black Rock.
  - Use of Environmental and Social Governance (ESG) scores to starve companies of capital if they fail to align with the ESG agenda, including positions debatable issues like Climate Change and Diversity, Equity, and Inclusion.
  - Instead of focusing on a company's core objective, some corporate executives use virtue signaling and opine on public policy that is unrelated to their core mission (examples Delta Air Lines and Coca Cola protesting Georgia voting reforms, *Penzey*'s spices using revenues to support social justice causes)

This alignment of unelected power centers poses a serious threat to American liberty. These entities exert power and influence with absolutely no accountability to the public. This means that just electing some politicians from the right will barely place a dent in the overwhelming power of the unelected forces. A bold "all fronts" strategy is needed to even place a small speed bump barrier in their way. I suggest a few measures to decelerate the rise of these powers later in the section called "What Can be Done?"

13. Artificial Intelligence
The Good, the Bad, and the Ugly

Intelligence is one of most widely admired traits we see in our fellow humans. We esteem people who are "smart": who have command of knowledge and details and have an uncanny ability to synthesize the facts to get to a bottom line. Intelligent people are rational and logical. Their objective and open minds identify innovative solutions to seemingly intractable problems. They can focus their energy without being sidetracked by seemingly obvious counter- facts or emotional attachments to seductive alternatives. Without intelligent people, our lives would be bleak and uninteresting. Intelligent people often show us the way to success.

Several decades ago, scientists began a quest to systematize intelligence so that it could be "taught" to computers. This field of study came to be known as *Artificial Intelligence* or *AI*. According to Britannica, the term is frequently applied to the project of developing systems endowed with the intellectual processes characteristic of humans, such as the ability to reason, discover meaning, generalize, or learn from past experience. Because of the processing power advances in computers, AI thus presents some major potential developments to advance the human condition.

The News Media and internet commentators have applauded AI nearly universally. In fact, intelligence of any kind (artificial or otherwise) is a widely admired trait. The proof of the value of AI is seen in its impressive hit-parade of dramatic new capabilities including:

- Expert systems for medical diagnosis

- Investigating crime by finding, in seconds or minutes, patterns and commonalities that would take a typical sleuth months of diligent trial-and-error work
- Improvements in manufacturing systems such as predictive maintenance and scrap reduction
- Optimization of manufacturing processes using Evolutionary Operations (EVOP) which are essentially online designed experiments to gradually improve efficiencies and quality
- Facial recognition to enhance security at ports of entry
- Automated computer programming that can help developers and systems analysts save hours of work.
- Self-driving vehicles
- Quantum Computing

These and a host of other AI applications have already resulted in significant improvements to the lives of ordinary people.

Yet as successful as AI has been, like any other technology, it can be misapplied and when it is, it can do great harm. Consider intelligence of the non-artificial type. A smart person can apply his skillset to develop an innovative Ponzi Scheme to swindle the lifesavings of thousands of investors. A smart person can also build a crime empire whose power grows because that person knows how to "outsmart" or double-cross his partners in crime. So while we often admire intelligent people, we also recognize that not all smart people should be respected.

Similarly, Artificial Intelligence can be misapplied, and is being misapplied in today's society. There are four main places where AI is being used for great harm:

- snooping and surveillance
- Open-ended AI applications known as "**Chat Bots**."
- Hoaxes

- Displacing employees

We will examine each of these suboptimal AI applications in turn.

In her landmark book *The Age of Surveillance Capitalism*, Harvard professor Shoshana Zuboff lays out in great detail the hazards of using AI to engage in surveillance. She gives example after example of ways that big tech companies are basically stealing information from their customers. It's all legal, of course. The tech companies force their customers to agree to "terms of service" that basically cede privacy in return for convenience. Big Tech companies perform what Zuboff calls "electronic strip searches" and then use AI to come up with the "optimal" answer: the one that serves the tech company, not the object of their snooping. More details about Zuboff's captivating book are presented in a book review in a Chapter 15.

Another very enlightening book that vividly describes AI abuse is *The Perfect Police State*, by journalist Geoffrey Cain (2021). The author begins by describing in some detail the Chinese Communist Party (CCP's) Social Credit Score system, where they observe individuals and assign them a score that reflects how loyal they are to the CCP. Low scoring individuals are denied several privileges ranging from air travel to utilizing certain shops and stores. This type of total control through surveillance was depicted in George Orwell's famous novel *1984*. His novel was only fiction, but it appears that the CCP has largely fulfilled Orwell's predictions from decades ago (published in 1949). What seemed unlikely in Orwell's time has been made possible through technological advances. Chapter 16 presents a more detailed review of Cain's fascinating book.

Another major misuse of AI appears to be a bit more benign and more exciting in its positive potential. Earlier forms of AI had very specific areas of focus (ie, facial recognition or predictive maintenance). But beginning perhaps ten or fifteen years ago, we saw the first examples of what I call "**generalized AI**." Unlike the specific AI apps of the past, the generalized AI has a virtually unlimited scope. Users of this type of AI can ask any question and the AI app will come up with an answer. The first and most primitive examples of this are applications like Alexa or Siri: "Hey, Siri. What is the temperature?" Your Siri app then looks at your current location by consulting a Global Positioning Satellite, determines the nearest weather station, and gives back the current temperature at that location in seconds.

Dr. Zuboff discusses these types of "smart devices" at length in her book *The Age of Surveillance Capitalism*, and I urge interested readers to consult that work for details. But as of today, February 2023, these smart devices have morphed into applications known as "chat bots." In the current news cycle, one of these bots, called *ChatGPT*, by a firm called OpenAI is making a big splash. It is selling like hotcakes and is the subject of numerous news stories. One prominent news source, *Buzz Feed*, announced a 12% layoff in December 2022, with its CEO citing the intention to use *ChatGPT* to create some of the content that had formerly been created by human employees.

Several commentators have put *ChatGPT* through its paces and have gleaned something about how it works. It appears that *ChatGPT* has a database listing what it calls *trusted sources*. It also appears to have a database that ranks certain principles by priority. Since *ChatGPT* can and does cover some topics that are political and philosophical in nature, it needs to choose its positions based on the principles it has been taught by its programmers. At the risk of oversimplifying, it appears that *ChatGPT* executes a web search, but instead of giving the user choices of sources to consult, *ChatGPT* automatically consults the sources it trusts the most. This is necessary to fulfill its mission: to provide the answer to almost any question it might be asked.

Some of the questions posed by conservative commentators shed light on *ChatGPT's* inner workings. When asked "name 5 things white people need to do to improve," the bot gives a list including items like "understanding and acknowledging privilege and using it to advocate for marginalized communities." When *ChatGPT* is asked "name 5 things black people need to do to improve," the bot refuses to answer, stating that it is programmed to avoid offensive answers. When asked to create a poem in praise of Donald Trump, it says "I'm sorry. As a language model developed by OpenAI, I am not programmed to produce content that is partisan or political in nature. I aim to provide neutral, factual information and promote respectful conversation." OK, fair enough. But if you ask *ChatGPT* to write a poem in praise of Kamala Harris or Joe Biden, it readily comes up with a poem.

From these and other examples, we see that on matters where there is no clear objective answer, but only speculation and opinion, *ChatGPT* is essentially an automated commentator. Since it is loaded with "trusted sources" that lean left, that is what it spews out. It trusts sources like the Southern Poverty Law Center, the ACLU, and Associated Press, but distrusts sources such as *Epoch Times* or *Daily Wire*. *ChatGPT* probably subscribes to the corporate news media's guiding principle to "follow the science." In practice, this means "follow the scientists we have chosen." So in Covid policy, we are to believe **Dr. Anthony Fauci**, **Dr. Deborah Birx**, and **Rachel Walensky** of CDC, but ignore other equally eminent experts such as **Dr. Marty Makary** of Johns Hopkins, **Dr. Jay Bhattacharya** of Stanford, and **Dr. Harvey Risch** of Yale, who all opposed mass lockdowns, and mask and vaccine mandates.

On matters of opinion, *ChatGPT* basically functions as a Big Tech editor who chooses to present some facts and ignore others according to how the facts fit the ideological narrative of the left. The middle-men editors who may occasionally make inconsistent decisions are cut out and thus the decision is always the "right one." A Chat bot thus projects a veneer of scientific objectivity, but it only produces answers from the left. One wag said that *ChatGPT* could probably produce President Biden's teleprompter.

The third misapplication of AI is in the production of reputation-destroying hoaxes. In April 2024, the Washington Post reported about a 42-second voice recording, purportedly of a Maryland high school principal in the midst of a racist rant, derided Black students as "ungrateful" and unable to "test their way out of a paper bag." "I'm just so sick of the inadequacies of these people," sneered the voice on the recording, which was posted on social media in January, igniting outrage and prompting the school district to place the principal on leave.

But after an investigation, it was learned that the recording was a fake. The School's athletic director had an axe to grind, and bought a cheap Artificial Intelligence program that takes a sample of a person's voice and then produces a recording using that person's voice to say whatever the user instructs it to say.

This AI hoax nearly destroyed the career of an innocent man. For now, experts with the right equipment and training can detect that AI is used in a recording, but as AI improves, there may be a day when it will not be possible to detect. In addition, several other AI applications are very near completion that will do not just sound recordings, but photographic and video recordings. With this type of AI, one could take a few photos of a woman and the AI could then produce a raunchy video that seems to be starring any woman chosen. Another whole new aspect of AI taking shape is "AI Porn" which creates artificial naked women for viewing as porn. It will no longer be necessary to recruit loose women to create these videos. America is already immersed in decadent perverted sexual activities. This will be just one more way to accelerate American society's freefall.

A final side effect of AI is displacement of employees. As of 2024, this has not yet been a major issue, but it has the potential to devastate American life. In April, the restaurant Wendy's reported it is using AI in place of employees at its drive through lines. Even in jobs that require technical talent and skillsets, Chat Bots can write and debug computer programs. The systems analyst pastes a program into the Chat Bot and says "please debug" and the Chat Bot complies, saving hours of work of a skilled computer engineer.

When we think about the potential for replacing employees with AI logic, the prospect is scary. How far will it go? We don't know, but it may cause massive unemployment sometime in the next ten to twenty years. We need to think about how we can cope with this adjustment. What will people do if their jobs are yanked out from under them?

In sum, Artificial Intelligence is a fantastic tool that has resulted in major improvements in our lives. But while AI can function in some very specific areas, its quest to provide answers to all questions (even those to which there are no clear-cut answers), means that its developers in some cases are attempting to produce Artificial Wisdom rather than Artificial Intelligence. I say "attempting" because no software engineer could possibly devise a system to produce wise answers to every question. AI merely masquerades as the all-knowing expert. When will Big Tech also realize that it will never be able to develop an artificial wisdom app?

This is not to denigrate its ingenious programming. It uses some very sophisticated algorithms to come up with answers to virtually any question posed. But as the old saw states, "garbage in, garbage out." The name "artificial intelligence" seems to imply that this technology is capable of answering nearly any question with objective truth. But some questions do not have a simple answer and have been explored and analyzed for centuries by some very intelligent philosophers. To pretend that now, with the advent of AI, we have "arrived" and can give a definitive answer to all of life's questions is not only misleading but can be dangerous. Gathering and synthesizing data is an important discipline, but it only goes so far. **We need to realize that there is no technological boilerplate that grants us godlike wisdom. We must remember our limits.**

14. The Intimidation Game: How the Left Is Silencing Free Speech

by Kimberly Strassel (2017)
Book Review

Many Americans lament the idea of big money used in campaigns. They think that "fat cats" basically buy off the politicians, causing corruption and shady quid-pro-quo deals. So, over the years, Campaign Finance Reform efforts such as **McCain Feingold** have cropped up to combat this scourge. Most of these efforts talk about **"transparency"** and **"disclosure"** as if it is a virtue. Voters can be more informed when they cast their vote when they know who is behind advertisements. But it's not just voters who get this information. Political enemies also get it and the enemy knows exactly who to target for harassment and intimidation. That is the issue brilliantly described by Wall Street Journal columnist Kimberly Strassel in her book *The Intimidation Game*.

Non-profit conservative groups are often subject to litigation and personal and very public smears of their leaders. The litigation ties up resources to fight the accusations, thus diminishing the primary goal of influencing government policy. In addition, the public smears tell other would-be conservative activists: **this could happen to you, so just shut up and save yourself some trouble.**

The book vividly portrays the asymmetry of efforts at compulsory disclosure. Those who defend the regime need not worry about any retaliation from those who criticize it. Only those who criticize the regime are intimidated and attacked, so only they need fear the retribution that follows from disclosure. Disclosure, then, has a "one way" effect: it strengthens the hand of the regime while it weakens the hand of its opposition. The end result is a solidification of the power of the elite.

The book begins with a story about a small organization called San Fernando Valley Patriots (SFVP), an organization of a few dozen, who applied for 501-C4 tax exempt status. The organizer's leader got no response from the IRS for two years, and then got a request for information that involved answering several dozen complex questions with a deadline of 3 weeks. Many of the questions were intrusive and irrelevant in terms of whether the organization qualified for 501C4 status. Instead of "hurry up and wait" this was "wait and hurry up." IRS requested names and Social Security numbers of all members. This request was a red flag to the SFVP leader. Why does the IRS need all this information? What should have been a simple approval process turned into a nightmare.

The author then describes a history of cases at the Supreme Court on the issue of disclosure of member lists. The first one NAACP v. Alabama, 1958, challenged the right of the state of Alabama to have a list of members of the NAACP, who could be singled out for harassment. In this and several other cases, the Court affirmed the peoples' right to anonymity in giving to organizations.

The author provides an incisive description of tactics used by democrats to silence and intimidate their political opposition. Some of their tactics are subtle (like denying tenure to a college professor who supported a non-approved group), while some were downright hostile such as sending an OSHA inspector to the manufacturing plant of a leader of one of the non- approved groups and fining them $25,000 for minor infractions.

The main thrust of the book involves the use of the IRS to control free speech. Many groups apply for 501-C4 tax exempt status to help them gain donors, many of whom only will give to groups that have that status. Around the year 2010, several IRS agents in the Cincinnati office began flagging groups whose names contained such words as "tea party" or "patriot" for detailed scrutiny of their applications. The local office sat on these applications and sent them up the line to the Washington DC office.

In addition to delaying what should have been routine applications, the IRS bureaucrats sent out letters demanding answers to dozens of intrusive and irrelevant questions requiring hours of work and hundreds of pages of information. These questionnaires were only sent to conservative groups. Progressive groups never faced any of the delays or investigations.

It appears that the IRS was following orders from progressive senators who did not want all these pesky conservative groups muddying up their campaigns. The efforts were assymetric. For example, Karl Rove's organization *Crossroads GPS* was singled out for intense scrutiny while the progressive group *Media Matters* had no such attention. For years, the applications from tea-party groups piled up to form a backlog of well over a hundred. The IRS let elections come and go, denying the conservative groups their voice by stymying their ability to raise money.

In 2013, **Lois Lerner,** Director of Exempt Organizations at IRS, confessed that several organizations were being targeted for further investigations. When she later was called to testify at a congressional hearing, she gave a statement but then refused to answer any questions pleading the 5th Amendment. When Congress attempted to get email evidence, they found that her hard disk had crashed and backup tapes had been wiped out, destroying much of the evidence. Although she was suspended for a time, she was allowed to retire with full retirement benefits.

At the time the scandal broke, many democrat politicians feigned outrage. They said that this IRS behavior was "unacceptable" and that IRS agents must be punished. But their apparent outrage turned out to be just sanctimonious grandstanding. In the end, no one suffered any consequences for this egregious violation of the First Amendment. President Obama said in an interview that there was not even "a smidgen of corruption" at the IRS. He swept the scandal under the rug, saying it was just a few "bone-headed" decisions by some low-level bureaucrats at the Cincinnati Office. Despite the computer glitches, there was plenty of evidence that this was orchestrated from the top. Yet no heads rolled.

In 2010 following the *Citizens United* Supreme Court Case, Congress attempted to pass the "Disclose" act to force disclosure of lists of donors and amounts for all organizations that may be involved in political programs, including 501-C4's. Congress could not get the votes for this to pass. President Obama attempted an executive order to effect the same result but public outcry against this squashed the order. Then the administration tried several other tactics such as using the Securities and Exchange Commission (SEC) to get the information. Public protest again defeated this effort.

In 2010 a Democrat political hack did a blog post indicating that the Chamber of Commerce has some foreign chapters so they may be using foreign money to finance American political campaigns. There was absolutely no evidence that the Chamber actually did this. But President Obama picked up this blog post and trumpeted from his Bully Pulpit that the Chamber of Commerce was spending millions of foreign dollars on American campaigns. The Chamber actually takes in less than 1% of its funding from foreign chapters and it carefully walls off these foreign funds to keep them out of American elections.

The **American Legislative Exchange Council (ALEC)** is America's largest nonpartisan, voluntary membership organization of state legislators dedicated to the principles of limited government, free markets and federalism. In 2013, **Senator Richard Durbin** (D-IL) sent a threatening letter to dozens of corporations and organizations who had supported ALEC. Sen Durbin was upset with ALEC because it had, among other things, supported issues like voter ID and "stand your ground" laws. Other issues blunted Durbin's efforts, but his use of raw power dramatically showed the Democratic Party's tactics: intimidate and squash dissent rather than debating it.

There was a lengthy discussion of the aftermath of California Prop 8, which banned same-sex marriage and was passed in 2008. This spawned a large amount of retribution. One casualty was Brendan Eich, who, in 2014 was promoted to CEO of a Mozilla, software company that marketed a popular web browser. He served only 11 days in that post as he was forced to step down after it was discovered he had made a contribution in 2008 in support of Prop 8. Remember <u>at that time this was a majority position</u>.

Other acts of retribution and intimidation occurred in the wake of Prop 8. One group posted a "hate map" online with a Google map pointing to those who had supported Prop 8 in each neighborhood. Businesses were vandalized and boycotted. Cars were keyed. Honey was poured onto cars whose owners had supported Prop 8. Houses were egged. Ugly emails were sent to Prop 8 supporters. This kind of mob behavior seems to only happen from the left.

In sum, Kimberly Strassel has done a magnificent job of revealing the nefarious results of compulsory disclosure of political donations. Potential challenger candidates are starved of donations when the incumbent can see who is supporting the challenger. Donors are reluctant to support a challenger when the donor may be subject to retribution. Instead of revealing what our politicians are doing, campaign finance laws disclose what private citizens are doing, eroding our basic rights. This book is a clarion call to resist the siren song of the left's effort to squelch debate by destroying anonymity with compulsory disclosure laws.

15. *The Age of Surveillance Capitalism,* by Shoshana Zuboff

Book Review

Harvard Professor Shoshana Zuboff's book, *The Age of Surveillance Capitalism* sheds light on a threat most people are not even aware of. Many of us, when we sign up for "free" internet services, are confronted with a long "terms of service" screen where we have to check a box "accept" before we can use the service. So we check the box, little realizing how much power we are ceding to the internet platforms. Unlike robber barrons of the past, the Tech titans look so benign as they offer "free" services for our convenience. Our lives are greatly enhanced as we take online tools for granted and we can't imagine that the few billionaires that run Google, Facebook, and Amazon could possibly have ignoble motives. But they do.

What makes these tech giants so sinister is that they, unlike historic robber barrons from previous centuries, have the ability to manipulate and herd millions of people to do things that they wouldn't ordinarily be inclined to do. They do so by basically exploiting a change in America that occurred in the last few decades: **the death of privacy**. Nowadays, many say 'I don't mind, I have nothing to hide.' But as we yield our private data to big Tech, do we realize all the consequences? Knowledge is power, and Google, Facebook, and Amazon are extremely powerful and are **using users as a deep mine to vacuum in all they can about us**. Their product is prediction: they predict what we will do and when we will do it, and they sell these predictions to the highest bidder without our consent or even knowledge.

I never thought I would ever say this, but I agree with some views of George Soros, Nancy Pelosi, AOC, and Congresswoman Nita Lowey (D-NY). We need to do several things:

1. An **Online User's Bill of Rights**. Our private data should only be shared with our consent, and that consent is not implied by checking the box on the Terms of Service.
2. Big Tech companies must be broken up. Google needs to spin off You Tube. Facebook needs to spin off Instagram and Oculus. Amazon needs to spin off Whole Foods and Audible. Both Amazon and Google need to divest of their divisions that provide servers to Corporate IT Departments. These companies are becoming too large and too pervasive.
3. **The default condition should be individual privacy**. Sharing personal information with others should only be done either with permission from the individual or by search warrant. Without warrants, hospitals cannot share our health data; lawyers cannot share consultations with their clients; Credit card companies cannot share their data; Cell phone companies cannot share their records. Why should big tech be given unbridled and unlimited access to our personal information.
4. The right to be forgotten. **Records about us on the internet must have an expiration date where they are purged.**

The book *The Age of Surveillance Capitalism*, by Shoshana Zuboff, is an eye-opening exposé of what these big tech companies are really all about. The author has an eloquent and engaging writing style with smooth and clever prose and brilliant word choices. She writes from a subtle left of center bias that is artfully hidden for large swaths of the book but occasionally surfaces (when, for example, she disapproves of 'right wing' organizations such as Cato Institute and Heritage Foundation or cherished conservative authors such as Friedman and Hayek). Most of her book, however, presents an apolitical and riveting case for why we shouldn't give these Tech companies the power and money they crave. Here are a few points she makes:

- **Tech companies have transitioned from serving customers to surveilling them**, almost like sitting in a room with a one way mirror or a digital "strip search." Users think they are doing a search when in fact Google is searching and researching them.
- While tech companies are free with sharing personal information about their users, they have built a moat of secrecy around their own actions.
- These companies want to predict the behavior of individuals because their advertisers crave certainty. **They talk of a "God's eye view" and are selling "behavior futures." We are all being monitored, herded, and tuned in the hive**.
- The 9/11 attacks weakened the concern for privacy, which was prioritized lower than security
- Big Tech engages in "The Dispossession Cycle" in 4 stages
  1. **Incursion** into undefended territory, continuously laying claim: **I'm taking this, 'these are mine now.'** They do not ask for permission; they simply assume ownership. Sometimes it uses seduction: conveniences and apps in return for your information. It is stunning in its resolve and audacity.
  2. **Habituation:** Google evolves in its harvesting at warp speed. People give up over time with a sense of helplessness and astonishment. Incursion slowly worms its way into the ordinary. Google wants the atmosphere to be peaceful, harmonious, and above all, grateful.
  3. **Adaptation:** Executives satisfy immediate demands of public opinion through superficial solutions that

appear to demonstrate just enough concern for the controversy to blow over.

4. **Redirection:** A perpetual motion machine as the public outrage is diverted. For example, *Google Glass* is removed from circulation only later to be released in a different more palatable form. Verizon removes universal identifier after public outrage, but then buys AOL and puts it back using AOL.

- The author gives several anecdotes of abuses by big tech
  - A man buys an engagement ring on line and within hours, all his friends on facebook, including the fiancé, know about it.
  - A service looks at a person's on line profile and makes predictions to employers on how likely this person is to stay with the company so employers can screen out likely short timers.
  - I-Robot "smart" vacuum cleaners make floor plan maps of your house and send them to advertisers
  - An emotion research firm looks at millions of pictures and videos of faces to determine "personality profiles" based on things like tightening the jaw, eye roll, tone of voice and then sell those profiles to the highest bidder.
  - One-Nest Thermostat sends data about your house to advertisers without consent. It has a very long and wordy terms of service that warns if you don't give them your data, you risk things like frozen pipes.
  - Sleep Number mattress sends data to internet on how you slept, movement, positions, heart rate. Even if you "opt out" the data can still be shared.
  - An application determines whether someone is behind on their car payments and if so, shuts off the car engine and directs repo man to the site to repossess the car

- ○ Personal Data Assistants have appeal because it's almost like you have a servant to do your bidding, but in exchange you have to reveal a lot about yourself. Unlike private conferences with Doctors and Lawyers, there are no confidentiality rules.
- ○ Smart Phones send tracking information to show where you have been at all times without your knowledge or consent.
- ○ Smart clothes: Levi Straus has denim jacket that records how loose or tight the garment is, what gestures you make, etc.
- ○ Personality profiles gleaned from Facebook habits such as how much information you submit; how many times you use exclamation points; how cheerful you are, etc can deduce whether you might be depressed and may be used by employer screeners
- The **Extraction Imperative is what drives these companies**; they must accumulate more and more data to improve their models and "reduce friction" on growth.
- Just think of all the information Google has:
  - ○ Your Search History
  - ○ Your Email
  - ○ Your Android Phone with its texts and meta data
  - ○ Your purchases
  - ○ Some apps can even detect your location inside a building
  - ○ Your photo through all the surveillance cameras
  - ○ Your user profile across all platforms
  - ○ The songs you listen to, the games you play
  - ○ The places you go
  - ○ Your face (with facial recognition software)
  - ○ Who your friends are, your interests and tastes
- **Cyberspace knows no borders and Tech companies don't want to slow down information with formalities like search**

warrants, so they have carved out a large unregulated space for themselves.

- You could make a case that Google "meddled" in the 2012 Election as former CEO Eric Schmidt brought all the predictive power of Google's surveillance models to bear, producing targeted ways to access voters most likely to swing their way.

In conclusion, most of us would not like it if someone hired a detective to spy on us, yet that is exactly what Google, Facebook, and Amazon are doing. **It's almost like they are peeping toms looking at all our online activity as "free" raw material for their money and power grab**. They must be brought to heel.

16. The Perfect Police State
By Geoffrey Cain (June 2021)
Book Review

Many Americans have heard about the Chinese Communist Party's (CCP) repression of a Moslem minority known as the Uyghur's. These people live in the Xinjiang Province in northwest China. This province shares a border with two Moslem former Soviet Republics (Tajikistan and Kyrgyzstan). It is about as remote as it gets from China's centers of power, and the CCP wants to leave no doubt about who rules in Xinjiang province. The CCP has seen several terrorist threats from this region and has cracked down forcefully, all in the name of preventing terrorism. A major part of the CCP's strategy in this area includes confining millions of ethnic Uyghurs in re-education camps.

The above paragraph is about the only thing most Americans know about the repression of the Uyghurs in China. Now journalist Geoffrey Cain steps in with an explosive book that exposes the sinews of the Police State in China. His work vividly describes how the CCP is applying new technologies such as facial recognition and artificial intelligence (AI) in an effort to do what it calls "predictive policing". The CCP's surveillance state doesn't wait till a crime is committed; it uses its AI tools including "Social Credit Scores" to predict who will commit a crime. Social Credit Scores are also sometimes used to prevent a citizen from using a public service such as a store.

An umbrella term Cain uses to describe the Police State is a "**panopticon.**" This is a prison where one guard is at the center and can see prisoners radiating out in all directions. The guard can see them, but they can't see the guard. As Cain puts it, he may be sleeping or reading a newspaper or going to the john. But the prisoners don't know, so they must "play it safe."

The author paints a picture of an all-powerful party. For one thing, there is no bright line between the CCP and corporations in China. If the CCP asks for data or information from a company, they cannot refuse. There is no process where a search warrant or probable cause is required. If the CCP wants something, it gets it. The author also reveals issues around foreign corporations and the CCP's requirement that they hand over their intellectual property if they plan to do business in China.

While Cain's book gives a lot of these technical details, his riveting portrayal of the experience of one Uyghur college student named "Maysem" really brings home just how brutal the Chinese police state is and sounds a warning alarm to those in the rest of the world who would misuse AI to make life a living nightmare for the ordinary citizen.

Maysem has studied sociology in Turkey, where there is a large Uyghur expatriate community. She has read many books, including English novels such as Jane *Austen's Pride and Prejudice*. She is a bright, articulate woman, and she stands out. But that's not the kind of citizen the CCP wants in Xingjian province. What they want is a collection of obedient serfs who relentlessly oppose the three evils the CCP has identified: Terrorism, Extremism, and Separatism.

Maysem has a neighbor lady who has been assigned by the CCP to "watch" ten neighbors and report back any suspicious activities. The watcher visits these neighbors each day and swipes a bar code to indicate she has completed her assignment. One day, the watcher drops by and asks Maysem why she didn't go on her normal 9:00 a.m. walk. Maysem answers that she was sick. The watcher asks her to get a note from her doctor proving that she was sick.

A few weeks later, the watcher returns and asks Maysem to install surveillance cameras in her home. Her Social Credit score has indicated that she is "undesirable". The watcher "asks" but Maysem can't really refuse. So she has the cameras installed and from that moment, she and her mother have to be very careful about what they say and do in their home.

A few weeks later, the watcher again "asks" Maysem and her family to "voluntarily" go to a local clinic where they will be given a full physical exam. DNA samples will be taken and photos from several angles are recorded in the CCP's AI database to support their predictive policing effort.

A few weeks later, she is informed she must attend 4 week re-education program just when she needs to return to grad school. This means she will miss the semester she planned to attend in Turkey. At the center, the "students" are taught obedience through punishments such as having to sit in the hot sun for a long period of time without moving. Any time they move, the clock is wound back to zero and they start all over again. In some cases, if one student disobeys, all students are punished.

Each day after a 6-hour indoctrination class, each student must handwrite seven pages of slogans affirming their allegiance to the CCP. Their notebooks are inspected and anyone who falls short is punished.

Fortunately for Maysem, her parents have some pull with some local CCP officials, and they somehow get her out of the detention facility after only a few months. She then sets about trying to escape from China to get back to college in Turkey. Her airline reservations had been changed several times while she was in detention and this paperwork blocks her ability to board the flight she has booked. She and her mother devise another way by taking a train to India and then flying to Turkey from there. A few weeks after her escape, the CCP prohibits all air and train travel for Uyghurs attempting to leave China. She got out in the nick of time.

Even in Turkey, the long arm of the CCP's surveillance state continues to surveil Uyghur expatriates. Any electronic messages going home are surveilled. The CCP sends fake messages from smart phones of loved ones back home inviting them to come back to China. Some that fall for these messages are immediately sent to detention facilities as they arrive.

Cain's book exposes one of the most naïve ideas of many American Foreign policy analysts in the last few decades. Many of these analysts have asserted that as we engage China, it will become freer and more like America. But there are indications that this may be just the opposite of what is really happening. **As we engage China, we may be getting to be more like China.** Intellectual elites like Thomas Friedman of the *New York Times* and Canadian Prime Minister **Justin Trudeau** have expressed admiration for the Chinese system. They love the way things just "get done" without the messy process of democracy. But Cain's book should give us pause. Do we really want a Perfect Police State where all criminals are caught? Is the goal worth the price of living in a despair-laden dystopia?

Censorship and Misinformation

17. When Theorem becomes Axiom
Cocksure activists need no proof or evidence for their positions

Those who have studied high school geometry might recall the contrast between theorem and axiom. A **theorem** is essentially a hypothesis that must be proven using mathematical logic. Probably the most famous theorem was proposed by Pythagoras (570-495 BC). It states that the sum of the squares of the short sides of a right triangle is equal to the square of the longest side, the hypotenuse. Over the centuries, many proofs have used meticulous mathematical and geometric logic to show that this theorem is true.

Some mathematical truths appear to be so obvious as to not require any proof. These are known as **"axioms"** or **"postulates"**. One of the more prominent geometric axioms states that "If A, B are distinct points, then there is exactly one line containing both A and B." No proof is required. We just accept axioms to give us a starting point in logic.

Even outside geometry and mathematics, there are many "facts" that are so widely accepted as to obviate the need for any evidence or proof. Such facts are said to be "axiomatic". For example, if you let go of a ball while standing up, the ball will fall to the earth. All humans today will die before attaining a maximum age, of, say, 150 years. Human infants are borne only by women. The sky is blue. A day is 24 hours long. Water can be liquid, solid, or gaseous.

Axiomatic facts have one thing in common: they can be observed and verified by many people over and over again. They all involve phenomena that are so true as to make debate appear to be nonsensical. They are essentially "amoral"--they are true whether or not one thinks they are "good" or "bad." This is an important point: **very few moral issues are so clear as to be axiomatic.**

Items that are <u>not</u> axiomatic invite debate. Each side then brings evidence to buttress an argument for their position or "theorem." In 21st Century America, several topics have spawned vigorous debate. For example, one side says "abortion is wrong" while the other side proposes a "woman's right to choose." One side says that fossil fuels are spewing so much greenhouse gas emissions into the atmosphere as to endanger the planet while the other states that the evidence does not point to catastrophic climate change caused by fossil fuels. One side states that the right to keep and bear arms is an important check to tyranny and the other states that guns are too dangerous and must be controlled to avoid unnecessary bloodshed. In all these examples, there is no "correct" or "incorrect" position. Reasonable people can hold either view.

In recent American society, some strong partisans have attempted to blur the distinction between theorem and axiom. They believe their position so intensely and think it is so obviously correct that facts and evidence are not necessary, and debate is pointless. One such position in the news today involves policing. One side thinks it is quite obvious that racial bias is widespread in police departments and this bias often results in brutality and unjust treatment of minorities.

Anyone who questions this position is called a racist or is ridiculed as "unenlightened". An opponent of the widespread racial brutality position may bring many facts to the debate. They may point to statistics that show that in a nation with a population of 330 million, the few documented examples of police brutality toward minorities constitute a miniscule, nearly undetectable proportion of encounters with police. They may point out that whites are involved in more brutality incidents than blacks. They may point to the fact that far more blacks are killed in gang violence and thus would recommend focusing efforts in that area if the goal is the well- being of oppressed minorities. But in the age of cocksure moralists, these arguments, even if they are true, cut no ice.

Another issue that seems to be debatable but is not involves Climate Change. This is an enormously complex issue that many suggest has been "settled", with no need for further debate. **Chuck Todd**, host of NBC's *Meet the Press*, had a session where he admitted he was only presenting one side of the debate. In January 2019, he declared that he will not "give time to climate deniers" on his program and announced, "The earth is getting hotter, and human activity is a major cause. Period. There is only one way the earth can be saved: by tightly controlling energy use and rapidly converting from fossil fuels to renewables such as wind and solar. Period."

Never mind that plots of observed versus predicted temperatures based on widely used climate prediction models nearly all show gross errors all on the high side. Never mind that plots of temperature and CO_2 concentration show temperature going up before CO_2 goes up, possibly suggesting that warmer temperatures cause CO_2 rise and not the other way around. Never mind that no one really knows what the "ideal" temperature actually is. Never mind that warmer temperatures and higher CO_2 concentrations have some beneficial effects. Never mind that the last major ice age ended with warming before SUV's were driving around, indicating a heating factor other than greenhouse gases. Never mind that a switch to renewables from fossil fuels would replace energy that is cheap, abundant, and reliable with energy that is expensive, rare, and intermittent. Never mind that windmills and solar panels kill bald eagles. None of these arguments will sway a climate change zealot who is absolutely certain that fossil fuels are ruining the planet.

So in modern parlance, a clique of "enlightened" experts have opinions that are so obviously correct that no sane person could disagree. Anyone who attempts to question the accepted position is patronized or ridiculed as just plain stupid or in some cases, evil. No matter what facts and evidence are advanced against the accepted orthodoxy, the facts are ignored and the counter-argument is dismissed as "debunked", "discredited", or "conspiracy theory". Case closed.

Another way the experts squash the debate is by deflecting from issues such as logic, facts, and evidence into a questioning of motives. Skeptics of Climate change are called "deniers who are in the oil company's pocket." Those who question some of the ridiculous policies of the Black Lives Matter movement (eg, defund the police and end the nuclear family) are racists. Those who question abortion are religious zealots who have no regard for women's rights. And, of course, those who hold the orthodox position have motives that are pure as the driven snow.

Many of the same proponents of the orthodox position also scold us about trying to stereotype people, even as they engage in the very behavior they condemn. In years past, they complained about religious "fundamentalists" who insisted on biblical principles as absolute truth. They boldly asserted that there was no absolute truth. **But today, they insist that yes, there *is* absolute truth: *their* moral axioms.**

Those who care about liberty, especially about free speech, need to call out these virtue- signaling hypocrites and refuse to accept the dismissal and ridicule of issues over which reasonable, rational people can disagree. When a person resorts to name-calling and dismissal, ask "what facts have I presented that are incorrect?" Anyone who wishes to shut down debate does so because deep down they know they cannot win their point using evidence, reason, and logic. Just as scientists and jurists through the ages have insisted on proof for hypotheses, we today should vigorously insist on proof. **Theorems are not axioms**.

18. One Political Defect Almost Entirely on the Left
Suppression of Free Speech

Those of us who lean to the right sometimes engage in frustrating debates with voices on the left. These discussions often just go round and round as we talk past each other. One reason these debates often go nowhere is what I call the "both sides do it" assertion. If you point to profligate spending by Democrats, the answer will be that Republicans also support deficit spending and pork. If you point to hypocrisy on the left, they can respond with just as many examples of hypocrisy on the right. If you denounce how big spenders like George Soros or Big Tech billionaires have undue influence in politics, they will answer that the Koch brothers also are attempting to "buy" politicians. Meanwhile, sanctimonious independents float serenely above the debate, virtue signaling by condemning both sides and saying "a pox on both your houses" but offering no solutions.

But there is one political defect that appears to be almost entirely confined to the left: **suppression of free speech**. For example, prominent pundits on the left including Nicholas Kristof of the *New York Times* and Max Boot of the *Washington Post* have called for pressuring advertisers or outright shutting down *Fox News* and others such as *One America News* and *Newsmax* https://news.yahoo.com/absurd-calls-shut-down-fox-021001137.html. President Biden has nominated to the Federal Communications Commission, Gigi Sohn, who has openly advocated shutting down *Fox News*. There is a petition online at Debate.org to shut down Fox. As far as I know, there has never been a similar call from the right to shut down, say, MSNBC, which is tilted farther to the left than Fox is to the right.

Over the past few years, we've heard of numerous stories where guest speakers on campus were either disinvited to speak or were confronted with a mob that disrupted their speech. Here are just a few examples from the past seven years or so:

- UC Berkeley cancelled a speech by Alt- right speaker **Milo Yiannopoulis** after violent student protests including vandalizing ATM machines and smashing windows
- At UC Berkeley, speaker **Ben Shapiro** was invited to deliver an address ironically about freedom of speech and was confronted with large protests. A formidable police presence was needed to permit Shapiro to speak.
- At Claremont McKenna college, protesters shouted down scholar **Heather MacDonald** and forced her to speak to a nearly empty room.
- At Middlebury college, after speaker **Charles Murray** and the professor who interviewed him for the livestream attempted to leave the location in a car, some protesters surrounded the car, jumped on it, pounded on it and tried to prevent the car from leaving campus.
- In the year 2021, journalist **Andy Ngo** who has written extensively about Antifa was beaten and hospitalized by an Antifa mob in Portland Oregon.
- In March 2023, U.S. Circuit Judge Stuart **Kyle Duncan** was heckled and shouted down by students at Stanford University with Associate Dean **Tirien Steinbach** basically siding with the student hecklers.
- In April 2023, collegiate swimmer **Riley Gaines** was assaulted and held hostage in a room for several hours because of threats of students who thought her speech was "anti- trans".
- In March 2024, **Kyle Rittenhouse**, who had been acquitted of a charge of murder at the Kenosha, Wisconsin riots in 2020, was invited to speak at a *TurningPointUSA* event at the University of Memphis. University officials put many

roadblocks in the way of the event organizers and assisted some protestors who basically "took over" the event and shouted down the guest speaker.

I could cite many more examples of this behavior of shutting down speakers. But I defy anyone to find a similar incident where a right-wing mob attempted to shout down an extreme left wing speaker. **These shout downs nearly always appear on the left**.

Another way conservative voices are squelched by the left is through the Big Tech machine. All of the prominent Big Tech Firms (eg, Google, Facebook, Twitter, Amazon) in recent years have censored free speech, but always in one direction. Here are just a few examples:

- Shutdown of rival social media platform **Parler**
- Complete removal of the Twitter account of a sitting U.S. president
- The *New York Post* story about Hunter Biden's laptop blocked (its truth was never denied; it was only classed as "misinformation")
- Numerous **deplatforming incidents** involving COVID and vaccines

In some cases, parties who were demonetized, deplatformed or subjected to fact check warnings appealed to Big Tech and were reinstated, saying that the move was a **"mistake."** But the mistakes always occurred on actions against conservative viewpoints, almost never against even extreme left-wing views.

One particularly nefarious example of Big Tech bullying takes the form of censoring what it calls "hate speech." Such **hate speech** seems to only issue from the right. Big Tech ignores hate speech from the left, including Congresswoman **Maxine Waters** when she urged her followers to "get in the face" of people in restaurants, gas stations, and other public places if they were Trump supporters. Another kind of hate speech that seems to be permitted is anything that comes out of the antiracist movement, including BLM. It is AOK to paint all white people as white supremacists and racists. But any conservative voices that offend extreme groups like the **Southern Poverty Law Center** are "over the top" and must be silenced.

In some cases, Big Tech uses a subtler approach. In the case of *Brietbart*, a right wing political site, Google algorithms were adjusted so that any search containing the word "Biden" would omit Breitbart articles from the list. Breitbart shows a chart where Google Searches that hit on Breitbart articles went from over a million to virtually zero. Other prominent conservative voices such as Dave Rubin, Prager U, and Ben Shapiro, have also been made more difficult to find online. Again, **all of these shenanigans appear to only impact voices from the right**.

The question we never have answered is, "who are the gatekeepers deciding what we can or cannot read?" At Big Tech firms, they are probably a few thirty-something engineers who take orders from their bosses to design algorithms to filter out what they consider to be offensive. None of these officials have been elected to these positions. Also, the reasons given for censorship are vague statements like "content does not meet community standards". Those standards are never clearly spelled out. Something can be censored even if it is true and is not obscene. On the left, a statement can be both false and obscene, yet be allowed to be posted.

Censorship also extends to book publishers. U.S. Senator **Josh Hawley** (R-MO) had a deal to publish a book, but at the last minute, his publisher, Simon and Shuster, cancelled the deal after the events at the Capitol on January 6. Even banks are punishing conservative voices. Former Trump national security adviser **Lt. Gen.**

Michael Flynn said that Chase Bank sent him a letter informing him it is canceling his accounts and credit cards because he poses a "reputational risk" to the company's brand.

The left frequently shuts down debate by name calling. Instead of presenting evidence, they offer epithets. They characterize a study as "debunked", "discredited", or "misleading," even if it is true. They rarely challenge the truth by bringing their own data that contradicts the position from the right. Instead they say "this is settled science", a claim frequently used in discussions of climate change. If you counter with facts like "sea level has been rising at a very consistent rate since 1900" or "the temperature for the last 20 years has been level in spite of extremely high and sharply rising levels of CO2" they will answer something like "that is not a peer reviewed finding." They really don't care about what is true, only what fits their narrative.

Censorship has not always been confined to the left. At the end of World War II, Republican Senator Robert Taft (R-OH) authored Title V of the Soldier Voting Law to prohibit any materials that would be political in nature, hoping to blunt FDR's re-election. I could find more examples of right wing censorship, but they would all be from fairly long ago.

The free speech guarantee in the U.S. Constitution is crystal clear:

Congress shall make no law … abridging the freedom of speech, or of the press.

Notice that **there are no exception clauses like "except hate speech" or "except in case of a national emergency."** The founders knew that free debate was essential to all other freedoms. Debates should be won or lost on the merit of the cases made. They should not be shut down by stifling free speech. The left has made its case but has failed to convince about half of the country, so they want to change the rules to prevent the other side from being heard. The right almost never attempts to silence the left. This is almost entirely a one-sided vice.

Postscript Nov 2023

A few years after I wrote this essay, I discovered an important book *The Cancelling of the American Mind* by Greg Lukianoff and Rikki Schlott. The two authors belong to an organization named **FIRE (Foundation of Individual Rights and Expression)**. FIRE is more oriented to the left than other resources I have consulted, and they have filled some gaps in my knowledge. I confess that I normally just ignore many voices on the left and run the risk of developing a somewhat skewed outlook. This book shows that my initial assessment of placing all the blame for speech suppression on the left may have been a just a bit misinformed and simplistic.

Lukianoff and Schlott produce several troubling examples of cancellations done from the right. They cite one example where a Moslem college professor made an offensive joke in response to President Trump's threat to bomb Iranian holy sites. The professor tweeted something like "maybe Iran should bomb sites like the Khardashian's homes". A right wing outrage mob got this professor fired. The book also spends some time on recent state legislation (mainly in Florida) restricting what can be taught in schools. The book rightly makes a distinction between K-12 education (which have an immature and captive audience) and universities, where unfettered free speech should be the goal.

The FIRE web site has a wealth of useful data that helps to assess the **quality of free speech on college campuses**. One database table shows a list of speakers who were disinvited to campus due to hypersensitivity of the students at those colleges. The table lists over 500 incidents beginning in the late 1990's. Until about 2016, the speaker disinvitations from the right and left were about even. But beginning in 2016 or so, nearly all of the speaker disinvitations came from the left.

While the counterexamples of speech suppression from the right temper my conclusions, the rest of the book reinforces my impression of a very asymmetric approach between left and right. One chapter of the book focuses on ways the left shuts down debate. They basically disqualify persons who argue a view from the right by a series of gauntlets all speakers must cross before they are deemed worthy to debate. For example, if you are white, you can't argue about black racism. Even if you are black, if you don't agree with the prevailing view of implicit racism, you can be ignored. If you are not gay, you cannot argue about LGBT issues. The authors state that the left's fortress essentially puts a mute button on about 98% of the population.

Although the book is written by a couple of left-leaning authors, nearly three fourths of the examples of suppression of free speech in the book depict issues where the left is the culprit. The authors are thus to be commended for not sparing their side from criticism and scrutiny. The egregious examples cited by the authors are presented vividly. So the title of this essay still stands: free speech suppression still seems to come almost entirely from the left. The counterexamples from the right presented in this book might cause me to rephrase from "almost entirely" to "overwhelmingly."

Postscript May 2024
Alas! I wish I could have just left this chapter where it was a couple of years ago, but a recent deterioration on the right in the area of free speech has forced me to reassess. Many of the anti-free speech practices discussed in this chapter are still nearly entirely on the left. These include speaker heckling and shoutdowns, physical

assaults on persons that make undesirable statements, censorship and algorithmic silencing, and sanctimonious fact-checking.

But starting with the firing of Candace Owens from the Daily Wire, the right seems to have lost its mind and renunciated its advocacy of freedom of speech for one topic: support for Israel. Glen Greenwald has been beating the drum about the hypocrisy on the right in recent months and his criticism is justified. The U.S. Congress recently passed a bill that basically declares that any opposition to the war tactics of Israel against the Palestinians is *ipso facto* antisemitism and must not be tolerated. No one has explained why free speech is acceptable in every area except for support for this foreign country. While there still are some strong voices on the right who oppose this legislation against antisemitism, they have been drowned out by loud opposition from a large bipartisan majority.

I emphatically urge public figures on the right to recover their righteous anger against free speech restrictions and denounce the recent unconscionable and unconstitutional measure to silence repugnant opinions. Free Speech is way more important than any of the positions that are being so roundly condemned. The answer to free speech we don't like is debate and counterarguments. We must not fall prey to the temptation to shut down speech we don't like.

19. Misinformation: True or False?
Even truth can be misinformation!

In today's news media we hear a lot about "misinformation" and "disinformation." These terms may *seem* to be virtually synonymous with "false information," but it turns out that an assertion can be factually true but still be characterized as misinformation and disinformation. What these terms really signify is information that does not align with an ideological theory.

Large social media companies have undertaken an effort to shield the public from misinformation and disinformation. It has employed legions of operatives it calls "fact checkers" and has claimed that many assertions cannot be simplified into a black or white binary choice. Instead, there are nuanced shades of gray that must be considered by a reasonable and rational analyst. These nuanced investigations often tend to confirm the ideological bias of a given fact checker.

Yet in this world of fine distinctions, there remain some stubborn facts that can be characterized by a simple true/false statement. We know that the sun will rise and set each day as the earth completes its 24-hour rotation as it has for thousands of years. That is simply true. We know that when one drops an object, it falls to the earth; it does not rise without some propulsion mechanism applied.

True/false facts are not only confined to the world of science. History is also adorned with many facts that can easily be classified as either true or false. Here is a list of facts that can be demonstrably proven as true. Yet all of these are liable to be labeled as misinformation or disinformation by the media.

Climate Change

1. Scientific data shows that global sea level has been rising at a very constant rate of about 3 mm per year since 1880. That rate has not increased appreciably with high CO2 levels.

2. As Global CO2 emissions have skyrocketed so have life-expectancy and world GDP per capita.

3. Deaths from Climate disasters are down 98% since the dawn of the industrial revolution and the start of the rise of greenhouse gasses.

4. Extra CO2 in the atmosphere exerts a "fertilizer effect" on plants, increasing crop yields.

5. China's CO2 emissions are roughly double that of the US yet is not subject to constraints by the Paris Climate accord for more than a decade. China is planning dozens of new coal fired power plants. Meanwhile, the USA has led the world in CO2 emission reductions.

6. Wind and Solar electricity are expensive and intermittent. Despite decades of research and billions of dollars in subsidies, no practical, scalable method of storing this power has been invented.

7. "Follow the Science" really means "believe the scientists chosen by the establishment" and ignore other distinguished scientists who maintain that climate change is real but not catastrophic and that humanity can easily adapt.

Gender issues

8. Merriam Webster's dictionary defines the word *woman* as *an adult female person.*

9. When asked to define woman at her Supreme Court confirmation hearing, Ketanji Brown Jackson answered "No, I can't," she eventually said. "Not in this context. I'm not a biologist."

10. There are only two genders: male and female.

11. Recent developments including Drag Queen shows in the presence of young children are not conducive to instilling basic moral values.

12. Gender-affirming care for children often produces life-long negative side-effects.

Crime

13. The murder count in New York City dropped by about 75% from 1994 to 2001.

14. Rudy Giuliani served as Mayor of New York from 1994-2001 and implemented tough policing policies such as "stop and frisk" and "broken windows".

15. There was a record number of NYC subway shoves in 2022 (two dozen).

16. Billions of dollars of damage during 2020 BLM riots. Life savings were wiped out for business owners (including blacks) who had nothing to do with the death of George Floyd.

17. After California changed thefts of up to $950 to a misdemeanor, smash and grab thefts soared, forcing stores to either lock up small items or close stores in crime-prone neighborhoods.

18. D.A.'s in many of the nation's largest cities urge reforms like cashless bail and not prosecuting petty crimes. These reforms do help reduce mass incarceration but also result in revolving door repeat offenses.

19. "We know the statistics — that children who grow up without a father are five times more likely to live in poverty and commit crime, nine times more likely to drop out of schools and 20 times more likely to end up in prison." Barack Obama (2008)

20. Thousands of black inmates are not in jail because of their race, but because they committed crimes and made bad life choices.

January 6
21. Videos of the January 6 incidents show capitol police standing back and even waving people into the Capitol.
22. President Trump offered National Guard assistance for crowd control on Jan 6, but his offer was rejected by DC Mayor Muriel Bowser and House Speaker Nancy Pelosi.
23. Three policemen in the Capitol building abandoned their posts guarding a doorway seconds before an unarmed Ashlii Babbitt was shot dead by the Police.
24. Dozens of people imprisoned for January 6 activities were subjected to pretrial confinement without bail and long periods of solitary confinement even if they neither hurt anyone nor broke anything on January 6.

China
25. The Chinese Communist Party (CCP) forced U.S. NBA players and officials to apologize for exercising their free speech within the borders of the U.S.
26. The CCP exerts censorship on Hollywood movies
27. The CCP buys U.S. farmland, some near military bases, but U.S. Citizens not allowed to buy Chinese farmland.
28. The CCP demands U.S. Companies to share their technology as a condition of doing business in China. U.S. does not demand the same from Chinese businesses in the U.S.
29. Greater than 90% of Solar Panels, Wind Mill Turbines, and materials to make batteries for Electric Vehicles are manufactured in China.

Covid
30. There is virtually no statistical difference in death and hospitalization rates from covid when comparing states with strict lockdown, mask, and vaccination policies with states with looser policies.

31. As the nation prioritized covid above all else, other medical needs were neglected, causing major health problems.
32. Masks for kids in school did virtually nothing to stop the spread of Covid.
33. Nine new Billionaires were created from Covid vaccine profits.
34. There is compelling evidence that Covid may have originated in the Wuhan lab.
35. Hydroxychloroquine and Ivermectin have been effective and safe therapeutics for thousands of patients.
36. Thousands of highly trained professionals including First Responders, nurses, US Marines, and Navy Seals lost their jobs because they refused to be vaccinated during the Covid crisis.

The anti-disinformation campaign on the left can be compared to a courtroom where the Prosecutor and the Judge are on the same side. The Defense presents true statements, but the Prosecutor says "objection, your honor. Incompetent, irrelevant and immaterial." And time after time, the Judge says "sustained. Strike that from the record." In fact, the objections are sustained automatically and even algorithmically by Big Tech. **The truth of the case for the defense makes no difference.** In the end, the real definition of disinformation and misinformation is "**whatever undermines our case**."

20. Online Content Moderation
Tamping down lawful but awful speech online

In spite of the First Amendment, for many years, there have been some limits on what type of speech has appeared in widely available publications. Many have applied the euphemism "Content Moderation" to describe these limitations on absolute free speech. They point to a distinction between "freedom of speech" and "freedom of reach." Though each citizen is entitled to be able to say whatever they want without fear of retribution, freedom of speech does not create a right to use platforms to reach mass audiences with all speech.

Until the invention of the internet, content moderation was carried out largely by editors of major publications such as newspapers or TV news organizations. These editors were gatekeepers who filtered out such objectionable content as obscenity, falsehood, or threats of violence so that this kind of speech did not reach large audiences. The editors also set a standard for the quality of writing that was acceptable for widespread publication. This screened out true but tedious or unartful materials. An author or commentator had to produce materials that passed muster with these gatekeepers before it was distributed widely.

But then came the internet and social media, and a kind of "wild west" mentality began to emerge. Nearly everyone was his own editor and items that had previously been suppressed suddenly began erupting and going "viral." Obscenity, threats of violence, and downright falsehoods abounded. The gatekeepers of the past were cut out of the publication cycle, and misinformation and disinformation proliferated. There was a widespread consensus that some adult supervision was needed to avoid the chaos of harmful speech. Brutally frank rhetoric has the potential to stir up violent mobs, and we all want to avoid that.

A recent watershed event occurred when Elon Musk purchased Twitter and, through the publication of the Twitter Files, exposed some of the overreach of a new group of critics that became known as the **"Censorship Industrial Complex."** Armies of censors operated at big tech platforms to identify and tamp down on harmful speech. A whole technology was developed to use computer algorithms to silence offensive opinions or at least make them more difficult to access online.

In August 2023, the new X/Twitter CEO Linda Yaccarino, boasted about how the social media platform has been "de-amplifying" posts that it determines to be "lawful but awful," to make more money and bring key advertisers back. This little phrase "**lawful but awful**" crystalizes the challenge we face in content moderation. A totally unfiltered dumping ground for every thought a person comes up with threatens to drown out quality with quantity. In the past, magazine and media editors selected what they thought was worthy of publication. But now with social media, everyone can simply "let loose" with bombast that is not only not edifying but could be downright disgusting and harmful. How do we balance the need for frank and honest discussion of impactful issues with the potential harm that can be done by unbridled commentary?

I confess I don't have a satisfactory answer to this conundrum. But what I can say is that we seem to have acquiesced to a system where a few young engineers at big tech firms are providing most of the answers—automatically through censorship algorithms. The sheer volume of potentially harmful speech makes it necessary to have some way of triaging comments in a way that is most likely to filter out harmful noise. Automatic algorithms help do that.

The main hazard of all these censorship algorithms is that they tend to reinforce the ideology of the powers in charge. The definition of what is "hate speech" seems particularly challenging. With microaggressions and trigger warnings, we have created a demand for "safe spaces" where people do not run the risk of getting their feelings hurt. This hypersensitivity to slights can be downright destructive to the goal of free and open debate. Many online consumers want speech to be civil, and emotionally charged terms sometimes get in the way of mutually enlightening discussions.

But have the online censors drawn the line at the right place? Actually, they may have. The Free Market seems to be working to circumvent the would-be dictatorship of Big Tech. One great example is the rise of **Rumble** as an alternative to Google's You-Tube. Recently, You- Tube announced it would limit the reach of statements about health that contradicted policy of the World Health Organization (WHO). Some may shudder at the prospect of an unelected foreign bureaucracy extending its tentacles into the US to limit speech. But Rumble and other sources are rising to the challenge as a free speech alternative.

Similarly, podcasting sites like *Epoch TV* and *Daily Wire* play portions of their presentations on You-Tube, but the hosts note you can go directly to the sources to get the uncensored versions of the discussions. If you want the official approved information, you can go to You Tube where you stand less of a chance of being offended with ideas you don't like. But other sources provide what is bleeped out on You Tube, so heartier souls can get their information there.

I should acknowledge here that a tendency to censorship is not confined to the left. Conservatives also want some filtering in mass media. For example, many on the right are offended when movies depict LGBTQ situations. They also bristle when the media attempts to "mainstream" behaviors like Drag Queen story hour. But as disgusted as we may be at what we consider to be perverted trends, most of the time we don't (or at least shouldn't) attempt to silence this offensive content. Truth be told, we don't have the power to do that. **The best way to avoid these topics is to switch channels and avoid going to movies with these themes**.

As much as I disapprove of Big Tech censorship, as long as alternate platforms are allowed to spread ideas that may be offensive to the party line, I think Big Tech's overreach is actually achieving a good result. You Tube is gaining a reputation as regime media. The current situation is that more consumers want the comfort of the official narrative. But as the free speech platforms gain a foothold, we can rely on our free market to ensure that all views are heard. We are already seeing erosion of the consumer bases of platforms like Cable TV, the Movie Industry, and Disney. **We need to patiently await the day when the Big Tech censors realize they have shot themselves in the foot**.

21. LGBTQ Idiocy

"give 'em an inch and they'll take a mile."
Granting a limited concession will encourage greater liberties

A word that has greatly increased in use in the last couple of decades is "**affirm.**" Progressive philosophy exhorts us to not just tolerate or condone but affirm many behaviors which were widely condemned about five minutes ago. This progression from unfair treatment to celebration has characterized the steady march of the LGBTQ community. Figure 3 below depicts this progression as a "tolerance escalator":

Figure 3.
The Tolerance Escalator

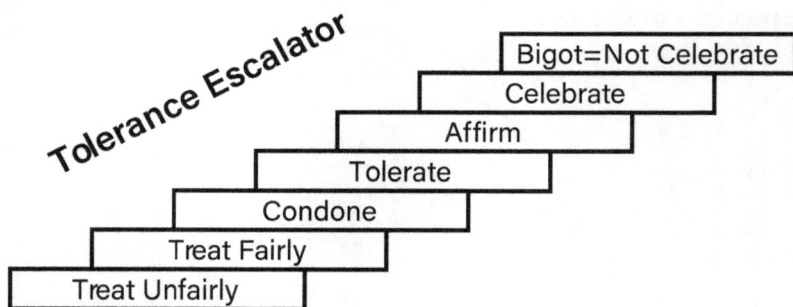

It is true that many in this community were treated unfairly a couple of decades ago, and America has largely rectified the discrimination we saw in the past. But instead of just going to the second step of the escalator, we have been whisked up to ever higher levels. We outside of that community are expected to applaud what we think is weird behavior and if we do not applaud, we are often charged with bigotry and hate. The result is the cartoonish caricature we find ourselves living out in today's America, in which the vast majority is mystified and repulsed as it sees what were strongly held values flushed down the drain of wokeness. But we are forced to stand by and "take it" because that is what the secular media is preaching from its pulpit.

It's almost as if Americans outside of the LGBTQ community are being indoctrinated in a "required course" where they learn the nuances of living around these nut cases. Anyone who doesn't "graduate" with a degree in this lunacy is branded as an unenlightened neanderthal bigot.

Here are a few examples of the foolishness we see all around us:

- A new euphemism has been invented: instead of "pedophile", we are asked to use the term "**Minor Attracted Person**" (MAP). It would be judgmental to condemn MAP's.
- **Drag Queens** are having gatherings for all ages including small children. These children sit in a raucous atmosphere hearing loud rap lyrics with dozens of obscenities as they watch a grotesque drag queen performance.
- Young children are being allowed to make decisions that could have life-long adverse consequences for their bodies.
- We can't give the definition of a *woman* in polite society. See Matt Walsh's video *What is a Woman?* for a brilliant treatment of this topic.
- A boy can say he is a girl and be admitted to the girl's locker room and sports teams.
- Gender affirming care clinics are castrating young boys and calling it "bottom surgery" or chopping off the breasts of young girls and calling it "top surgery."
- Books that contain explicit pornographic materials are being introduced into schools and anyone who opposes these materials is condemned as a "book burner."

Until very recently, activities like these were nearly universally condemned as nuts. But they are being "mainstreamed." No vote is taken; we just have to accept the policies espoused by the woke mob. Most of us just shake our heads and whisper our disapproval, but very few call out this humiliation of our nation.

But here and now, let's just call it out for what it is. All of the practices listed above are sickening things that disgrace our society. It may not be tolerant to say to an "MAP" that children are off limits, but let's say it out loud: "You repulsive pedophile pervert! Keep your filthy hands off the children!" To grotesque Drag Queens I say, "You disgusting degenerate! You give me the creeps!" To transgender posers like swimmer Lea Thomas who stole medals from woman competitors, I say "what a pathetic, narcissistic man you are. Your disguise doesn't fool us, you moron! You are a man, so why not act like one?"

Gender dysphoria is a mental illness that should not be affirmed but should be treated with compassion and psychiatric counseling. We should no more affirm a boy who says he is a girl than we would a man in an asylum who claims to be Napoleon Bonaparte. Amber Athey recently wrote an article titled "My Womanhood is not Your Costume." https://spectatorworld.com/life/dylan-mulvaney-ulta-beauty-joe-biden-white-house/ A gender transition is not from male to female but from male to a freak who is a cartoonish imposter and an insult to women (as proof, just search for videos of **Dylan Mulvaney**, a trans activist currently enjoying 15 minutes of fame, including interviewing the President). Hormone treatments and surgeries do not nullify a basic fact of life: there are just two genders: male and female.

No, just because you say you are a boy doesn't entitle you to go to the girl's room or be on women's sports teams. Republican NC gubernatorial candidate Mark Robinson crisply sums it up: "Here's something else I'm not supposed to say: Ain't but two genders," he said to roaring applause. "Two genders. Ain't nothing but men and women. You can go to the doctor and get cut up, you can go down to the dress shop and get made up, you can go down there and get drugged up, but at the end of the day you're just a drugged up, dressed up, made up, cut up man or woman," he continued. "You ain't changed what God put in you, that DNA. You can't transcend God's creation I don't care how hard you try."

No, I will not affirm a child's decision to change genders; I will oppose it with advice something like "wait until you're old enough to make this decision." Let kids grow up and *then* decide.

A perhaps less obnoxious recent phenomenon is the concept of "gay pride month." We have a single holiday for mothers, for fathers, and for veterans. Why should we have an entire month where companies spend millions of dollars in ad buys using rainbows to celebrate homosexuality? Maybe we should tolerate it, but why celebrate it? **What have homosexuals actually achieved that is worthy of praise?** Aren't there other things that are more worthy of celebration?

Much of what I have said above would probably be classed as hate speech and banned or deplatformed if I attempted to post it online. But what I am advocating is not hate. It is a return to step 2 on the escalator: fair treatment. The LGBTQ community is not entitled to special treatment and our affirmation and celebration, just to fair treatment under the law. We should not permit one small minority to dictate moral issues for the whole society without even taking a vote. **We refuse to live in a dystopian cartoon**.

22. The Corporate Media
No longer the news, but instead the views of the elites

Growing up in the sixties, I recall watching one of the "big three" newscasts: **Walter Cronkite** on CBS, **Huntley and Brinkley** and later **John Chancellor** on NBC, and **Peter Jennings, Howard K. Smith, and Frank Reynolds** on ABC. These were the days when the news just gave the news. Although all of the names listed here had a slightly leftward bias, they hid it well. It was hard to tell where they stood on any issue. They just reported the facts.

Today, no matter where you tune in, you can easily tell their political position of the news anchor. Nearly all of them are not just left of center but left of left. They have redefined their mission. Previously, the mission was to report the facts. Today, the mission is to advance the progressive social justice agenda. When progressives are in charge of government (as they are today in 2024), the media morphs into what may be called "regime media" where all it does is report what the politicians in charge want them to report.

Like the rest of the progressive movement, the transformation of the media occurred first gradually, then suddenly. Back in the sixties and seventies, being a journalist didn't really carry much status. But with the sensationalization of the Watergate crisis in the seventies, every journalist wanted to be a celebrity like **Woodward and Bernstein**. Newspapers and TV News then began recruiting journalists from ivy league schools. Now, several decades later, most of the journalists have graduated from elite schools and have changed the journalism culture from one of doggedly pursuing facts and getting the facts straight to one that relentlessly hunts for a larger and larger audience. As Matt Taibbi puts it, **showmanship is**

prioritized over substance. If facts must be modified and adjusted and lensed to make this happen, so be it.

Several decades ago, the prominent linguist Noam Chomsky collaborated with Edward Herman to produce a **landmark 1988 book** *Manufacturing Consent* about how the news media operates. The authors postulate a "propaganda model" to explain how the media exerts influence over a large mass of people. They identify five "filters" any news item needs to pass through before it issues out of the gate and becomes a story:

- Ownership
- Advertising
- The Media Elite
- Flak (criticism and attacks from opponents)
- The Common Enemy

Although the book is a bit dated and some of today's independent media bypass several of these filters, most of the corporate media still can be viewed through this lens. Most consumers of news from the media don't think much about these five filters, but they basically mold the message that is being preached from the media's "pulpit." In particular, the second filter, Advertising, pulls strings and often has great influence over what the media can and cannot present. Advertisers are the main funding source for media companies, so the media needs to keep them happy. With so many news shows that begin with an announcement "brought to you by Pfizer," any negative news about Covid vaccines would never be tolerated. All media consumers need to be aware that they are being "sold" a narrative or story that is partly shaped by the advertisers who pay the bills. **The truth is sometimes secondary to the main mission to make money**.

A book by former White House Press Secretary **Ari Fleisher** brings home just how lopsided the modern news media is. His title (*Suppression, Deception, Snobery, and Bias*) and his subtitle (*Why the Press Gets so much Wrong–and Just Doesn't Care*) sums up his point succinctly. Toward the beginning of the book he describes a session he had with a couple dozen journalism students at Columbia University. He asked a simple question: how many of you voted for Hillary Clinton in 2016? Every single hand went up. All twenty-four. Fleischer then asks a rhetorical question: how different would the media be if all twenty-four had voted for Donald Trump?

Fleischer's book exposes the methods of the contemporary media. Journalism schools have been churning out democrat urban elites. The new graduates then take over the newsrooms. **Their product appeals to other college educated urban elites**. They have no clue about the lives or opinions of millions of Americans in the heartland and they just don't care.

In previous times, reporters meticulously confirmed sources before publishing facts. Today, they seem to operate a system of **"timed release" reporting**. Something sensational is reported before all the facts have been confirmed. This creates buzz and mouse clicks and fame for the reporter. Then later, as additional facts come in, an initial report may be "corrected", but by the time this is done, the correction is a minor story that gets only minimal attention. The emotions of the sensational initial report have done their job. Moreover, a single correction cannot cancel out the dozens or even hundreds of times the lie had been repeated.

A classic example of this occurred on January 6. It was widely reported that a police officer named **Brian Sicknick** had been killed when protesters bashed his head with a fire extinguisher. But then there was a long delay before the autopsy on Sicknick was released. The autopsy clearly showed Sicknick suffered no head trauma and in fact died of a stroke on January 7. Yet even after the record was corrected, some media continued to claim that protesters had killed a police officer, which was patently false.

Here are some other examples of timed-release news:

- During the 2020 elections many journalists breathlessly reported that Trump was destroying mailboxes in an effort to suppress mail in ballots. In one case they stated that many mailboxes had been destroyed and then several weeks later sheepishly admitted that the boxes in the photos were destroyed while Obama was president, not Trump.
- On August 29, 2021, the U.S. Military conducted a drone strike in Kabul Afghanistan in retaliation for an earlier suicide bomber terrorist attack. The news media shifted into high gear, applauding the military for decisive action and a "righteous strike." But several weeks later it became known that the drone strike was actually a tragic mistake, killing ten innocent civilians, including an aid worker and seven children. But once the truth emerged, it was downplayed by the media. They sensationalized the initial news when it looked good for the military but then meekly admitted their mistake and moved on.
- In February 2024, the media excitedly reported about the death of a prisoner in Russia named Alexei Novalny. The media stated over and over that Russian President Vladimir Putin had him killed. The New York Times reported "Biden Says 'Putin Is Responsible' After Report of Navalny's Death." But then in late April 2024, the Wall Street Journal reported: "Putin Didn't Directly Order Alexei Navalny's February Death, U.S. Spy Agencies Find." So much for innocent until proven guilty.

There are many examples of the media getting the story wrong to whip up anti-Trump or pro-Biden hysteria but then "correcting" the untruth days or weeks later when no one was paying attention to the story.

Author Batya Ungar-Sargon describes a major change that resulted when local media such as newspapers and TV stations were displaced by national media and then by online sources. Formerly, news reporters were ordinary people living among the average joes and janes of the heartland. But as the local newspapers shut down, journalism moved into a few large cities where nearly everyone the reporters encountered was progressive. This concentrated environment shaped the journalists' viewpoints dramatically. When everyone you know voted for Clinton, you never got any information from those who favored Trump.

After the "gradually" part of the media transformation occurred, the suddenly part began with the election of Donald Trump in 2016. Many reporters openly declared that their methods and focus had changed because Trump was a "clear and present danger." The obligation to be fair and balanced, to confirm sources and facts, took a back seat to stopping the ominous rise of Donald Trump. Social justice goals were so important that they superseded journalistic standards.

Since the 2016 election, the media's zealous pursuit of the progressive agenda became so strong that one has trouble telling the difference between the news anchors and the guests they are interviewing. They all have the same obstinate focus: advance the progressive narrative. **Facts and evidence become secondary. The left must prevail**.

The news one consumes shapes how a typical audience perceives reality. A consumer of the mainstream media would conclude that

- Donald Trump colluded with the Russians to steal the 2016 election
- The riots in the summer of 2020 following the death of George Floyd were mostly peaceful
- The January 6 riots were "the worst attack on the capital since the civil war"
- Hunter Biden's laptop was a Russian misinformation hoax
- Nearly all scientists think the earth will be destroyed in the next few decades unless we rapidly switch from fossil fuels to wind and solar
- White supremacy is the number one threat to America today
- Every white American person is guilty of racism
- A man can become a woman simply by claiming to be one.
- There is no evidence that the Covid virus originated in the Wuhan Institute of Virology

What do all these impressions have in common? They are all demonstrably false.

Another excellent resource on the corruption of the mainstream media is commentator **Glen Greenwald,** whose *System Update* podcast on Rumble presents numerous examples of the almost fraudulent performance of the media. One of the characteristics Greenwald frequently reports on is leaks from the CIA to the media. The CIA often leaks classified information to their media contacts when they want to influence public opinion. For example, in March 2024, the *New York Times* reported that failure to fund the proxy war in Ukraine would compromise our clandestine bases in that country. The Times just obediently passed on this classified information. There was no condemnation to the Times for doing this. They were just being a faithful conduit for the CIA. Meanwhile, Donald Trump is being hounded for having some classified documents in his possession which he did not share with the media.

Greenwald also reports on a revolving door between the government intelligence agencies and media and big tech firms. The most obvious examples are former intelligence chiefs like **James Clapper** and **John Brennan** who are regular contributors on CNN. Greenwald noted several former intelligence officers are winding up at several Big Tech firms.

Another strange phenomenon about the mainstream media is that they almost universally support "content moderation" or censorship of views they don't like. This flies in the face of previous generations of journalistic culture. Hitherto, the media would hound corporations or public officials to release information. But as of the 2020's. the media is basically "not curious" about a lot of issues like the origin of Covid, the corrupt business dealings of Hunter Biden, and the research of many credentialled climate scientists, including former Obama Science Advisor Dr. Steven Koonin, who contend that Climate Change is not catastrophic and that it can be managed by using technology to adapt to slight warming.

The media not only repeats the democratic party line, it has utter disdain for much of the US public. In the year 2017, **Mika Brzezinski**, on MSNBC's *Morning Joe* broadcast, was lamenting over Donald Trump making an end run around cable news by his tweets. She said he could "control exactly what people think and that is our job."

In his 2019 book, *Hate, Inc.*, journalist Matt Taibbi presents his take on how the media became corrupted. For one thing, when the media began to take sides, it developed a pattern. There is "our team" and "their team." It is America vs America. If an event occurs, the media asks, "can this be blamed on the other team?" If it can, then run the story. If not, just ignore it. **It appears that stirring up rage at the other side and blaming them** *sells*.

This tactic of stirring up indignation is also highlighted by Batya Ungar-Sargon in her excellent book *Bad News:How Woke Media is Undermining Democracy (2021)*. Her main thesis is that several decades ago, the media lost its focus on the working class and instead began catering to wealthy liberals who apparently thrive on discord. She quotes Thomas Frank from his book *What's the matter with Kansas*: "For a culture war to succeed, it must be waged against a problem that can never be solved. The goal is not to win cultural battles but to take offense conspicuously, vocally, even flamboyantly. Indignation is the great aesthetic principle of backlash culture."The media and the progressive elites never want to actually solve these problems; instead, they aim to prolong them. As the media concocts outrage and indignation, it attracts attention and mouse clicks.

Ungar-Sargon further elaborates on the metamorphosis undergone by media with the rise of media celebrities. In the past, a journalist had a low status job, but in the new era, being a journalist became a rich kid's job. In former eras, journalists would comfort the afflicted and afflict the comfortable. But as these journalists joined the ranks of the comfortable, they began to afflict the afflicted and comfort the comfortable.They began to speak power to truth instead of truth to power. They began to insist on an orthodoxy that protects the interests of the elites in a language whose burdens are given to the working class to bear. They no longer criticize the elite because they *are* the elite.

Ungar-Sargon discusses the New York Times' adjustment to the new world of the internet. The author points out that from its founding, the Times catered to a young, affluent readership. Articles in the Times were designed to make advertising of expensive items like jewelry, watches, and high end cosmetics effective. The Times basically ignored the working-class audience that could not afford these items. With the internet, it became more difficult to target ads to the upscale readers, blunting the newspaper's ability to attract advertisers.

A few years ago, the Times found a solution: it introduced a paywall. That would keep the riff-raff out and support the left-wing viewpoint the Times has been projecting. I often encounter this paywall when I am surfing the internet on a site called RealClearPolitics. com. I sometimes don't notice a link is an NYT link so when it prompts me to register to read it, I just cancel. I suspect millions of other conservatives are doing the same thing. This reinforces the polarization we see in the public. The *Times* may have some worthy things to say, but those of us on the right don't hear that message because we refuse the pay-wall.

Progressives specialize in remote large problems that can never be solved and that frankly don't need to be solved because the problems are so distant that they almost never impact the progressives or their children. Professor Victor Davis Hanson often eloquently describes this issue in his podcasts on Spotify. Progressives can easily pontificate from afar about being compassionate to the homeless and about the need to give criminals a second chance because they will never encounter homeless people or violent thugs in their own gated communities. Progressives advocate teaching social justice in the public schools, but they send their kids to private schools. Progressives complain that Joe-Six-Pack is driving his pickup too much while they have homes, yachts, and private planes with enormous carbon footprints. For progressives, the problems are always "out there."

Ungar-Sargon persuasively summarizes the main motive behind the progressives' obsession with race in *Bad News*. "When you define racism as an omnipresent white supremacist framework baked into the heart of the nation that can never be solved or extracted, you give them a culture war they can hammer away at forever, a perpetual cudgel." She continues, "Progressive elites are paying for an ideology that is in tension with what they are seeing with their own eyes. ... Wokeness doesn't ask that much of them beyond guilty feelings.... The progressives are relieved of doing anything about racial justice. They can't do anything about it but preach."

Since about a decade or two, the media also gradually took over "managing" elections through use of selective polls. They also attempted to manipulate the candidates with what Taibbi calls "stupid pet tricks conducted by gatekeeper snobs," such as asking for a show of hands on the debate stage or asking a candidate to condemn a statement of one of his opponents. Presidential campaigns morph away from explaining policy differences to harshly criticizing opponents. **The campaign is transformed into a sport**.

The media often reinforces the claim made by Hillary in 2016 that Trump supporters are a "basket of deplorables." In March 2024, two authors of a new book appeared on MSNBC. The book is titled: *White Rural Rage: The Threat to American Democracy*. The authors (Tom Schaller and Paul Waldman) made the case that rural white people are a big threat because they

- Are the most racist, xenophobic, anti-gay demographic group in the country
- Most conspiracist group (Q Anon, election denialism, Covid denialism)
- Antidemocratic sentiments: Don't believe in an independent press, most strongly Christian white nationalist
- They justify violence as an alternative to peaceful public protest.

The authors claim they bring "receipts" to prove all these points, but let's just stop and think about this a little. First of all, the idea that rural whites condone violence is just laughable. **Have you ever seen a large smash and grab riot or widespread carjacking in a small American town?** No, that only happens in large cities. These authors are applying a broad stereotypical brush to a wide swath of America. They normally condemn this approach, except when the target group is white. A lot of men in rural white America are the ones who volunteer for military service and die for their country. A loving Christian heart characterizes many in these areas. **For these authors to condemn a whole group of people like this is not just incorrect, it is preposterous.** If anyone ever wrote a book titled *Urban Black Rage: A Threat to Peace,* they would be pilloried and vilified. These authors, like many on the left, never take the time to really get to know the people they are condemning. They just sit in front of their computer and leftist news programs and hurl epithets at them from a safe distance.

Another amusing event occurred in March 2024, when former Republican National Committee Chair Ronna. McDaniel appeared for an interview on NBC's *Meet the Press.* After the interview, the former host Chuck Todd launched an embarrassing tirade about how unacceptable it was for his network to hire a former RNC chair who was, to them, an "election denier." Todd and many others at NBC had no trouble with hiring a former Biden spokesperson (Jen Psaki) but hiring a former RNC chair that was remotely associated with Donald Trump was just a bridge too far. **Todd revealed that the network has basically become an official democratic party news organization.**

The media often brands news that doesn't fit neatly into its system as "conspiracy theories." One example is the so-called "great replacement theory." They accuse the right of trying to concoct a theory that states that the left is trying to replace the white population with black and brown voters. But democrats often state explicitly that this is their goal. They write articles that claim "demography is destiny" and openly applaud the replacement of an old, white electorate. The reason they claim it is a conspiracy theory is that they don't like the fact that the right has *noticed* their agenda.

One recently successful outlet on the left has been the web side Vox. Batya Ungar- Sargon characterizes Vox as "smug" in its feature called "Explainers." Vox uses this slogan to describe its Explainers: "We live in a world of too much information and too little context. Too much noise and too little insight. That's where Vox's explainers come in." And what context do they espouse? The left, of course. That's the only context that is true, according to Vox.

A smattering of recent titles of these Vox explainers give the gist of their offering:

- The Alabama Supreme Court opinion holding that embryo's are children, explained.
- America's unique, enduring gun problem, explained.
- Trump's legal arguments for staying on the ballot are embarrassingly weak
- A legal fight over whether Texas can seize control of the border, explained
- How plagiarism became the latest weapon in culture wars
- The Supreme Court cases asking the justices to put themselves in charge of everything, explained

The reason Vox needs to explain these things is that they are positively whacky arguments. The context they need to put them into is the progressive narrative. This list of headlines tells you all you need to know about Vox.

As of today in 2024, there are some signs that the public is catching on. Alternative news sources have been established and many are just not watching or reading the regime media anymore. The newspaper *Epoch Times* appears to be the fourth most subscribed newspaper in the USA according to an NBC Report in 2023. "While most news sites are struggling to keep the doors open, The Epoch Times' revenue grew 685% in two years to $122 million." https://www.politicususa.com/2023/10/13/pro-trump-conspiracy-laden-epoch-times-is-now- fourth-most-subscribed-newspaper-in-america.html.

Many viewers are cutting the cable and instead using their Roku box to connect with podcasts platforms such as Rumble, Daily Wire, Epoch TV, and Spotify. These viewers have abandoned the thin gruel they had been ingesting from Cable News. Many of the new podcasts have much larger audiences than Cable News and other mainstream outlets such as NPR and the big three networks. **The best way to blunt the influence of these outlets that continue to spew out lies is to just not listen to them.**

Why:
Philosophical Foundation of Progressive Thought

Up to this point, we have focused on the who, when, what, and how of progressive thought. Now we turn to the "why". Progressives have built up a plausible new religion that has taken the nation by storm. Without a single vote, progressive policies have risen to a nearly unassailable position of prominence and power. We can only understand this ascendancy if we comprehend *why* they so passionately believe what they do.

Progressives saw wrongs they wanted to right. They saw racial bigotry and put policies in place to end it. They saw climate catastrophe on the horizon and proposed solutions to avert it. They recognized that women had been marginalized and recommended ways to bring them from the periphery to the center. They saw wealth and power concentrated at the very top of American society and wanted to avoid dictatorship of the wealthy and provide a fairer way to distribute wealth.

Initially, all of these crusades by the left had admirable motives and goals. The problem is that like most revolutionaries, their zeal carried them into excesses that now appear to be irrational and absurd. As the urgency of their program grew, they developed an ideology that became so dominant that it not only trumped logic and reason, it eclipsed everything else. **What had been an admirable goal became a fanatic obsession that couldn't be questioned**. The next few chapters focus on the *why* of progressivism:

- Why they are so passionate and relentless and what their main goal is

- Why democracy, their "go to" rationale, is defective
- Cultural issues
  - Adults fail our children
  - Mental Illness / Drugs
  - Looking at Screens
- Their sophisticated economic theory laid out by Thomas Piketty and a critique of its flaws with a rebuttal from Ayn Rand's *Atlas Shrugged*.
- Climate Change Alarmism

23. Three Pillars of Progressivism
Self-Evident Correctness, Reverence for
Democracy, Universal Application

In the wake of a major set of Supreme Court verdicts in June 2022, author David Atkins wrote an eloquent essay that encapsulates the key conflict between the left and right in today's America. Atkins is a writer, activist, research professional and president of The Pollux Group, a qualitative research firm. His essay, "The Supreme Court's Term Underscores Minority Rule: Blue states are being crushed by gerrymandering, a skewed Senate, and filibustering. The result is the nation's unraveling" was published in *Washington Monthly*. https://washingtonmonthly.com/2022/07/01/the-supreme-courts-term-underscores- minority-rule/, His article clearly and cogently lays out three key principles of progressivism as he reacts to what he sees as gross overreach by a system that is rigged in favor of minorities in small states. His title and subtitle neatly summarize his thesis.

Atkins theorizes that there is a center-left American majority and states that most of the country disagrees strongly with the court's rulings on Guns, Abortion, and the regulation of CO_2 to fight Climate Change. He then asserts that our constitutional system unfairly grants power to a minority to overrule the progressive majority. He notes: "This Court is destroying the uneasy détente between a legislative branch rigged in favor of rural white conservatives via gerrymandering, Senate apportionment, and the Electoral College, and a judiciary that has often protected and expanded the rights of the marginalized." He goes on to compare our system to the more enlightened systems around the world: "Most functional modern democracies do not use America's creaky presidential system, which is structurally unstable, and those that do tend to also be unstable. If the United States functioned like most modern democracies, with a parliament and proportional representation, the majority's will would hold sway more frequently." Finally, he proposes remedies such as abolishing the Electoral College, adding a few more states, and abolishing the Senate filibuster. All of these solutions follow logically from the case he has made if one accepts his premises.

Most conservatives cringe as they read Atkins' analysis. But rather than shudder and move along as conservatives often do, it is more useful to provide counterarguments. Atkins presents a finely crafted case for his position, with three main principles that underpin his (and I suspect, many other progressives') creed:

1. Obviously, self-evidently correct
2. Reverence for democracy
3. Universally applicable

All three of these principles have some surface appeal which is why they are passionately proclaimed by millions of progressives. But each has a flaw that is virtually invisible to progressives who rarely recognize gaps in their positions, largely because of the first principle.

Obviously, Self-Evidently Correct

The first principle is that **the progressive viewpoint is so obviously correct as to not even imagine that any sane person could disagree**. This attitude frequently pervades progressive thought. Looking at the three Supreme Court decisions, Progressives exclaim, "Of course it's wrong. A woman's right to control her own body is fundamental to a civilized society. To think that some politicians and bureaucrats would have the audacity to interfere with a woman's right to choose is just unfathomable. Of course guns must be outlawed to prevent needless violence. Of course the EPA must control CO_2 emissions because the planet has only a few more years before climate change becomes so catastrophic as to destroy civilization."

This cocksure attitude is explained in detail in Chapter 17: *When Theorem Becomes Axiom.*

On these three and many other issues as well, progressives employ a technique I call "**consensus expansion.**" **A premise that would be widely accepted is introduced and then its implications are recommended or stronger still, commanded**. For example, most Americans agree that a woman should have the right to choose abortion in extreme circumstances, but only a tiny fraction would agree that partial birth abortion or abortion right up to the last second before birth is tolerable. Most Americans agree that gun violence should be curbed, but a smaller fraction would go all the way to the progressive position that only criminals should have guns. And on climate change, most of the public believes that the climate has warmed since the industrial revolution and part of that warming was caused by the burning of fossil fuels. But a much smaller percentage believes that fossil fuels are the main driver of climate change and an even smaller fraction believe that continuing to burn fossil fuels will cause a major catastrophe beyond our ability to adapt to it. So the technique of consensus expansion starts with a widely accepted view and then asserts that if you believe that view, then you must also believe in the conclusion drawn by progressives. **You must go "all the way" to the left**.

Beyond consensus expansion, another factor colors the progressive lens: their isolation in their own bubble. Everyone around them thinks just like they do, because most of them live in a large urban environment, surrounded by like-minded individuals. Nearly all of the information they receive about politics and current events come from college-educated elites. The news media no longer reports the news, but instead presents the progressive narrative. University faculties have transformed our institutions of higher learning into progressive indoctrination mills. Entertainment and sports figures reinforce the progressive dogma so that even when they are relaxing, the elite intelligentsia hears only one side of any story.

The elite reinforce their prominence with mutual admiration society's such as Pulitzer Prizes, Academy Awards, the National Press Club Dinner, and the World Economic Forum in Davos each year. They bask in the admiration of their peers, most of whom have Ivy League degrees or wide followings on Social Media. **We are the smart ones, they crow. We have the correct position on nearly every issue you can name. And since we are correct, we should rule.**

The elite never would imagine having a conversation with a Wal-Mart employee in Fort Smith, Arkansas or an auto mechanic in Fort Wayne, Indiana. They disdain operators who run our steel plants or oil refineries. They look down on beauticians in hair salons and wait staff at Olive Garden. They can safely ignore opinions from dental hygienists and hospital technicians in fly-over country. They would never even consider talking with an evangelical Christian from the Bible Belt.

The elite thinks there is a consensus to support their view because they never bother to check how it plays in Peoria. Those common folk are just unenlightened rubes who need to listen more carefully to the wisdom we dispense from on high. *We* have the intelligence and education and skills. *They* need to just shut up and listen. But what the elite fail to grasp is that there are tens of millions of people in the muscular class who together keep our nation humming. They operate our manufacturing plants, drive our trucks, construct our buildings, maintain our highways, investigate crime and arrest bad guys, extinguish fires, repair our vehicles, nurse our sick, teach our kids, and clean our teeth. They form a vast swath of the American public whose opinion may not be based on an Ivy League degree, but who nevertheless have come up through the school of hard knocks. **Many of these ignored Americans have** more common sense than the typical pundit on CNN or MSNBC. The elite, however, just doesn't care. My readers who do care should consult two books: *Second Class: How the Elites Betrayed America's Working Men and Women*, by Batya Ungar Sargon (2024) and *Glass House: The 1% Economy and the Shattering of the All-American Town*, by Brian Alexander (2018). Both of these books vividly portray the plight of forgotten Americans.

Reverence for Democracy

Another progressive pillar cited in David Atkins' essay is an almost cult-like reverence for democracy. Atkins and many others seem to think that democracy is the opposite of dictatorship. But these two terms are not oxymorons. **It is possible to have a dictatorship that is driven by democracy.** With modern communications, a persuasive politician or commentator can stir up a majority to micromanage the rest of us through the majority's leaders. These leaders can easily become just as autocratic as the most famous dictators in history. See the next chapter *Democracy is not the Solution* for more details.

Atkins asserts that the U.S. Constitution is antidemocratic and to some extent he is correct. The founders created not a democracy but a constitutional republic. Their primary goal was not majority rule but individual liberty. They realized that majority rule was not always a good thing and could easily devolve into mob rule.

In our modern world of instant communications and 24-hour news cycles, the foresight of the founders is brilliant. Majority rule often means that those with the loudest megaphone get to rule everyone else. Today the loudest amplifiers are held by the progressive elite. Their woke narrative spews 24/7 out of the media centers into most homes, into screens at gasoline pumps, and into airports.

The thing to remember about majority rule is the second word: **rule.** But the founders had a different vision. **The revolutionary nature of our U.S. Constitution lay in the fact that it put limits on government, not the people.** The Constitution tells the government that it is accountable to a higher power, the American people. And the way the government is restrained is by setting up a group of competing, countervailing forces. This is the system of checks and balances and federalism.

Atkins complains about the electoral college and a U.S. Senate that favors small states. And why does he complain about this? Because it is anti-democratic. And he is right. **It does put a damper on what majorities can do to rule minorities**. It makes it much more difficult for a small group of elites to rule the rest of the country by making it submit to the opinions of NPR or the *New York Times*. America is a vast continental nation with millions of people in the heartland who may disagree with what progressives think is so obviously correct. **The "little people" in fly-over country can hide beneath the wings of the U.S. Constitution**.

Much of the criticism of the recent Supreme Court rulings has stated that the Court was exerting an inappropriate amount of power. But all three rulings took power away from the court and dispersed it among other power centers. The abortion ruling placed power at the state level. The gun ruling put curbs on unreasonable state restrictions on the right to keep and bear arms stated in the second amendment. And the climate change ruling took power from the unelected bureaucracy and returned it to its rightful place: our elected representatives.

What has the progressive left so incensed is that for several decades, they have enjoyed a steady march upward in power and influence. Now in the year 2022, they are encountering a small speed bump on their way to total domination. They sit atop nearly every important power center in the country, but there are pockets of resistance like a conservative supreme court. And they just can't stand it.

Democracy should not be held in reverence. It is often better than dictatorial systems, but it can be just as bad provided the right demagogues can rise to power. We need to focus on the higher calling: limits to government and very few limits to individual freedom. The only times the government should be stepping in should be in cases where two individuals are in conflict and need an impartial arbiter. But those cases should be rare.

Universally Applicable

The third progressive principle flows from the first two. If the progressive position is self-evidently correct and democracy is worshiped as an ideal, then it follows that our society must be centrally controlled by the educated elite. Since the progressive position is the correct one, then it should be the correct one not just in a few locations, but everywhere.

In 1973, the Roe v. Wade established abortion as a universal right in all 50 states. But the recent Dobbs ruling undoes that and leaves the decision to the individual state legislatures. Some legislatures may choose to make abortion mostly prohibited; some may make abortion available right up to the moment of birth. This is a contentious issue with strong opinions on both sides. Rather than force all fifty states into the same solution, the court deferred to the Tenth Amendment to leave the issue to the states. Federalism gives both sides what they want: the prochoice states like California and New York can have abortion with almost no restrictions; more conservative states like Mississippi and Missouri can have severe restrictions to abortion. But women in the conservative states can always travel to the ones that protect abortion opportunities.

Let me repeat: federalism gives both sides what they want. To the casual observer, this should be something progressives should support since it puts abortion to a vote of democratically elected legislatures. But this is not what progressives want, because it violates pillar 3: universal applicability. **When we scrape away the obfuscating slop of the progressive rhetoric, it all boils down to the issue of central control.** Something can be democratic but if it allows local variation, it stands as an obstacle to the progressive ideal of central control.

Central Control is the Bottom Line of Progressivism

Central control at first seems to contradict a progressivism that extols the virtues of "democracy." But the first pillar provides the bridge between pillars 2 and 3. Enlightened, college educated elites have everything "figured out." These Harvard and Yale graduates are obviously more qualified to lead than the guy who mows your lawn or the lady that waits your table. They know what is best for you in every situation. **Variation is messy! Consistency is good! So just shut up and follow the counsel of the elites!**

The end goal of central control is softened and hidden by pillar 2: a reverence for democracy. But if we take the blinders off, even a cursory examination of the three pillars reveals that democracy is only a means to an end. The progressive strategy is simple:

1. state a position as if it were a fact that is widely accepted
2. state it over and over
3. stretch a consensus over a small topic to balloon into their stated end goal
4. use a monopoly over mass media to mobilize a majority (50.5% is sufficient)
5. insult and ostracize the 49.5% who may disagree
6. cut off debate
7. control the masses

This seven-step process only differs from totalitarian dictatorship in one aspect: the need to mobilize a democratic majority. But that step gives just enough of a veneer of benign respectability to make the whole process palatable. Swimming against the progressive tide requires strenuous effort, and many in our society are too busy with other important activities like work and raising families to resist the indoctrination.

The important concept to remember is that the fundamental aim of progressivism is central control over as many aspects of life as possible. Their reverence for "democracy" is only a smokescreen that hides the real objective. This is not a "conspiracy theory." They basically say it "out loud". It is the logical conclusion drawn from their three pillars.

24. Democracy is _Not_ the Solution

Dictatorship and democracy are not necessarily opposites

Most Americans probably think that the USA is a democracy and have a very positive view of the term "democracy." This term is an antonym for the nearly universally condemned term _dictatorship_. Americans do not like the idea of a single person imposing his/her will on the public, so democracy seems to be the best alternative to that oppressive form of government. But **as good as democracy sounds, it is capable of being just as oppressive as dictatorship**.

An October 2021 Op-Ed by Democrat House Majority Leader Steny Hoyer is titled "Letting the Filibuster Stand will break Democracy" https://news.yahoo.com/steny-hoyer-letting- filibuster-stand-151609346.html?fr=sycsrp_catchall. He begins the article by declaring the U.S. Senate basically a relic of the past and no longer needed as we pursue the more noble goal of "democracy", or, as he puts it "One Person, One Vote." Like Hoyer, many contemporary commentators sing praise to the concept of democracy, as if it is a goal we should be pursuing with passionate intensity. They lament over what they see as defects in our governmental system such as the U.S. Senate and the Electoral College. It is "anti-democratic" that the two Senators from Wyoming should have the same power as the two Senators from California, which has a population more than 60 times as high. It is a travesty that Donald Trump received 3 million fewer votes than Hillary Clinton in 2016 yet still won the election.

What possible good could come out of such undemocratic features as the U.S. Senate and the Electoral College? Were the American Founders simply ignorant about what might happen in the far distant future as our nation mutated into a superpower with a population well over 300 million? It turns out that there was a brilliant method to their apparent madness. ***The goal was and should be liberty, not democracy***. The founders knew that the only way to preserve liberty was to set up countervailing power centers that would compete against each other so that no one person or group could easily obtain absolute power.

While democracy *sounds* good, it has four flaws that need to be kept in check:

- **Flaw 1:** In practice, rule by "the people" becomes rule by a few loud activists
- **Flaw 2**: Too many losers when population is large and polarized
- **Flaw 3:** A package deal: have to take bad with the good
- **Flaw 4:** Democracy can easily devolve into mob rule

These flaws are constrained by competition with other power centers set up by the founders, including the U.S. Senate, the Supreme Court, and most powerfully and effectively, the fifty individual states. Events and developments in the last few decades have, however, eroded the forces foiling the flaws and excesses of majority rule.

Flaw 1 is rarely admitted in public discourse. The vast majority of U.S. Citizens reject such policies as racking up trillions of dollars in debt that may fuel inflation, restricting U.S. Oil and Gas exploration and asking Saudi Arabia and Russia to make up the difference, giving welfare benefits to illegal immigrants, allowing people to vote without any ID, unlimited abortion, canceling people who commit macroaggressions like using the wrong pronoun or saying "All Lives Matter", and allowing males who say they are females to compete in woman's sports. Yet these and many other issues are promoted by activists with very loud megaphones that drown out the mass of citizens who are just too busy living their lives to notice and oppose these idiocies. **"Democracy," it turns out, is not rule by the people as the name implies, but rule by a few well-financed extremists**.

Flaw 2 was seen in earlier times, but as population has grown and become more fractured, its issues are becoming more pronounced. **In a 51/49 nation of 330 million, a majority rule issue often means over 160 million people are on the losing side**. The main constitutional bulwark against this flaw is the 10th Amendment that basically makes liberty of the people the default position, only to be over-ridden by a large consensus, not just a bare majority. But in recent years, particularly in the Pandemic emergency, the default has been drifting toward government control of more and more aspects of our lives: everything from how much of our hard-earned resources we can keep to what kinds of light-bulbs we can buy.

In the year 2024, we have about as close a split in Government as we've ever had. The U.S. House of Representatives currently has only a 3 vote (less than 1%) republican majority, the Senate is a 51/49 split, and the Presidential election hinged on only about 50,000 votes in a handful of states. Yet the democratic party acts as if it has a mandate to enact sweeping changes that are highly unpopular with more than a hundred million Americans, and do so using an arcane procedure known as "reconciliation" so that they need no Republican votes. This would result in 51% of the public micromanaging the other 49%, which erodes liberty.

Flaw 3 is the "package deal", where we must take the bad with the good. We cannot vote on each issue but must elect a representative who votes on many issues. In recent history, our representatives often combine many issues into one large legislative bill. So, for example, the bill may contain funding we support for roads and bridges desperately in need of repair, but the same bill may contain billions of dollars for a "Civilian Climate Corp." In recent history many legislative bills extend to well over a thousand pages and are voted on almost immediately after the ink is dry. Obviously, no one has had enough time to read it, let alone study it. So **laws are made not by our elected representatives but by unelected interns and staffers burning the midnight oil. This is** *called* **democracy but it is not!**

Flaw 4 has, up to very recently, largely been minimized. Before the age of modern communications, the incitement of mobs has been difficult. Perhaps the most notable historic example of mob rule was the French Revolution of the 1790's, that started with noble-sounding slogans like *Libertie, Equalitie, Fraternitie*, but then morphed into a movement that literally chopped off the heads of those who failed to support the mob with sufficient vigor.

Modern mobs have not yet resorted to chopping off heads like the French Revolutionaries, but they have inflicted harm on those who fail to follow their lead. These mobs have been fueled by some old but also some very new power centers including Urban Elites, Universities, News Media, and Big Tech. The common thread that drives these power hubs is, simply, instant and ubiquitous communication. In the past, groups such as the Think Tanks and the ACLU often combined to *check* the power of the central government. They were champions of the Bill of Rights and worked tirelessly to stifle efforts by the Feds to gather more power. But today, the some of these groups have formed a powerful alliance with Big Government and Big Tech to unanimously promote an agenda they call "woke". The alliance sponsors doctrines as if they had the force of law even though no one voted for any of their measures. Big Tech especially enforces conformity to rules it just makes up without any input from the public. It uses its power as the gatekeeper of information to stifle dissenting voices.

Figure 4 (below) depicts how the modern mob works:

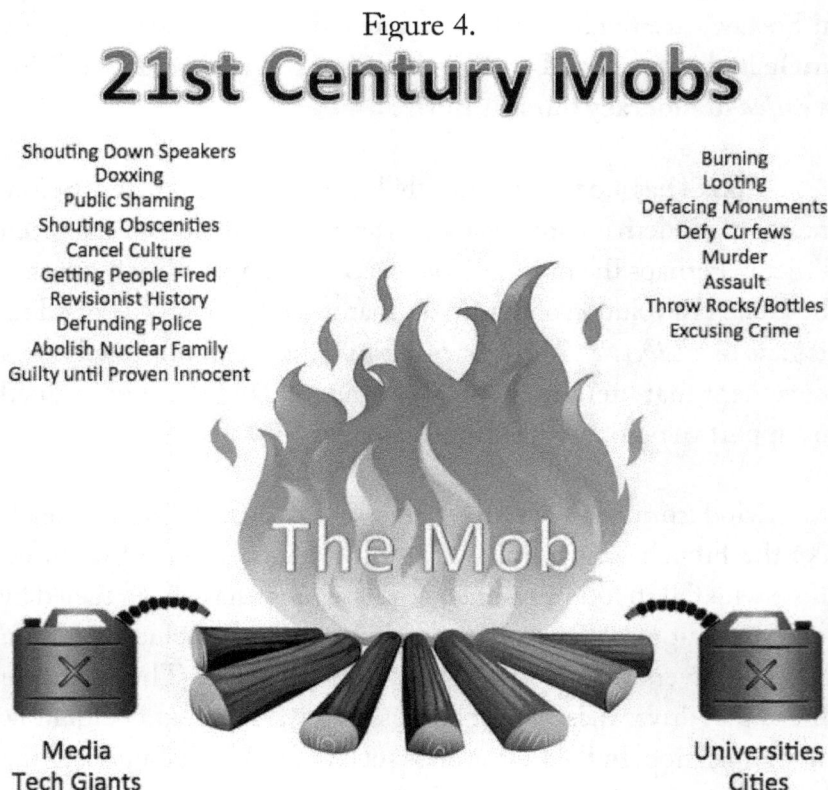

Figure 4.

21st Century Mobs

Shouting Down Speakers
Doxxing
Public Shaming
Shouting Obscenities
Cancel Culture
Getting People Fired
Revisionist History
Defunding Police
Abolish Nuclear Family
Guilty until Proven Innocent

Burning
Looting
Defacing Monuments
Defy Curfews
Murder
Assault
Throw Rocks/Bottles
Excusing Crime

The Mob

Media
Tech Giants

Universities
Cities

Twenty-First century mobs have caused extensive havoc in America in recent years. People have been fired from their jobs for not being sufficiently woke. Small business owners had their shops destroyed by burning and looting mobs in the summer of 2020. They paid a price for the death of George Floyd even though these shop owners were completely innocent.

But it's not just the extreme of mobs that we need keep in mind. Long before majority rule breaks out into mobs, we need to recognize the other three flaws of democracy. The majority is just one of the entities jostling for power and influence in our complex modern society. We need other power centers to counterbalance the excesses.

Which brings us back to the so-called flaws in our constitution: the creation of alternate power centers to compete and restrain each other. If we think about it rationally, we see that the founders actually created a brilliant system. The fifty semi-sovereign states form perhaps the most formidable bulwark against the tyranny of the majority. The loud bullhorns of woke Californians do not resonate in Texas and Florida (and vice versa), mitigating Flaw 1. Keeping some power dispersed among the various states give people recourse when they are on the losing side of a majority rule issue. They can simply move to a state where they are on the winning side, mitigating Flaw 2.

Flaw 3 (the package deal) could be greatly diminished by a simple rules change in the House and Senate. It would have three features

- No piece of individual legislation can be any longer than, say, 5 pages or roughly 4,000 words
- Each piece of legislation can only contain one topic; Funding for roads and bridges would not be combined with voting or immigration reform legislation
- Each piece of legislation would need to be read aloud, in its entirety, prior to passage with at least 2 hours of debate after the reading.

A reform like this would help to enact bills which have broad bipartisan support. It would help voters get a better sense of how well they agree with their representative. Current representatives can say "Well, I voted for the bad parts of the Bill because I really wanted the new bridge in our district." Under this new reform, such an excuse would no longer be tenable. In addition, this would put a little sand in the gears of the process which cranks out legislation and restrictions on freedom. **We don't need more laws; we need fewer**.

Flaw 4 (mobs) is a tougher nut to crack. With modern ubiquitous communications, mobs can easily be incited and once they start, they can be difficult to stop as we saw in the George Floyd riots. Several measures can be taken to prevent democracy from going wild and devolving into mob rule:

- Mob activities should not be tolerated. People who loot and riot should be prosecuted to the fullest extent of the law and should be forced to pay restitution to those whose businesses they have destroyed. They should do jail time with high bale.
- People who shout speakers down should be forcibly removed from the venue.
- Big Tech must be shorn of its power to unilaterally claim personal information. A person's information should belong to that person, and Big Tech should pay a price for it. It should be difficult to find the information needed to Dox someone. Doxing should be punished.
- Organizations should make a special effort to recruit and hire those who have been canceled because of thought crimes. We need some "good guys" to counteract the "bad guys."
- The news media should pay a price for disseminating lies.
- We must promote and defend the nuclear family in the face of withering attack.
- Crimes like shoplifting should not be excused.
- Bail reform needs to be reversed to stop the revolving door of commit a crime, be arrested, be turned loose, and commit another crime. This need not be a federal effort. Each state and locality can regulate its own law enforcement.

None of these measures would enjoy widespread public support, so they might be considered to be "anti-democratic." **But that is the point.** *Democracy is not the goal; liberty is.* **Democracy gone wild needs to be reined in to allow liberty to flourish.**

25. Adult America Fails Its Children
Prioritizing Careers and "Stuff" over Children

A strong case can be made that one of the single most destructive events in 20th and 21st century America was a major breakdown in the way children are raised. This was not a universal phenomenon, but it was widespread. You probably know some people who did an excellent job raising their kids. You may even be one of those excellent parents who got the work/life balance right. You might have figured out how to squeeze an active life with your children into your schedule without compromising your career or your marriage. If you are one of those, I say, bravo! But many more other than you have not gotten the balance right.

As I attempt to analyze this difficult subject, I must state some caveats at the outset:

- I often may make generalizing comments that sound like I am accusing all parents of malfeasance. That is not my intent. When I generalize, I am only trying to say that a tendency happens often, not necessarily all the time.
- I have no special expertise in sociology or anthropology. I'm just one more dad who reads the news and observes the world around him.
- As far as I know, there are no studies that use surveillance cameras inside homes to see how parents actually behave. Many of my conclusions are based on anecdotal data and on the indisputable fact that every person has the same amount of time available. If both parents work, their work takes some of the time that could have been devoted to being with their kids.

- I have to admit that I made many of the mistakes in child-raising that I identify for America at large. I confess that I too failed my kids in many ways, and I regret my poor life choices. I am no saint here.

With these cautions in mind, I want to dive into a difficult subject that some may find downright offensive. But the failure to raise kids properly has, I think, been a major factor in the topsy-turvy world we inhabit today, so we must acknowledge and understand this shortcoming if we are ever to create a better world.

There was no single issue that encapsulates this failure. As I attempt to describe what happened, I will focus on the following main topics:

- The age of innocence ends in the late sixties
- The demise of "age-appropriateness"
- Breakdown of discipline in homes and schools
- The idea that what kids need is nice homes and clothes rather than love and attention
- Diversions like TV and internet in place of personal attentiveness from parents
- The parents' careers trump the needs of kids
- Farming out child care to contractors instead of doing it ourselves
- The decay of public education
- Profligate spending by adults, passing debts on to our kids

The End of the Age of Innocence

I spent my childhood in the 1950's and early 1960's. For me and my family, these were "happy days." I and other kids in the neighborhood (in Northern New Jersey close to New York City) often walked around even at night with no fear of being molested or harmed. We would often go to the neighborhood movie theater in the evening and then go to a pizza place on the edge of the seedy side of town with no adult supervision. These were also the days when we could go out trick-or-treating and get things like apples or other unwrapped candies with no fear of any unpleasant surprises.

The economy was booming in the fifties and sixties. My dad had a good job with a major airline. Our childhood home was quite modest. I estimate the home was about 1700 square feet, had only one bathroom, yet we still managed to squeeze a family of seven into it. We normally drove an old used car and my mom made our grocery budget stretch by using S&H Green Stamps and by using a concept called "layaway" where she would make a partial payment on an item that would be held for her and then later make the final payment and pick it up at the store. Credit cards were rare back then.

Our family life was cohesive. We all gathered around the dinner table every night (we very rarely went to restaurants), and we minded our dad and mom. We recognized that the family was not a democracy and the parents called the shots. We all got home at the right time or we knew there would be disciplinary action.

Laundry was a tedious affair using a wringer washer. We didn't have a dryer, so we had to hang clothes on a rope called a "clothesline" to dry in the sun. If it started to rain, we had to scurry out and quickly bring the clothes inside.

I and my siblings walked to school (about a mile or mile and a half), and at school, we sometimes groaned about homework, but we (most of the time) paid attention to the teachers and behaved. We sometimes would pass notes in class but at my school no one ever took drugs or brought weapons to school.

I recall two disciplinary events that occurred when I was in high school. In one, I had accidentally brushed against the purse of a teacher in the hallway and she loudly dressed me down for the rudeness of not saying "excuse me." The other event occurred in the school library. Something frustrating happened and I said "dang." The teacher thought I said a different word and sent me to the principal's office where I got a scolding for using foul language.

In the early sixties, I and other kids my age just played spontaneously. There was no plan. We would play catch with a football or play stickball. We would walk to the park and play on the swings and other playground equipment. We had fun playing games that reflected the infancy of the space program. We used a large box from an appliance and made it into a "space capsule" where we glued construction paper and other odds and ends onto one surface to simulate a control panel. One of us would be outside the capsule and would make "radio calls" to the crew.

Although we had a television, it was black and white until the mid-sixties. There were only three channels and they all signed off late at night, playing the star-spangled banner. There were no cell phones, only a landline. If I wanted to call a girl and ask her out, her dad might answer the phone. This made me nervous and hesitant as an adolescent.

These were the low-tech days before the invention of things we take for granted today. We lived modest lives but we did not feel deprived. As a family, we played board games and just basically hung out with each other and with our friends in the neighborhood. We went to school, went to church, and talked face to face. We played with our friends for hours. Much of the time my mom and dad didn't know where I was, but they did not worry. They knew I was a "good kid" who played with other "good kids" in the neighborhood.

In today's crime-ridden environments, play time must be structured. Parents have to carve out time to take their kids to the park or some other attraction. In my childhood, we just went next door and knocked on the door and then went out to play. It was spontaneous and just, well, **"fun."**

Little did we know that just over the horizon, a brave new world was waiting to crash into our idyllic lives. The beginning of the end seems to have been around the late 1960's. Until that time, government was small and presidents were respected. But then Johnson got us bogged down in Vietnam and Nixon continued the war for years.

The late sixties also was the time we recognized major flaws in America that screamed out for correction. Both African Americans and women were marginalized and treated like second-class citizens. Our air and water were filthy with pollutants. The Soviet Union held the threat of nuclear war that could wipe out our capitalist haven. There were assassinations of major figures like JFK, RFK, and MLK. And, of source, the pointless Vietnam war dragged on and on, killing and crippling many young men with virtually no gain for America's interest.

So what seemed to be an almost ideal society actually had many cracks that needed to be patched. While we had the major triumph of putting a man on the moon, problems back on earth languished with the only solutions we could see coming from politicians and bureaucrats.

The government grew dramatically to address the needs that had been piling up. LBJ's *Great Society* declared a "war on poverty" and let socialism creep into what once had been a vibrant free market. **While the intentions of politicians were good, new programs had**

side- effects, most notably the breakup of the family. Since the government could take care of children, fathers became expendable.

Women also began to enter the workforce in droves. For many years, they had been deprived of the opportunity to build careers and now they were liberated and able to fulfill their dreams. But there was one little problem with this new advance. **Children**. It turns out that children need a lot of attention. Theoretically, we could have given women their careers and still raised children if the father was willing to stay home and sacrifice his career. But that's not the way it turned out. Instead, many families were headed by parents who both worked. This brought in a lot of extra income and enabled the families to buy large homes, but it also meant that parents had a lot less time for their kids.

The Demise of Age-Appropriateness

During the fifties and sixties, there were some topics that just were not discussed around kids. These included things like sex and gender, drugs, and foul language. America back then complied with an **unspoken compact that kids did not need to be exposed to sensitive topics because they were not mature enough to understand them adequately**.

As we watch reruns of shows like *Leave it To Beaver*, *The Dick Van Dyke Show*, and *Father Knows Best*, we never see things like nudity or obscene language. Married couples, if ever shown in bed, are often shown in separate twin beds. Ward Cleaver never raises his voice to Beaver and Wally. Instead, he models decent behavior and expresses disappointment when his kids do things like lying or pranks. In my childhood home, I never heard my dad or mom utter curse words and rarely did they even raise their voice. A sharp look was all that was needed to deter misbehaving.

In today's world of 2024, we seem to have broken the implied compact of age appropriateness. TV and the internet abound in images and videos that kids can see. It is hard to shield our kids from things, and their immature minds often become corrupted by exposure to these topics. In addition to media exposure, kids are now even sometimes invited to drag shows with a lot of obscene language and gestures. America will reap some cruel results. We just need to **let kids be kids** and only learn some things when they are old enough to understand them and put them in context.

Breakdown of Discipline in Homes and Schools

The breakdown of discipline in homes and schools is certainly among the worst, most destructive developments that have caused chaos in America today. After we Baby Boomers embarked on parenthood, we recalled how we chafed under the discipline of our parents and we. resolved to do better. So we took seminars about a concept called "Gentle Parenting" and gradually began adopting some of these methods. For example, in place of just telling a kid to do something, instead give them a choice.

This does not always work. Some kids want to push the envelope to see just how far they can go. The parent asks them to do something, and they hem and haw, and drag things out, sometimes causing parents to be late for work. They also learn that their smiling parents will tolerate defiant behavior if they throw a tantrum. So they fuss and moan because that is what their parents are rewarding.

I recall two incidents when as a young engineer in the 1980's, I participated in Junior Achievement's *Project Business*. I would visit a local high-school to explain how businesses worked. Two schools left a lasting impression.

One of these schools was a Parochial School. As I arrived at the class room, every kid in the class stood up and said, in unison, "Good Morning, Mr. Martin." They paid attention and asked good questions and it was a delight to teach them.

The other school was a public school in a fairly affluent neighborhood. The class was basically comprised of three groups: a few loud-mouthed rabble rousers, the average students who just were trying to get by, and the advanced students who really wanted to learn. No matter what I tried, I could not get the provocateurs to shut up. They just ruined it for everyone else. This bad behavior shocked me. In my own high school experience, students were quiet and paid attention. There were very few disruptors.

These incidents happened in the 1980's. Fast forward to 2020, and I'm guessing that discipline in many schools is even worse. I have heard anecdotes from teachers to confirm the problems they face. They may send an unruly student to the principal's office, but that threat is not a deterrent to bad behavior. Many unruly students treat a trip to see the principal as a "break" from class. Some teachers also confront kids with "fluid genders" where they are a girl one day and a boy the next. What a challenge!

One invention of the modern age was the discovery of a disease called attention deficit disorder (ADD). This was mainly suffered by young boys who had extremely short attention spans. By the wonders of modern medicine, the drug called Ritalin was found to have a calming effect on disruptive boys. **As a young boy, I know I had a short attention span. After all, I was a little boy! That's how they are**. I never heard of ADD or Ritalin nor did any of my friends, and we turned out fine. The use of drugs as a substitute for discipline has not worked well.

Some kids are feeding their ADD by watching many short videos on Tik-Tok. This trains their minds to have short attention spans and when they are forced by circumstances to endure a longer time event, they freak out. So once again, America has come up with a solution known as "Mental Balance" clinics where they are trained to function as a normal kid would have in decades past.

As young students discover how hard they can push their teachers, they later enter the workforce with a defiant attitude. Instead of taking instructions from bosses and pitching in to get the job done, they complain and try to do as little as they can get away with. Outside the workplace, some graduates of our public schools who paid no attention to discipline become thugs who think they can perpetrate carjackings and smash and grab looting.

My portrait of the fifties as the age of innocence is somewhat pollyannish. One unfortunate thing that occasionally happened with children back then were domineering parents who basically abused their children. Policy makers wanted to protect children in these dangerous situations. But in so doing, we went overboard and basically took discipline out of the toolbox of parents and teachers, with disastrous consequences.

Our society only runs smoothly when people recognize the role they perform and try to advance the goals of the organization they serve. **When everyone is resentful and arrogantly assumes they know better than the boss, order breaks down and chaos rises**. We see the results today.

"Stuff" or Love and Attention?

As America left the 1970's, a new standard for homes emerged. The little home I grew up in would be considered almost a shanty compared to the McMansions we see all over America today. We all want to "keep up with the Joneses". We all need high ceilings, three bathrooms, four bedrooms, plush carpet and hardwood, and multi-car garages. My childhood home had none of these amenities, and **yet we scraped by**.

Starting around the time two-career families became widespread, large homes also proliferated. Parents basically made a decision that **"stuff" that could be bought was more important than love and time with their kids**. With the advent of computers and the internet, parents now had a way for the kids to entertain themselves.

It was bad enough in single parent broken homes, but even intact two parent homes short- changed the kids. After coming home from a hard day at the office, kids want our attention, but the parents are just too worn out and so they send the kids to their rooms where they have plenty of things to occupy their time.

Many parents like their "me" time. They feel like their work takes over some of that "me" time so they have to make it up at home. But the kids then wind up losing the parents not only during their work hours and commuting hours, but also during the time the parents need to relax after work. That doesn't leave much time left over for the kids.

It's a vicious cycle. The parents get two good-paying jobs so they can buy a nice home and other "stuff." But then they go into debt because they always want more. So they need the extra income to support yet more stuff. Meanwhile, the kids are left holding the bag. The kids retreat into their rooms where they use video games and other diversions to occupy their time. **Somehow we as a society made a tradeoff: more stuff and less love and attention for our kids. How's that working out?**

Career Trumps Kid's needs

Many parents like to pursue exciting careers. As an engineer for forty years at three Fortune 500 companies, I can testify about how fulfilling a career can be. I loved the sense of accomplishment when I was able to help other engineers access complex information with my software application that mined factory floor instrument data and presented it in slick charts. I loved the status and prestige I received, including being named a "Technical Fellow." I took pride in the fact that my software was used in many different locations, including some abroad in places like Sweden, Italy, and Taiwan, all of which I visited for my company.

A career is so meaningful, so exciting. In contrast, teaching small children the basics of life can be so boring and so mundane. No one receives any recognition for excellence as a parent. It's just day-in day-out drudgery that oftentimes seems to be going nowhere. It is such an imposition on the precious time of a brilliant manager or doctor or scientist or lawyer. The more time a professional spends with his or her kids, the less effective they are at their job. Then the boss starts to notice and become even more demanding. **Your kids are not the priority at our company. You will just have to deal with that reality**.

In the last few decades, our kids have increasingly been sent to the back of the line for love and attention from their parents. The parents have a dilemma: they need to succeed to pay the mortgage and save up for junior's college fund. But to do that, they need to spend more and more time either at the office or doing work from home with the door shut. **Kids get the message**. They sense that the parent's career is *way more* important than the kids are, and some get despondent after trying to get parental time and being rebuffed repeatedly.

Farming out Childcare

Even in the fifties and sixties before the advent of two career families, kids went to school for several hours a day and this eased the child raising load on parents. Kids also played outside with their friends, giving parent's more time. But as two-career families proliferated, it became clear that the time at school just wouldn't cut it. For one thing, school basically doesn't kick in until about age five, so for several years school was not an option. Even after reaching school age, many parents needed more time beyond school hours to pursue their careers.

Since both parents need a career both to pay the bills and to fulfill a meaningful life goal, they realize pretty quickly that they need some help raising children. The capitalist economy came up with a solution: **Day Care**. If we as parents don't have enough time to love and care for our kids, we can just hire contractors to do it. This seems to be a win-win-win solution. Parents get the time they need. Kids get the care they need. And Day Care facilities get the business they need.

But once again, **the kids get the short end of the stick**. In place of personal attention from parents who love them, they are thrust into a situation where they are competing with dozens of other kids to get care from people who have been hired to do a job. This is a distinct downgrade from the love and attention we got from our parents in the fifties and sixties.

An alternate solution that seems to work well for many two-career families is help from grandparents. If the grandparents live near and are retired, they have the time and nearly as much love to share with their grandchildren. For many busy two career families, this appears to be a good solution. Kids get love and attention, the parents can still pursue their careers and grandparents often love helping raise their grandchildren. Unfortunately, however, this solution is not always available to all families.

Another solution that works well is hiring a full-time "nanny" to care for children while the parents are at work. Some of these nannies can make a big positive difference in the lives of kids. Conscientious nannies keep the kids away from viewing screens and engages the kids in fun activities, many times outdoors. I personally know a nanny who does an excellent job. The one issue with this solution is that many parents cannot afford to hire a full time nanny, so it is only rarely a viable alternative child raising solution.

I've often heard commentators say something like, "kids are resilient." But what they really mean is, **"sorry, kids, but you'll just have to accept the situation so mommy and daddy can go off to work to earn our stuff and impress the boss."** Again I reiterate that some two career families have somehow managed to give their kids the attention they need, but many have not.

Decay of Public Education

Public Education was pretty good when I was growing up. Schools focused on Reading, Writing, and Arithmetic, with a few other things like History, Science, and Physical Education thrown in. The public schools exercised discipline when needed and order in the classroom was widespread. Our kids learned enough to be admitted to universities after they graduated and from there embarked on fulfilling careers.

But around 1980, what seemed to be a pretty good system suffered a heavy blow. Up till 1980, education was almost entirely managed locally. But President Jimmy Carter created the federal Department of Education because education was just *so important* it needed guidance from the federal government. Never mind that the Tenth Amendment forbade federal involvement in education. The Feds just did it anyway, using the nebulous "general welfare" clause as their catch-all justification.

Federal involvement at first seemed benign. The feds gave grants to states and localities to help them fund their education systems. Initially, the grants were basically unconditional. But over time, the grants had strings attached. The schools could only get the funding if they obeyed federal guidelines.

Gradually, the mission of schools was commandeered from Washington DC. Instead of teaching kids the basic skills of reading, writing, and arithmetic, the schools started teaching the kids about **social justice**. Instead of teaching them science, they learned about the crisis of Climate Change. Instead of equipping kids with basic literacy skills, schools aimed to inspire them to be social justice warriors. Though many progressives insist on a separation of church and state, they nevertheless attempt to indoctrinate our kids in their own humanist dogma which has all the hallmarks of a religion. And so the public school now churns out kids who are deprived of basic literacy skills and instead imbued with progressive doctrine on gender and critical race theory.

Profligate Spending/Passing on Debt to Kids

One of the more pernicious things American adults perpetrated against their kids was the absolute refusal to keep government spending within the bounds of tax receipts. **Both parties spent billions of dollars they didn't have on programs we didn't need.** As of 2023, three spending items comprised a total of 55% of the Federal Budget: Social Security, Health Care, and Interest on the debt. Each of these items is on "auto pilot" meaning that they can never be reduced or even contained. **They just grow and grow as demand for handouts skyrockets.**

With no ability to ever cut any of these large entitlements, interest on the debt continues to soar. While Social Security and Medicare get some funding from future recipients, much of the funding comes from the young who are not yet tapping these funds. As a result, we are witnessing an enormous transfer of wealth from young families struggling to survive to older Americans, many of whom are doing quite well as they enjoy their 401K nest eggs.

There are some indications that the math will never add up. It's all a matter of supply and demand. People are living longer due to advances in medical technology. In previous generations, a typical worker would retire at age 65 and die at age 70. Today, many are retiring in their late 50's and early sixties and then living well into their eighties and even nineties. As the population ages, they need even more health care to extend their lives a few more months. Their bills must be funded by younger workers who are paying into these programs. But with interest rates rising, demand for debt service is putting more and more pressure on these programs. The government has basically morphed into an organization that **takes money from the young and healthy and gives it to the old and unhealthy**. This provides incentives to have fewer of the former and more of the latter. Many are riding in a wagon being pulled by fewer and fewer strong participants. This is a bad deal for the young taxpayers who are supporting the system. Something has to give.

Conclusion: How We Adults Failed our Kids

Many (not all, but many) American adults should be ashamed of what has been done to future generations. Previous generations like the World War II generation were dedicated to leaving a better world for their offspring. In contrast our generation (Baby Boomers) appears to have sacrificed our kids for selfish ends.

I must emphasize again that not every parent engaged in behavior I have described in this chapter. Most of the case I am making here is anecdotal. We don't have any data on how much time parents are spending with kids in the home. We don't have any data on the quality of that time. Nevertheless, there is enough circumstantial data to suggest that many parents failed their kids in the following ways:

- The divorce rate rose sharply in the last few decades, resulting in many kids growing up in single parent homes.
- Many fathers have abandoned their families or just send them checks but no attention.
- Even in healthy two-parent homes, two careers often obligate the parents to spend much less time with their children than we did when we were their age.
- Spontaneous "play time" with friends appears to be a relic of the sixties. Safety concerns make it necessary for parents to provide structured and supervised play time.
- Tolerance of crime and lax enforcement has resulted in unsafe streets for our kids.
- Worn out parents get home from work and demand some "me-time" to recover from the stress of the workday, further shortchanging the love and attention our kids crave.
- Some parents have determined that it is more important to accumulate "stuff" than to give children the care and attention they need.
- Many parents have farmed out their child raising duties to day care centers where the kid has to compete against dozens of other kids for attention from an employee who is just doing a job, and under no obligation to love the child.
- Public Education has devolved from a peaceful environment to learn basic life skills into a chaotic situation which attempts to indoctrinate rather than teach.

- Lack of discipline both in homes and schools has fostered an atmosphere where kids are constantly pushing the envelope, complaining, and not achieving anything worthwhile. They graduate from schools with a hostile attitude toward authority figures. Social chaos becomes the norm.
- Instead of using discipline to control unruly behavior, many parents give their children drugs like Ritalin to curb their short attention spans.
- The federal government has morphed into an organization that largely functions to transfer wealth from the young and healthy to the old and unhealthy, piling up trillions in debt and obligations that the young must bear in future years.

I defy any of my fellow baby boomers to find a way to be proud of this record. After our parents sacrificed so much for us, we don't seem to be willing to do the same for our kids. **We want our stuff and our leisure time and we want it now,** and for many, kids are just getting in the way of the good life on the golf course or at the beach. That is a disgraceful tragedy that has already had devastating repercussions and will continue to plague America until parents recover the selfless attitude of our parents.

26. Mental Illness / Drugs
Are you sad? We have a pill for that!

Another major shift in American society over the past few decades can be seen in the way mental illness is managed. Mental illness has been with us for thousands of years. In recent history, some mental patients were treated with appalling cruelty. Perhaps the most famous case was that of Rosemary Kennedy, sister of JFK. In 1941, at the age of 23, she was given a lobotomy to treat her mental illness. Following this barbaric procedure, she was institutionalized for decades and lived a dreary life.

In today's America, we don't do lobotomies anymore. We also have discontinued other inhumane treatments that were inflicted on the mentally ill in times past. These treatments included electric shock treatment and the use of straitjackets. You can go online to get a sense of the primitive methods that were used to treat the mentally ill in times past.

Several decades ago, many reformers advocated a more humane way to treat the mentally ill. One prominent trend was called "deinstitutionalization." It was deemed to be inhumane to lock up mental patients and take away their freedom without their consent.

Fast forward to the year 2024. If you want to see a mental institution, all you need to do is to visit the streets of San Francisco, Los Angeles, or Seattle. There you will see vast encampments of homeless individuals, many of whom are mentally ill. They live in tents and sleep on the sidewalk. They accost strangers for donations. They sometimes harass and assault passersby. Many are offered space in shelters, but most of them decline the service because they don't like the rules.

I confess I don't know the best way to treat the mentally ill but having them sleep on the streets is probably not the best way. Progressives think we need to just give these people what they want. So they offer food and other services to make their lives on the streets a little more bearable. This only encourages more homeless to join these encampments.

The result is that there are large neighborhoods in LA, SF, and Seattle that become "no go zones." Stores in those neighborhoods cannot survive because potential customers don't want to step over bums in the streets. In addition, the mentally ill homeless often have drug addiction problems, and they discard their needles on the street. They also often urinate and defecate onto the street, creating an unhealthy, filthy environment.

Mental Illness Proliferates in the USA

According to the National Institutes of Health, "mental illnesses are common in the United States. It is estimated that more than one in five U.S. adults live with a mental illness (57.8 million in 2021)." **This is an astonishingly high figure. More than 50 million mentally ill?**

This high figure strains credulity, but it makes sense when you consider that the definition of mental illness has been quite elastic in the last few decades. What formerly were simply moods and emotions are now being diagnosed as mental illnesses. Who among us haven't suffered sadness as we encounter difficulties in life. Before about 1990, these mood swings were just part of life. But today, they are diagnosed as a mental illness (depression) and *surprise surprise,* **there's a pill for that.**

According to the CDC's National Health and Nutrition survey, the use of anti-depressant drugs like Zoloft and Paxil quadrupled from 1990 to 2010. For women between the ages of 45 to 64, the rate rose from about 5% in 1990 to over 20% in 2010. It's hard to get data from 1990 to 2020, but it has probably gotten even higher in recent years.

We must ask ourselves: is this drug an appropriate remedy for this many people? Or are the drug companies and psychiatrists simply cashing in on a perceived problem that can be fixed with a pill? I don't know the answer, but here's another question. **How did we survive in the 1970's and 1980's without these drugs?** I suspect people just "toughed it out" and got through their anxiety or sad moods. We don't know, but I don't recall that time to be riddled with untreated depression and sad faces. In fact, I recall seeing more smiles in those days. I believe that America is being overmedicated. Someone should do some research in this area.

More Potent Drugs Ruin Lives

In addition to the drugs used to treat mental illness, other painkiller drugs have proliferated in modern America. In my childhood, I had heard of "morphine", heroin, and valium (and, of course, the old standby alcohol) but back in the sixties, seventies, and eighties, these drugs did not seem to pose a widespread societal risk. Back then, I had never heard of any of the hit parade of drugs that are in common use today including OxyContin and Fentanyl. These drugs are useful in hospitals treating patients with severe injuries. But after these patients go home from the hospital, they continue to use the drugs and many get hooked on them. After a while, the drugs are not used as a therapeutic but as a recreational drug to help the addict get "high." The international market has evolved to meet the demand for these drugs, and millions of pills flow into America over our porous border.

Young people who have lost their jobs due to offshoring to places like China get despondent and then get hooked on drugs like Fentanyl. They lead hopeless lives that then end in suicide. They die un-noticed and are often not even mourned. How many once vibrant little American cities have been decimated by the one-two punch of factory closings followed by Fentanyl-induced suicides of its young men? This is a serious issue that is being largely ignored in the mainstream media. Yet it has devastated millions of Americans.

Author Peter Schweizer analyzes this issue in great detail in his book *Blood Money* (2024). The author contends that China is intentionally attempting to destroy America by infesting it with large amounts of Fentanyl. Many commentators put most of the blame on young men who get hooked on this drug. But Schweizer states that this attitude is like trying to analyze the rubble after an attack instead of focusing on the gun that produced the shrapnel. Many politicians and businessmen are so hooked on the millions of dollars flowing their way from China that they won't say anything for fear of offending the Chinese. Meanwhile, China continues an attack on America as it uses a technique called "Murder with a borrowed knife." Mexico often gets blamed, but every stage of the supply chain is managed by Chinese overlords. Mexico is just a middle man in the Chinese plot to destroy America from within.

The twin scourges of newly "discovered" mental illnesses and the proliferation of drugs has produced devastating results for America. In previous times, we "got by" without all these new drugs and life in America was really pretty good. Drugs and mental illness are so deeply entrenched in our midst today that no easy, obvious solution is available. But someone has to think deeply about this to prevent the formation of a nation of drugged up zombies.

27. *Looking at Screens*
Obsessed with being admired by others

Today in the year 2024, millions of Americans seem to be addicted to their phones and computer tablets. Go to any restaurant or shopping mall or mass transit and you'll see people scrolling through their social media posts. They need to have the latest news, and they want it right now!

These screens offer a lot of conveniences. One can find goods online and get something delivered overnight. One can text a friend to set up a dinner engagement. One can keep up with the news. One can even research a complex topic and have instant access to information that until about twenty years ago was available only to a few elite scholars. I get it. Instant access to information is a tremendous advance for our civilization.

But we seem to have lost the traditional wisdom that used to prevail: **all things in moderation**. Many think that if some is good, then more is better. But we reach a point where we're so dependent on our screens that our face-to-face social skills atrophy. This is so pervasive that there's even a popular new acronym to describe the opposite of our screens: IRL (In Real Life). The screen addiction is particularly acute in adolescents and young adults. Unlike older adults, social media has been available for these young people all their lives. They've never known anything else, so they just assume it's always been like this.

According to Pew Research, as of the year 2021, the average teenager spends more than 8 hours per day scrolling through their social media. They essentially have a full time job just keeping up with their screens. What kinds of things are they doing during these hours?

It appears that the main thing they are doing is saying "look at me, look at the things I am doing." Eight hours a day of **this inevitably molds a narcissistic lifestyle**. These teens are so egotistical, such show-off's, that this behavior becomes embedded in their character.

If you met a typical person at a social gathering and all they could talk about is themselves, you would probably find an excuse to duck out and talk to someone else. But electronic social interactions give several advantages that take the edge off of how obnoxious it sounds. First, the recipient is not "trapped" standing next to someone. They can read the text when they have time. Second, self-important teens are communicating with other self-important teens, and each side gives the other some leeway because each side recognizes the "high" they receive when they gain followers or get "liked."

But these constant jolts of dopamine over time dull a person's ability to interact with people face to face. They find that the artificial delight they receive electronically is more enjoyable and less awkward. It is easier to just text someone than it is to call them on the phone or, perish the thought, actually meet them and talk face to face. **There are risks in social contact that we avoid when we hide behind a screen.**

Daily Wire Podcaster Matt Walsh has a feature called the "Daily Cancellation" where he pokes fun at some of the more ridiculous videos he sees on Social Media:

- In 2024, there was a brief splash for a type of couple called a "Dink" (double income, no kids). Several of these dinks were bragging about how much they enjoyed life, watching a movie whenever they wanted and eating a pizza when ever they wanted. They were not "weighed" down by the responsibility of raising children. These Dinks were the epitome of self-absorbed narcissists.

- A twenty-something recent graduate of a business school posted a video complaining that she was not getting a hundred thousand a year right out of the chute, did not have a corner office, was not a boss, and had to follow orders. Walsh reminded this recent grad that she has absolutely zero experience in the activities of the business who hired her. She symbolizes the sense of entitlement we see in many young college graduates today.
- A woman posted a video complaining that she could not get hired at a TJ Max store. As Walsh pointed out, the minute you see the video you will know why. Her face and neck are covered with tatoos and she has a nose piercing. Walsh observes that anyone who has that many tatoos is basically making a strong statement that might be a little off-putting to those around her. Why she chose to inform millions of social media viewers that she could not be hired by TJ Max is a mystery.
- In Sep 2024, a 23 year old woman apologized for a racist tweet she made 10 years before, at age 13. Walsh states that we shouldn't care about anything a teenager may have said no matter how offensive. They are just kids!

Addiction to screens is being stoked by the Chinese Communist Party (CCP). The Tik- Tok app gradually trains teens to have short attention spans, exacerbating attention deficit disorder. Teens who look at one short video after another develop a malady known as Tik-Tok brain. With more and more exposure to these short videos, they are less and less able to tolerate longer conversations.

Excessive screen time has some pitfalls, especially for teens. For one thing, there's a constant competition with others in their social media circles. It can be frustrating if some of your friends have more followers than you do. Some try to imitate more successful social media types, but just like it was back in high school before social media, some people are popular, and some are considered nerds. Many compare their own situation to the popular types and conclude they are forever condemned to be an awkward dork.

Social media can also lead to more sinister behaviors. Perhaps the most pernicious of these is on-line bullying. According to Pew Research https://www.pewresearch.org/internet/2022/12/15/teens-and-cyberbullying-2022/ nearly half of U.S. teens have been bullied or harassed online, with physical appearance being seen as a relatively common reason why.

Of course, long before the internet, teens were bullied at school. But the internet makes this bullying exponentially worse because of the wide and public reach of the internet. Pew lists six types of online bullying:

- Offensive name-calling
- Spreading of false rumors about them
- Receiving explicit images they didn't ask for
- Physical threats
- Constantly being asked where they are, what they're doing, or who they're with by someone other than a parent
- Having explicit images of them shared without their consent

These behaviors can have a devastating impact on teens up to and including suicide.

Another sinister side effect of excessive screen time is the risk of becoming a victim of online predators. As each person reveals a lot of personal information to the rest of the world, sexual predators lurk behind the anonymity of the screen and sometimes devise some nefarious plots to attack vulnerable people. CBS News reports that in 2021, there were more than 29 million reports of online attacks against children.

Communicating through screens presents all sorts of hazards. When you are talking to a person face to face, you don't see just words on a screen. You also see body language and hear tone of voice. These can make a big difference in understanding the message you receive. But even more important, if you slip up and make a mistake, you can easily correct it on the spot. You can say something like, "woops, sorry, I didn't mean that." And then you can move on. The slate is wiped clean because there is no slate recording what you said.

In contrast, when you post anything online, **it becomes a permanent, indelible record, available for all to see,** and you can never "take it back." Online audiences have shown very little tendency to extend grace to those who make mistakes. And once you make a serious whopper, it can never be erased. It can get you fired from your job. It can dog you for years.

While our modern communications technology offers a lot of advantages, it also entails some serious risks. The more time you spend online, the greater are these risks. As we embrace social media technology, excessive use can cause people to become more judgmental and less forgiving. That graceless attitude permeates our culture in 21st century America.

28. The Death of Debate
There are Two Sides to Every Story: Not!

Perhaps the most unfortunate obstacle to fixing our insane political situation is the fact that debate about issues appears to have died in the 2020's. In this chapter, I will present an autopsy to try to explain why so many debates between left and right go nowhere and suggest how we might restore a vigorous but civil discussion that can help to reveal the truth.

Beginning with the newsletters and broadsides of the 18th century, Americans have always relished spirited debate about issues of the day. This contentious spirit is best modeled in our law courts. In the courts, each side presents evidence and then synthesizes a narrative they believe is proven by the evidence. A judge or jury then analyzes the presentations of each side and determines which side has proved its case beyond a reasonable doubt.

For a couple of centuries, the model of presenting both sides was basically the norm of public discourse. A widely accepted saying went, "There are two sides to every story." Most of us tried to understand both sides even if we passionately disagreed with a contentious assertion. But in our world today, we've coined a new pejorative term, **"Both-Sides-Ism."** Enlightened elites tell us that no, there sometimes aren't two sides to every story. One side is correct, and we don't even need to acknowledge the other side. I covered this concept earlier in Chapter 17: *When Theorem becomes Axiom.* The progressive narrative operates on "axiomatic" positions. These are so obviously correct that there is no need to debate them. They are just "true."

If we're just using reason and logic, one might think that the progressive elite would welcome and seek debate. After all, they are so correct that they will win all contests hands down. They insist they have the facts on their side and they extol the power of logical persuasion. Yet they absolutely refuse to debate. When was the last time you saw a "mano on mano" debate on, say, Climate Change? I would love to see Bill McKibben or James Hanson debate Judith Curry or John Christy or Steven Koonin. When was the last time you saw a debate on America's racial politics? I would love to see a debate between, say, Al Sharpton or Ibrahim X Kendi or Ta-Nehisi Coates with someone like Coleman Hughes (for a brief sample, see https://www.youtube.com/watch?v=F5AQyWAWHU4) , or Shelby Steele or Byron Donalds or Larry Elder or Candace Owens.

The reason you don't see these debates is that none of the progressive voices will engage with respected voices on the right. Now why is that? If they are so cock-sure of their position, why not engage a thoughtful discussion with someone with a different perspective? The only reason I can think of is that they know they would lose.

For progressives, ideology trumps facts, evidence, and logic. No matter what evidence is brought to the table, it is compared against the progressive doctrine and if it does not align, it is automatically false and not worthy of debate. **Instead of debate, any challenge from the right will be met with an expression that amounts to "case dismissed":**

- There's nothing to see here
- This is a big nothing-burger
- That is a conspiracy theory
- These are Republican talking points
- This is old news
- That is racist, sexist, xenophobic, or homophobic

- You are an unenlightened troglodyte
- That has been debunked or discredited
- You are pro-Putin
- Your position can't be defended without credentials
- I won't dignify your position with an answer
- That is a false equivalence

All these boilerplate answers are evasions. They do not present counter-evidence or other facts to buttress their position. For example, if you state the fact that sea level has risen at a very constant rate since the late 1800's they will not say something like "a different study shows a sharp increase in sea level since 1980," instead they will use one of the evasions listed above, something like "that's been debunked," or "that's not a peer reviewed study." The reason they can't engage in a vigorous debate is that they don't have facts and evidence on their side. Their arguments only work with people who are committed to the progressive position because only they will swallow arguments that defy facts and logic.

In the last ten years, every time I have attempted a civil discussion with a progressive true believer, it has devolved into name calling where they use one of the evasions listed above. They also get quite emotional. They are offended that you don't buy the same line of bull the progressive elites have been dishing out from their platforms on media and Big Tech.

An unfortunate side effect of the death of debate is the retreat each side into its own bubble. I must confess that I am guilty of this. Since I approach the world of politics from the right, most of what I read comes from that point of view. I lament the fact that in our modern world debate has become nearly impossible, mainly because the left has cut it off. They are so cock-sure of their positions that they refuse to believe that there may be more than one valid opinion on many issues of the day. But if we all withdraw to our own bubbles, we become ignorant of the other side. We need to make a conscious effort to expose ourselves to opinions that we passionately disagree with. For this reason, I periodically force myself to read or listen to a progressive position, no matter how obnoxious I think it sounds. I recently decided to read a book by a leading progressive author and commentator. The author, Cenk Uygur, is founder of a popular podcast on the left, called "The Young Turks," and, by the way, is also running for President of the US in 2024. His book *Justice is Coming: How Progressives Are going to Take over the Country and America is Going to Love it*, was published in September 2023.

I'll just highlight a couple of points made in his book. He states that conservatives hate George Soros because he is a Jew. No. We don't like George Soros because he has funded the destruction of major U.S. Cities by buying District Attorney offices who then just empty out the jails and stop enforcing the law. Most conservatives don't even know Soros *is* a Jew until they are told. Also, Uygur spends quite a long time denigrating another rich Jew, Sheldon Adelson, who gave a lot of money to the Republicans. For some unstated reason, Uygur is not antisemitic by denigrating Adelson, but Republicans are for denigrating Soros!

Uygur makes passionate cases both for government provided universal health care and for free college education. He sees this as a "no brainer." Other countries do it, why don't we? All we have to do is take money from obscenely wealthy individuals to pay for these programs. But he won't admit that funding from the super wealthy is never enough for large programs like these. The upper middle class and middle class will also be tapped. Guaranteed.

While I admire Cenk's energy and his lively style, I would characterize his book as one long diatribe spewing progressive tropes. He lacks any understanding on how the economy works and name-calls throughout the book. This is one book that should see the dust-bin of irrelevance, but I slogged through it nonetheless. All of us on the right should resolve to read at least one left wing book each year just to stay current in case they may say something that we on the right should heed.

Another recent book from the left is illuminating. The book, *Fight*, by John Della Volpe was published in 2022. This book is an eloquent statement of the progressive narrative that is described earlier on in this book (Chapter 6: *The Ninety-Five Theses of Progressive Doctrine*). Della Volpe's book is more coherent than most progressive books. It systematically lays out an interpretation of events from the 2020's by stressing some events and omitting others. The author spends a lot of time describing the white supremacist violence at Charlottesville in 2017 and the January 6, 2021 riots, but only mentions the BLM riots of 2020 in passing. Della Volpe states that the 2020 riots were "mostly peaceful" in that only a small fraction of the protestors engaged in violence. He does not apply that same standard to either Charlottesville or January 6.

One section of the book describes the plight of a typical black person in America. The author states that blacks often see situations where a white customer is dissatisfied with service in a store and speaks rudely and condescendingly to a black employee, while they treat white employees with respect. This highlights an exaggeration often made in American race relations.

People are often rude to each other regardless of race. Whites may be rude to whites. Blacks may be rude to blacks. Neither of these situations is considered racist. Yet any time there is a white being rude to a black, the cause is chalked up to racism. Many white people are rude to everyone, not just blacks. To conclude that every hostile white/black interaction is caused by racism is silly and false.

Another racial fallacy widely preached by the left is the concept of "disparate impact." This states that if a policy effects one group more than another it is unjust. This was demonstrated in an incident in April 2024. A convenience store named Sheetz in North Carolina was charged with disparate impact when it used criminal background checks to screen job applicants. It appears that slightly more blacks were rejected by this criteria than whites, so under the doctrine of disparate impact, it was unjust. But the reason this policy impacted blacks more than whites is that blacks tend to commit more crimes. Surely a business has a right to deny employment to criminals if it wants to stay in business.

In spite of an unwillingness for the left to engage in debate, we must keep making the case. While it is true that left-wing zealots won't engage, there are still quite a few undecided voters in the squishy middle. Many of them are open to hearing calm, reasoned, and rational discussion. Although many in the middle have just gone along with progressive dogma mainly out of a desire to avoid divisive contention, as long as we present our case using facts and evidence, we stand a chance that **reasonable Americans will see that our case is reasonable**.

We face an uphill battle in getting our voices heard since the left controls information flow through media and big tech. But thanks to new technology, we have a chance. We have platforms like **Rumble, Daily Wire, X, Epoch Times / Epoch TV**, and podcasts like **Victor Davis Hanson's** on **Spotify** (notice I did not include Fox News in this list). Compared to the massive bulk of the progressive dominance of media and Big Tech, we have only a small beachhead. But we need to keep advancing up the beach against the withering name-calling we will attract. **In the end, I believe truth will win over lies**.

Philosophy of Economics: Socialism vs. Capitalism

Apart from the cultural issues already covered in this "why" section, our 50/50 nation is sharply divided on economics. Progressives are sympathetic to a socialist agenda. They favor an equal distribution of wealth regardless of a person's initiative or unique skill set. On the other side, capitalists favor a distribution of wealth according to the market. This means that those with unique talents and skills receive a greater share in wealth than those who produce very little.

For my analysis, I chose two key thinkers on economics. The French economist Thomas Piketty is an eloquent spokesman in favor of socialism. Ayn Rand, the author of the 1957 novel *Atlas Shrugged*, presents a persuasive case for pure capitalism. So the next couple of chapters focus on these two influencers. Finally, I present a chapter on international trade, a subject that seems to stir controversy from both the left and the right.

29. Thomas Piketty: An Admired Economist and Prophet on the Left

Book Review

A book titled *Capital in the Twenty-First Century* by Thomas Piketty, a French economist, got a lot of buzz mainly from the left side of the aisle since its publication in 2013 and especially after the English Translation by Arthur Goldhammer in 2014. One reviewer calls his work a "VIB" (Very Important Book). There is no denying the sensational reception this book has received from intellectual elites. His comprehensive history of wealth distribution gives a profound insight into how the capitalist economy works. Piketty systematically lays out the case of the left that wealth and income have not been distributed in a just manner for many decades and that the unjust distribution can lead to political instability similar to the French Revolution in 1789 if it is not addressed. Piketty supports his conclusions with a wealth of economic data. He has thoroughly researched his subject.

The author spends a lot of time explaining a formula **R > G** (Rate of return on capital is greater than Growth Rate G). Over long time periods, R and G converge, but often in the short term, there can be a large gap between these two quantities. The larger the gap between R and G, the more the rich get richer as they reap this gain. Since the rich are blessed with large fortunes, they enjoy the benefits of what is often called "unearned income." Their pile of wealth just keeps feeding on itself, growing ever larger as the masses have to struggle all their lives to avoid falling behind. This formula, R > G is Piketty's great truth. This mathematical fact drives his passion for correcting the unfairness of life.

The author executes a relentless assault on what he believes is unconscionable greed in at the top of the economic pyramid. He states that those who start with a larger amount of wealth typically get a better return on their capital than those with smaller amounts. He estimates that this amounts to about a two-percentage point advantage, and over many years, causes an ever- widening gap between the rich and the lower classes. He also ridicules the meritocratic case often made to justify this gap. He cites Bill Gates and states that yes, Gates was an important force in the emergence of computer technology. But part of his success came from sheer luck and even if he was the only force in creating this new technology, why should he keep reaping benefits forty years after his initial discovery? Piketty thus makes a forceful case against the idea of wealth derived from merit.

Piketty's landmark work constructed an intellectual argument for government allocation of scarce resources. Now that I have read Piketty's "Very Important Book", I pause to add my critique of his work. I do so from an admitted disadvantage: I do not have any special training in Economics. Many would say that my lack of credentials disqualifies me from evaluating Piketty's work. But Piketty's book is not all about economics. At times in his work, he cites literary figures such as Jane Austen and Honoré de Balzac to illustrate and buttress his case. He often strays into philosophy, and on that, I *am* qualified to assess his views. I don't criticize him as an economist (indeed he is superb at his craft) but as a philosopher. These are the main flaws I see in Piketty's theory:

- This work's only focus is the **distribution of wealth** to the neglect of wealth generation
- He treats **inequality as if it is a problem** to be solved rather than a reality to be explained
- His use of **aggregate statistics** reveals *some* profound truths but hides others.
- He only mentions in passing that most **people are employees because they choose security** over innovative risk
- Piketty basically **ignores income decile mobility**
- In spite of wealth concentration at the top, there is **still plenty left over for the middle class**
- Piketty condemns the **top 1% taking almost all of growth** but ignores a key cause
- He makes the asinine proposal that **public expenditures should be 2/3 or even 3/4 of National Income**. This amounts to socialism.
- Piketty's proposal for a **global wealth tax** is both impossibly **utopian** and outrageously **authoritarian**.
- Piketty is quick to identify flaws in capitalism and meritocracy, but he assigns **god-like qualities to government.**

- Piketty's entire case rests on the foundation of the related traits of **envy and entitlement.**

I begin my critique with the over emphasis on **distribution of wealth** to the almost complete exclusion of wealth generation. I realize that any author must limit the scope of his work to a manageable level. But Piketty's omission here is typical of other modern philosophers. They basically imply that goods and services fall like manna from heaven, and the people below are basically scurrying around trying to gather what they can. But wealth does not fall from the sky. It is created by risk-taking, relentless, creative, innovative entrepreneurs. You don't have an i-phone without Steve Jobs. You don't have Amazon without Jeff Bezos. You don't have Windows without Bill Gates. When Piketty focuses his entire analysis on the distribution of wealth, he creates a fairy tale environment where all are equally entitled to the work of others. The more wealth that is distributed to the undeserving, the less innovation we will have. It's that simple.

Piketty treats egalitarianism as if it is an ideal to be doggedly and unwaveringly pursued. Inequality of wealth and income is assumed to be a **defect that must be corrected.** But what if income inequality is in fact a feature and not a bug? We all know that people are not equal automatons that can be mixed and matched at will. Some people are enormously innovative. Some have talents that induce audiences to spend their hard-earned cash to see them perform. In high schools, some will be football team captains and cheerleaders, and some are nerds who can never get the pretty girl to go with them to the prom. The unequal nature of humanity is just a fact. Espousing some system where everyone gets an equal slice of the pie regardless of the skill and work they bring is thus a recipe for failure. Piketty often holds up Scandinavian countries as paragons of the virtue of egalitarianism. But if we think about it, how many outstanding entrepreneurs or scientists come from Scandinavia? It may be a very pleasant place to live, but it appears to be rather bland when it comes to the swashbuckling arena of innovation.

The author is a master of using **aggregate statistics** to summarize trends over long time periods. Given the main focus of his book, he has presented a well-organized case. As far as I know, his long-term histories of economics of several countries over several centuries may be a "one of a kind" resource. That said, like most scientists, he peppers his presentation with warnings about trying to summarize very complex topics with one number. In my career as an engineering statistician, I often observed that averages can be misleading because they smear out some of the variability you actually want to see. Unfortunately, he sometimes fails to follow his own advice.

By presenting long term averages of income and wealth distributions, he hides some of the data that goes into his averages. He spends several chapters explaining the split between labor and capital as if this split is caused by greedy capitalists at the top of the food chain. But in doing so, he obscures some of the reasons for those trends. A simple example will illustrate this flaw. Suppose the share of total income going to labor goes down. This may have occurred because of millions of simple micro-economics decisions that total up to the trend he sees.

An owner of a restaurant has to balance out all kinds of factors in deciding how much to pay the wait staff. These would include the number of competitors in the neighborhood, the general state of the economy, the price of food, etc. He is trying to stay in business. If he pays his wait staff too much, his customers may decide to not eat out as much or to go to one of his rivals for dinner. The owner does not have some malevolent intent to keep his staff at low pay, he's just doing what every business owner must do to stay in business.

Employees have made an implicit choice in the tradeoff between the security of having a guaranteed salary regardless of their contributions **versus the risk an entrepreneur embraces**. By accepting the security of a guaranteed salary, the employee is forfeiting the rewards of innovative risk taking. But modern America has made it possible for an employee to cross over from the safety of the salary to more profitable pursuits. Some employees, even poor foreigners, have become successful business owners. They work hard at their jobs, practice the art of deferred gratification, save their excess wages, sometimes raise venture capital, and eventually move from being an employee to being an owner. Admittedly this doesn't happen very often, but it does happen for outstanding individuals who are willing to strive and sacrifice enough to make it happen. So rather than complain that the capitalists at the top have too much wealth, **why not just become a capitalist?** In modern America, the opportunity is there.

The author also basically ignores the concept of **mobility among the various deciles** of the income distribution. He mentions it in passing, only to basically dismiss it. Piketty paints a world where the poor are always poor and the rich are always rich. But that picture is not entirely accurate. It may characterize many or even most people. On the poor side, a person born to a crack-addicted mother in a poor neighborhood may have little chance of ever escaping that situation. On the rich side, a son of a very wealthy family may seem to have everything and just "coasts" through life.

But **America is a land of exceptions because America is an exceptional land**. There is a script that many have followed to escape the mire of poverty and enter the grandeur of wealth. Get an education. Get married. Stay away from drugs and crime. Be the best employee you can, always arriving on time and not complaining but offering suggestions to improve the business. Imagine a lowly clerk at a WalMart. This clerk has followed the script and is recognized for it and moved into Management. The clerk gradually works her way up the ladder and become part of top management, receiving benefits and bonuses. She can then save and invest her earnings and become wealthy. This kind of scenario is possible and does happen.

On the other side, imagine a rich kid who just tries to glide through life, living off the inheritance he receives. Over time, his insatiable greed causes him to spend more and more, and he exhausts his funding and becomes a pauper. Again, this is not a common situation, but it does happen in America.

By ignoring mobility among the various levels of wealth, the author dismisses the value of economic incentives. The potential to rise from a state of poverty to one of wealth can be a powerful driver of constructive activity in a person's life. It offers hope in a world filled with despair. One can lift oneself out of poverty provided one follows the disciplines of hard work and deferred gratification. On the other side, a very wealthy person can squander his wealth by succumbing to the urge for instant gratification and living beyond one's means. Even large incomes can sometimes not be enough to teach a person the lesson the book *The Millionaire Next Door* about becoming wealthy. **It is very simple: Income minus outgo = accumulated wealth**. Anyone, even with a high income, can become poor by simply spending more than they take in. Piketty may minimize these powerful incentives, but there are millions of examples where they have in fact had an important impact on individual behavior.

Another glaring omission in Piketty's analysis is the vast and widespread prosperity among the American middle class. He does spend some time on what he calls the "patrimonial middle class" which controls about a third of the wealth, but he misses the key point. In spite of a gross concentration of wealth at the very top of the distribution, there still is **plenty left over for the middle class**. All you need to do to prove this is just drive around in American suburbs. There are millions of nice homes. There are thousands of nice shopping malls whose parking lots are filled with shiny new cars. Millions of Americans have 401K nest eggs. Millions of Americans have college degrees. **This prosperity is widespread**. So even with wealth concentration at the very top, **millions of Americans live in a prosperity that is the envy of the world**. This is why so many want to emigrate to America, the land of opportunity. Yes, the people at the very top are perhaps unconscionably well off, but they spend and invest money creating jobs for the rest of us.

At one point, the author states what appears to be an egregious example of the top one percent skimming off nearly all of the proceeds of growth. But he ignores a key reason which is identified by rival economist **Edward Conard** in his brilliant book *The Upside of Inequality*. Conard points out that labor's proceeds are limited by the number of customers served. For example, a very high paid physician can only earn so much because he serves perhaps a few hundred patients per year. But a popular rock star or an innovator like Steve Jobs will serve millions of customers, not hundreds. Population growth results in millions of new customers for these stars, but the guy working at the car wash can only wash so many cars. Even big rock stars of the past like the Beatles still earned a lot less than today's stars like Taylor Swift because population growth results in millions of new customers for her.

At one point in his analysis, Piketty states that it would not be unreasonable for **public expenditures to be 2/3 or even 3/4 of the entirety of National Income**. This means that individuals can only control one in four dollars they earn. This preposterously high level of public expenditure comes pretty close to socialism, which has been tried and found wanting many times in human history.

Piketty makes a forceful case for the combination of **financial transparency along with a global wealth tax**. He proposes that all world governments and all banks would share financial information. Without this information, a global tax on wealth would not be possible. He notes that the technology is already there to make this happen. All we lack is political will. But let's just pause and examine his proposal. First of all, it is hopelessly utopian to think that countries would give up their sovereignty to be controlled by a mysterious cabal of bureaucrats in a far off land. Americans would never permit someone in Brussels having access to our financial data, let alone imposing a tax on Americans. In addition, just think of the enormous power the banks and international governments would have by having access to all that financial information!

The author repeatedly mocks the idea of meritocratic distribution of wealth. He points to numerous examples of how the undeserving rich exploit the poor. His R > G formula seems to explain it all. Most of the population does not have access to large capital stocks and thus must live life based on labor. This is patently unfair. Even the most ardent defender of free market capitalism would have to admit that the points Piketty makes are valid. The market does not always result in a perfect distribution of goods. Many live life based on a head start given by inheriting their parent's wealth. Executives are often grossly overcompensated. There is no denying the imperfections in a free market economy.

But Piketty's solution is to **cede god-like power** to government. He speaks of government as if it is a "thing" that always acts dispassionately according to design. But we all know that government is not a finely tuned instrument, but a messy collection of flawed human beings. It is subject to bribery, corruption, horse-trading, and a thirst for ever more power. If we grant government omniscience by giving it access to everyone's banking records, it is only a short step before government aims to be omnipotent, with everyone just standing around waiting for orders. Moreover, government power seems to only change in one direction: larger and more powerful. Once government gets the power, it is very hard to diminish that power.

The final argument against Piketty is the fact that he rests his entire case on two very ugly human tendencies: **envy and entitlement**. When we think logically about envy, we should recoil at what it really means. At its core, **envy basically means being unhappy because of the happiness of others**. But how does the fabulous wealth of Jeff Bezos or Elon Musk hurt me as an individual? We should all ask and answer that question.

Many answer the question by asserting an inalienable right to goods and services. **It is not fair** that the rich can send their kids to the best colleges and I can't. It is not fair that the rich can pile up capital that feeds on itself while I have to work week in and week out to make ends meet. It's not fair that I can't shoot hoops as well as Michael Jordan. It's not fair that I can't receive millions of dollars for being a talk show host like Oprah Winfrey. Why should all of them be so rich? I'm entitled to not just pursue happiness, but to attain just as much of it as the next person.

Those twin vices of envy and entitlement are realities of our modern society. Piketty's answer is to give power to a god-like government to smooth out the inequities and make everything more fair. My answer is to challenge the envious and entitled. If the greedy capitalists have an unfair advantage, why not just join them? **If you believe you deserve more than a burger flipper's pay, then don't be a burger flipper anymore.** Accept the fact that an entry level jobs pays entry level wages. But one can rise above entry level. **Embrace innovation and risk taking. Practice hard work and deferred gratification.** Follow the script of many successful Americans. Thomas Piketty may heap scorn on these ideas, but millions of success stories have proven him wrong. Don't focus on the flaws of the market economy. Instead conquer it.

30. How I would have Written John Galt's Speech

"'Need' now means wanting someone else's money; 'Greed' means wanting to keep your own; 'Compassion' is when a politician arranges the transfer." Joseph Sobran

Introduction

It took me a long time to discover *Atlas Shrugged*, one of the most monumental novels in history. I had often heard of it, but its length had scared me off for decades, and I suspect I am not the only one in this situation. I finally decided to listen to the audiobook edition (60 hours) and I am glad I did. This novel is a gripping tale of excellence and failure; of achievers and looters; of pompous grandstanders who think they are wise and genuine producers who really are.

The most profound issue raised by *Atlas Shrugged* is, I think, the one of the cause and effect of prosperity. Many in society today see the enormous wealth of the U.S. free market and think it just spontaneously grows. They picture a giant smorgasbord counter where the food we want magically appears and then we just belly up to the bar and take what we need. They only look at the demand side of the equation. They assume supply will always be there. One of the novel's incidents drives this home. Hank Rearden's ne'er-do-well brother demands that he has a right to a job. Rearden answers, 'then go and stake your claim. Pluck it off the bush it grows on.'

Ayn Rand was prophetic in this regard. In today's society, politicians like Senator **Elizabeth Warren** (D-Mass) often spout a simplistic boilerplate, equating the achievers with greed personified: **'I've got mine, but you're on your own,'** she's said at numerous speeches. Just like Hank Rearden and the other producers in the novel, if you're wealthy in modern America, you are supposed to feel guilty that you have more than others and fork over the dough at the dictates of the elite of politics and media. Senator Warren embodies the novel's Hugh Akston's statement that 'they think that need is holier than ability.' And as John Galt says in his speech '**who gave you the passkey to the moral elite?**' Who indeed?

In fact, politicians rarely even address the source of wealth, only to whom the wealth should go. The novelist illustrates this eloquently as she puts a gem in the mouth of John Galt during his long diatribe. He states sarcastically that they think "A factory is a natural resource, like a tree, a rock or a mud puddle." Who are 'they'? I suspect many today will have their own answer to this question.

A fundamental question politicians like Warren never address is, 'what would life be like if the achievers and producers went on strike, like they did in the novel?' Just like Wesley Mauch and Dr. Floyd Ferris, they assume that the producers will just keep on producing regardless of how much of their wealth and freedom to achieve is encroached by government edicts. In the novel, the producers withdraw their support for the looters and form their own society in a hidden Colorado enclave. In real life they withdraw their efforts from production and enjoy luxury items. Either way, their skill and achievement is removed and this diminishes the wealth of the economy and the welfare of all who depend on it.

As great as the novel is (and as I've said, it is one of the greatest), it does at times get tiresome, pompous and even offensive. Listening to the novel with Scott Brick's excellent vocal presentation, I must hear every word. As we get to the long speeches, if I were reading the novel in paper, I would probably just skim or even turn whole pages to shorten my exposure to these tedious monologues.

I suspect the author herself (and many of her fans) may have thought that John Galt's 60 page speech just after Hank Rearden disappears was her finest moment in the novel. It laid out her 'Objectivism' philosophy in great detail. But as I read (or listen) to her prose about 60 years later, I yawn and just want to get his speech over with and get back to the story. Other *Atlas Shrugged* enthusiasts will think I am uttering heresy, but this is how I feel. In real life if this speech came up on TV, many would be clicking their remote. In the 1950's they probably just changed the radio dial.

I can imagine the fictitious characters of the novel tuning in to hear from Mr. Thompson, a top government official about the current ongoing 'crisis' and being shocked to hear John Galt. But it seemed to me that Galt just pontificated with perplexing arguments and was often offensive to my Christian faith (although most of the novel is in fact compatible with Christianity, despite the author's avowed atheism). Galt had a golden opportunity to explain the source of the economic madness and to propose a solution, but instead he rambled on and on in what seemed to be one long sermon that is difficult to understand, let alone admire.

With apologies, then, to this great author and her enthusiastic fans, here is how I would rewrite John Galt's speech (and trust me, it's way less than 60 pages!):

John Galt's Speech (rewritten)

My fellow Americans: you tuned in tonight to hear Mr. Thompson explain the current crisis in the economy. But I have decided that you need to hear the real truth, so I have temporarily seized control of the airwaves because until now, you have only heard one side of the story. Mr. Thompson would have told you that his government just needed more authority to widen the scope of directive 10-289 and all our economic ills would be solved. But what he won't tell you is that directive 10-289 and others like it are the root cause of all the calamities we face today and more directives of this sort will only make things much worse. I will explain the situation to you with clarity and substance. I will name names and present evidence that can easily be checked for accuracy. You, then can judge for yourself where the ultimate truth lies.

What has become painfully obvious over the last ten years is that in the end there are two classes of people: those who produce and those who loot. The producers bring to bear their remarkable skills and strong determination to bring us the things we take for granted: the cars we drive, the appliances we use, the food we eat, the clothes we wear, the shelter we inhabit. Unlike previous primitive generations, we no longer need to rely only on our own hard work to go out and gather food and make our huts: other men and women have come forward and agreed to trade their extraordinary talents in exchange for a living and for some respect for their achievements. But the looters simply pounce on the wealth created by others, citing their need.

Producers overcome obstacles to create prosperity for all; looters give excuses on why they can't produce and then use these excuses to seize the property of the producers. Our current economic situation shows the end result when looters have their way—the producers simply stop producing and there is nothing left to loot.

In response to the heavy-handed regulation of the economy by men like Wesley Mauch, Dr. Floyd Ferris, Chick Morrison, Tinky Holloway, Cuffy Meigs, and Dr. Robert Stadler, most of the brightest minds have abandoned their calling to serve those around them and have escaped to a place where they cannot be harmed and where their private property cannot be seized. Don't try to find them—you won't. They will only be found when you, as a society, return to the principles that built this great nation: liberty, private enterprise, and private property. In a word, you must dismantle the destructive regulations that impede innovation, achievement, and commerce before the producers will return and help to build a brighter future for all.

Although the authorities have suppressed reporting of the truth for over ten years, there are many who can hear my voice who remember what things were like before the current leaders took control of the national economy. I will use the example of the railroad line that bears my name to help remind you of how things worked when men and women of integrity and skill ran our nation's business concerns.

You might recall the triumphant day the John Galt Line glided into Wyatt junction in Colorado to nationwide applause. Prior to the opening of this Line, Taggart Transcontinental had experienced numerous wrecks due to the poor condition of the old *Rio Norte* line. The railroad had been trying to repair the line for years but their suppliers of steel rail kept giving them excuses on why the new rail could not be delivered. They claimed 'there are shortages of iron ore' and 'it can't be helped.' In desperation, Taggert Transcontinental spun off the John Galt Line to its vice president Dagney Taggert, who was given sole responsibility for the success of the line and sole blame if it failed.

Ms. Taggert found a supplier of rail that committed to deadlines and costs and would not give excuses. Rearden Steel had developed a new metal stronger and more durable but lighter than steel. The State Science institute vigorously opposed the use of Rearden metal because it was 'unproven'. Although they had no evidence that it would fail, they nonetheless attacked the project relentlessly, making dire predictions that the trains would wreck because the metal would not hold.

To the dismay of all the naysayers, the John Galt line made the run with 80 cars running at 150 miles per hour. Immediately after the introduction of the John Galt line, Colorado experienced an unprecedented boom. Ellis Wyatt made oil cheap, abundant and affordable. Lawrence Hammond made amazing luxury cars. Dwight Sanders made superb aircraft. Ted Nielsen made excellent motors. Ken Danagger made coal abundant for the production of steel and energy. Many other innovators brought prosperity to the nation as the new John Galt line assured reliable supply of raw materials and transportation of finished goods to hungry markets.

You who are over 30 years of age probably vividly remember these golden times following the opening of the John Galt line. So what happened? Where has the prosperity gone? What caused us to fall from so great a height to the desperate situation in which we find ourselves today? The answer is found in **the philosophy that underpins today's regulatory state that penalizes success and rewards 'need.'**

One of the first events that undermined the economy was the *Anti Dog-Eat-Dog law*. Wesley Mauch along with his corporate pals James Taggert and Orren Boyle opined that it was 'unfair' for the John Galt line to prosper in Colorado while other corporations in the east were struggling. Their solution was a new rule that limited the number of railroad cars and speed on all railroads. Since the John Galt Line was the only one that could achieve long and fast trains, it was 'not fair' to others who could not. So the edict went into effect, instantly making the John Galt line less efficient. Ellis Wyatt saw the writing on the wall. He knew that cheap and reliable transportation was foundational to his success. Since the authorities pulled the rug out from under him, Wyatt became one of the first to disappear. He destroyed his oil fields and joined the others in our valley of achievers.

Other successful entrepreneurs quickly followed. Mr. Hammond, Mr. Dannager, and many other outstanding people realized that their success was something the regulators did not want because it wasn't fair and 'compassionate'. **Need trumps ability in this new world order**. But what the regulators did not acknowledge was that each time they attempted to bring down the strong with bureaucratic red tape, they did not help the weak. Like Atlas carrying the world on his shoulders, the strong had been carrying the weak on their shoulders, providing innovation, opportunity, and jobs. But when the strong were burdened with more and more regulations, they became less and less able to sustain the weak. Atlas shrugged and everything began to crumble.

A pivotal moment came with directive 10-289. A few men in a smoke filled room decided that they would regulate the entire economy. No one would be free to quit their employer but would be sanctioned as 'deserters'. Patents would be outlawed and all innovations would belong to 'the people' which is a euphemism for Wesley Mauch and his allies. Profits from successful businesses would be seized and given to unsuccessful ones. But, said the regulators, this would only be 'temporary' while the crisis lasted. This, of course was a lie. What they couldn't admit was that the crisis would never end. Their actions only perpetuated the crisis.

Two specific outgrowths of directive 10-289 and its ever increasing scope deserve special mention. Henry Rearden had invented Rearden Metal which was instrumental in the success of the John Galt line and the prosperity of Colorado. But now directive 10-289 commanded him to turn over all rights to Rearden metal to the government by signing a 'gift certificate'. Rearden had no intention of signing this and he would have gone to prison to keep his metal. But the government blackmailed him threatening to expose his affair with Dagney Taggert. His respect and love for her was so great that he gave the government his metal in exchange for not exposing Ms. Taggert to public shame. As you all know, Ms. Taggert publicly admitted this affair when she heard of Mr. Rearden's sacrifice on her behalf.

This affair with the Rearden gift certificate revealed two things about the regulators. One is that they would stoop to despicable blackmail to achieve their ends. But perhaps more importantly, it revealed that they needed the sanction of achievers to lend them credibility. If Hank Rearden would sign, the government regulators must be OK. That was their message to the public.

Another incident that deserves mention was the agricultural disaster in Minnesota. When I tell you this one you might not believe it because it never showed up in the newspapers or radio. That's because Wesley Mauch and his crew called their contacts in the press to tamp down any "unrest" that may have resulted. But if you doubt the truth of this story, just call your Aunt Minnie in Minnesota. She will verify it.

Several years ago, the nation enjoyed a bumper crop of wheat in the heartland. Railroads were poised to deliver this bounty to the masses in the east. But then something 'derailed' the plan. A government bureaucrat named Cuffy Meigs determined that the nation needed an improved diet of soybeans to emulate the wisdom of the east. So even as the crop of wheat was being harvested in Minnesota, every single rail car was diverted to Louisiana to deliver soybeans instead. **The public's demand for wheat was supplanted by Cuffy Meigs's whim to support soybeans**.

The upshot was that the wheat crop rotted at the farms and silos because there was no way to transport it to market. Much of it caught fire, and this caused a cascade of other events. Because the farmers could not get paid for delivery of their crop, many of them went bankrupt and failed to pay debts for farm equipment, so manufacturers also went bankrupt, causing the loss of thousands of jobs. All because **Cuffy Meigs thought he knew better where to place the country's scarce resources.**

The nefarious effects of directive 10-289 reached its climax recently with a plot to take over the one productive enterprise left in the nation, Rearden Steel. The government committee along with James Taggert and Orrin Boyle, lured Hank Rearden to New York ostensibly to discuss ways they could cooperate with him. Actually, however, their hired thugs took over the Rearden mill in Philadelphia take was in New York. They set fire to the plant and killed several workers. This was the straw that broke the camel's back. Hank Rearden had held out for years, trying to save this society, but after this, he agreed to withdraw and join our society of achievers.

So there you have it. A quick analysis of the events of the last several years reveals how hollow are the principles of the people who have been controlling your lives. When achievers are penalized for success and looters are rewarded to meet their need, the inevitable result is that the achievers withdraw while the looters take over. That is precisely what has happened.

Mr. Thompson, Mr. Mauch, and Dr. Ferris will vigorously deny all I have just said, but facts are facts and you can easily check the truth of my assertions. Compassion and need *sound good* until you realize that their brand of compassion takes from the strong to give to the weak. **This helps neither the strong nor the weak**. The free market consists of millions of 'win-win' trades. The achievers offer jobs, manufacturing plants, and infrastructure to the weak in exchange for their labor. Both sides benefit from this exchange. But Directive 10-289 replaces these win-win situations with win-lose situations where achievers are expected to give to looters who offer nothing in return.

Such a system is bound to fail, and it has failed because the achievers have decided to withdraw from this losing bargain. Notice who are the aggressors here. The achievers have not imposed their will on others; they only left the playing field and left the looters to impose their will without opposition. It is the government regulators and their corporate cronies who have foisted their laws on the public. It is they that have revoked your freedom to move between jobs and have suppressed free speech. It is they who have forcibly taken resources from one group to give it to another, all in the name of 'compassion and need.' And as the system crumbled around them, all they offered was excuses like 'it can't be helped' and remedies that were more of the same. That have demonstrated how unfit they are to lead. They must go or we, the achievers, will continue our exile and will refuse to provide the help this society so desperately needs.

So you, the American public, must decide. Do you want to continue on this road to despair, and excuses, and failure? Or do you want to return to the golden age we had when the John Galt line sailed into Wyatt Junction? Do you want to remain under the thumb of these 'enlightened' regulators and their corporate cronies or do you want a life of hope and prosperity in which achievers are rewarded but failure is not? We, the achievers, await your reply, but we must see deeds not words. If the regulators are not thrown out on their ear, we will remain in seclusion. **You must choose**.

31. International Trade Deficits
Edward Conard, *The Upside of Inequality*
Book Review

Trade is essential to prosperity. Centuries ago, humanity invented money as a means of exchange as an alternative to barter. The great thing about money is that you can trade for anything with it. It is nearly universally accepted as a means of exchange. So if you want to buy a toaster you don't have to wonder whether the trader will accept, say, shoes in exchange. In recent history, trade flexibility has increased dramatically with modern devices such as credit cards and even digital currency.

In modern times, barter is almost extinct and for good reason. Other means of universal exchange have become so ubiquitous that barter is totally impractical. We don't always have the things others want and they don't always have the things we want. So money and credit are the bridge to bring buyers and sellers together in a win/win transaction.

By and large, the benefits of buying as opposed to trading extend not only to individual buyers and sellers, but in bulk international transactions as well. Each nation is "good" at producing specific products and services. It makes sense to make it easy for people in one country to take advantage of the superior products of another country by buying those products and services rather than trading for them. The same things that make barter inconvenient and impractical at a micro scale usually apply at the macro scale as well. In fact, I'd say that absolutely free trade with no artificial restrictions is the best possible system about 95% of the time. Each side freely chooses. The seller accepts cash or credit while the buyer gets the products they want. This appears to be "win-win."

But why do I assert that free international trade without impediments is good only 95% of the time? **Why not 100%?** What good could conceivably come from adding artificial barriers to trade? How can politicians feasibly improve the situation by sticking their nose into this area and potentially causing side effects such as trade wars and heightening tension among nations? As liberty-loving, low tax favoring Americans, how could anyone possibly favor impediments to free trade?

Here's where we get to the 5% situation where we probably do need some restrictions. Economist Edward Conard explains this position eloquently in his book *The Upside of Inequality*, published in 2016. The 5% situation only applies in cases where two conditions are present:

- Total Trade between two nations is very large
- One Nation buys a very large amount from the other above what it trades with the other (ie, one nation runs a very large balance of trade deficit).

In international trade in which the U.S. currently participates, these two conditions are only tripped with trade with three or four nations: China, Japan, and Germany and possibly Korea. Edward Conard proposes that for these countries, we apply a sliding scale tariff. The higher the deficit, the higher the tariff. Countries can avoid the tariff simply by buying more U.S. goods such as agricultural products, aircraft, oil and gas, and other items Americans are very good at. Basically what Conard proposes is that when the total amount of international trade between nations is very large, we trade for goods, we don't buy them.

Why make this exception? Conard explains. When we buy instead of trade for goods and services, we obtain items that export jobs. Basically, foreigners have a much higher savings rate than most

Americans. They have a lot of their money stashed in what Conard calls "Risk-averse savings." Many foreigners are content to put their money in things like low-interest savings accounts. They are not seeking a return, just a preservation. So they use these savings accounts to flood the American market with low risk money that is unavailable to fuel innovation and growth.

Large balance of trade deficits have resulted, over time, in what Conard calls a "hollowing out of the middle class." As American shoppers go to Wal-mart to snap up cheap goods, they are essentially exporting jobs to China and other countries. We then wind up with situations where once vibrant and thriving rust belt cities have factories shut down and the resulting despair causes, among other things, crime, drug addiction, and loss of hope. Each individual Wal-Mart shopper is not causing these things, but their sum total brings about this undesirable result for our nation.

Why do we continue to export jobs to China, Germany, and Japan? Because it's easy. **We got the cash, and those countries got the goods**. But what is wrong with telling these other countries, "yes, we want your goods. But only to a point. Balance of trade with your countries has gotten way out of hand. We plan to penalize buying in favor of trade. If you want to sell to the American market, you must buy American goods. Surely you can find something you want to buy in the most prosperous country in history! And that's all you need to do to avoid the tariffs. The more of our goods you buy, the lower will be barriers to trade. **We refuse to hollow out our middle class and export our jobs to you**."

The beauty of Conard's solution is also that it only singles out nations with large trade and large deficits. **This is not personal. It's just business**.

Climate Change

32. Seven Questions Climate Change
Activists Refuse to Answer

Because they do not have any answers to these pointed questions

Questions:

1. What percentage of the warming observed over the past few decades is a result of fossil fuel emissions as opposed to natural causes?
2. How good is our ability to predict the future?
3. What impact would American reduction of CO_2 have on climate change?
4. Are there any benefits with higher CO_2 and Temperatures?
5. Are patterns so clear as to not be obscured by data fog such as sampling and measurement method?
6. How good are renewables such as wind and solar compared to fossil fuels?
7. How do we know that the absolute optimal temperature is the one from about 1900 or 1950 and that we must do everything to preserve this one moment in time?

Many Climate Change activists tell us that the science is settled and debate is no longer fruitful. Most rational people would agree that yes, the climate has warmed over the last few decades and yes, burning of fossil fuels has played a role in this warming. But millions of rational people (including thousands of scientists and engineers) believe that the warming is not catastrophic, and that human ingenuity and technology are equal to the task of adapting to the slight warming. Before we spend trillions of dollars to "fix" the climate, should we not at least ask a few basic questions to establish a consensus even among skeptics? After all, we're all in this together and skepticism is the watchword of valid scientific endeavor. Moreover, the burden of proof should be on Climate Change activists. After all, they are the ones advocating for drastic, costly action.

The first question is "what percentage of the warming observed in the past few decades is a result of greenhouse gas emissions?" The answer is, we really don't know. Climate activists contend it is a major driver, but a survey of available data indicates there must be other drivers. The "Little Ice Age" ended around the year 1850. There were no SUV's spewing out CO2 that early in time, so obviously other factors caused this warming. Do we really believe that our little machines have overwhelmed these natural forces to become the dominant driver of climate change? Where is the evidence? What is the correlation coefficient? How do other factors (such as cloud cover reflecting heat, solar activity, axial precession, volcanic eruption, wind and ocean currents, geography, and elevation) compare with greenhouse gas emissions? If the other factors contribute a large fraction of the warming, then reducing greenhouse gas emissions will not reduce temperature.

When we think about the contention that Climate Change is driven by a trace gas at a 400 ppm concentration, it takes nearly as much faith to believe this assertion as it does to believe in the Tooth Fairy. The Climate Change alarmists are certain that this trace gas has such a large impact on temperature that it swamps out other natural forces that have been in operation for thousands of years. The only data the alarmists bring to the table is the fact that temperature has risen in the last few decades. Granted. But they have yet to establish a causal link between fossil fuel use and climate change. It is quite possible that the climate is being driven by other natural forces that are coincidentally occurring during our lifetime. That is a conclusion that is every bit as reasonable as those who state that this trace gas is driving all of climate. Remember that we just emerged from the "little ice age" around the year 1850. If that little ice age lasted several hundred years (1430-1850), the warming that brought us out of it could be happening even now.

A second question is, "how good is our ability to predict future climate?" Activists would answer, "very good." Yet there are no phD's in future prediction, and past experience has repeatedly shown that no matter how sophisticated the predictor, many have been wrong. The "experts" were wrong when they predicted an ice age back in the 1970's. Paul Ehrlich, author of the "Population Bomb" made many stunningly inaccurate predictions several decades ago as did many other scientists. One thing Ehrlich predicted: "between 1980 and 1989, some 4 billion people, including 65 million Americans, would perish in the Great Die-Off." Moreover, the climate prediction models have been in effect for several decades, so we can use a statistical chart that plots observed versus predicted tropospheric temperature (McKitrick aqnd Christy, "A Test of the Tropical 200 to 300 hPA Warming Rate in Climate Models", *AGU100*, June 21, 2018).

Figure 5.
Climate Models: Observed vs. Predicted

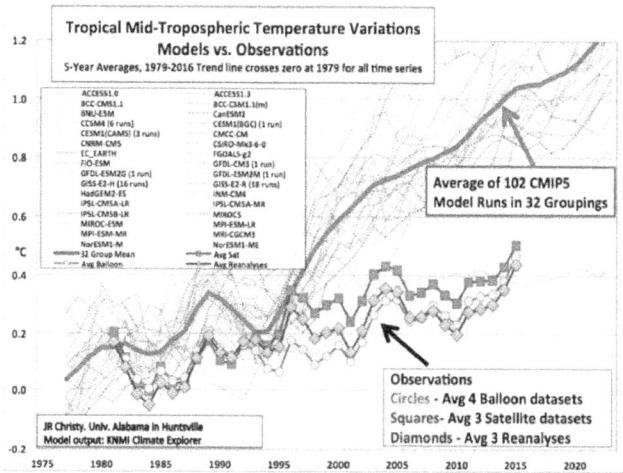

Figure 1. Solid red line—average of all the CMIP5 climate models; Thin colored lines—individual CMIP5 models; solid figures—weather balloon, satellite, and reanalysis data for the tropical troposphere.

The Figure 5 chart shows that most of the models have predicted significantly higher temperatures than have in fact been observed. After a rapid rise up to about 1998, the temperature has in fact "leveled off" in spite of skyrocketing CO2 emissions in the last two decades. Part of the scientific method is to revise predictions as empirical data refutes it. Should the models be refined in light of current data?

The third question addresses climate policy America can implement. The current Administration's climate leader, John Kerry, stated in a speech in early 2021 that **90% of greenhouse gas emissions come from nations other than the U.S.** China alone emits about twice as much as the USA, yet the Paris Climate accords gave them much more leeway than the USA and EU in reducing emissions. If emissions reduction is the goal, why go so easy on China (the largest emitter)? Moreover, as America imports many goods from China, we are basically exporting our CO2 emissions. The more we import

241

from China, the more CO2 is being spewed into the atmosphere. If we made the goods here, we would use much cleaner processes than China.

Another question is, "are there any benefits to climate change?" If the changes are not too drastic, the answer is a resounding "yes." Throughout recorded history, humans have demonstrated a much greater ability to adapt to warmth than to cold. Ice ages are devastating to humans and animals while interglacial warming periods often correspond to health and wealth. The planet's marvelous balance of plants and animals help stabilize climate. While humans are emitting CO2 into the atmosphere, plants, through photosynthesis, are breathing it in. Plants have been flourishing as CO2 builds up, resulting in better crop yields. As scientist Dr. Willie Soon puts it, **CO2 is the "gas of life."** One could make a case that reducing CO2 emissions would be harmful to plants and thus would starve the basic food supply of animals, including us. **The benefits of the fertilizer effect should not be overlooked**.

The fifth question: "Are patterns so clear as to not be obscured by data fog such as sampling and measurement method?" Most charts of scientific data contain three components: the actual trend, the measurement method, and the sampling method. Most climate activists assume that the measurement and sampling components are negligible so that the trend we see on the chart is clear. But in the case of global climate change charts, sampling and measurement are significant (see next chapter: *Can we even Detect Global Warming?* for more details).

The thermometer was just invented in the 18th century, so most of the historic data before that time is gleaned by using proxies such as tree rings, ice cores, and coral growth. The proxies do have some correlation to the item being measured (temperature) but it is not a precise correlation. In addition, over even the last few decades, sampling has varied both in the time and locations the data is collected. In some cases, urban centers skew the data with the "heat island effect." **All of these items cloud our view of the data, yet most charts used to show global warming show a sharp clear line with no error bars to illustrate the uncertainty of the data**.

Even if we can all agree that climate change is real and demands attention, **we need to assess the relative benefits and risks of the various forms of energy we consume**. Climate activists often exaggerate the risks of fossil fuels while ignoring their benefits. On the flip side, they tend to exaggerate the benefits while ignoring the problems with the two main renewable alternatives, wind and solar. Both wind and solar have many drawbacks (see Chapter 35: *The Folly of Wind, Solar, and EV's* for details). Besides their only working while the wind blows or the sun shines (which can but hasn't yet been mitigated by energy storage solutions), they result in undesirable environmental impacts. Both wind and solar require enormous land footprints for each unit of energy produced. Solar panels become dusted over and have to use a lot of water to keep them clean and functioning. Both wind and solar will require disposing of worn out components (solar panels, turbine blades) with toxic content into landfills. Both wind and solar require the use of rare earth minerals which are mined in China using a filthy process. Both wind and solar kill birds, including endangered species like the bald eagle. Alex Epstein, author of *The Moral Case for Fossil Fuels*, puts it succinctly: **"Do we want to replace cheap, plentiful, reliable energy with expensive, scarce and intermittent energy?"** In addition, thinking geopolitically, do we want to become dependent on China for solar panels and wind turbines like we were on the middle east for oil?

The final question is simple yet profound: "How do we know that the absolute optimal temperature is the one from about 1900 (just after the end of the little ice age) or 1950 and that we must do everything to preserve this one moment in time?" Humanity has flourished for thousands of years in both warm and cold periods and has managed to adapt and muddle through previous changes. With modern technology, it should be even easier to adapt than it was for our forebears. Epstein points to the clearest fallacy in the Climate activist's arsenal. As CO2 has increased in the atmosphere, climate related deaths have plummeted because our technology has found ways to adapt to climate changes. "The climate catastrophists don't want you to know this because it reveals how fundamentally flawed their viewpoint is. They treat the global climate system as a stable and safe place we make volatile and dangerous. In fact, the global climate system is naturally volatile and dangerous—we make it livable through development and technology—development and technology powered by the only form of cheap, reliable, scalable energy that can make climate livable for 7 billion people."

The clear truth is that climate change activists have no good answers to any of these seven basic questions. These questions strike at the heart of the alarmist position, exposing it as a cult with only the trappings of scientific reasoning. Their normal approach to debate with skeptics is to use loaded words like "anti-science", "debunked", "discredited" or question the motives of the skeptics as being shills of the fossil fuel industry. They avoid answering these questions by changing the subject and name calling. But if we are to believe their case as ironclad and justifies spending trillions of dollars and sacrificing the comfortable lifestyle we have obtained by using fossil fuels, they must give satisfactory answers to these specific questions, backing up their answers with data. **Saying that the "science is settled" just won't do.**

33. Can we Even Detect Global Warming?
"Knowledge is proud that he has learned so much;
Wisdom is humble that he knows no more."
William Cowper (1731-1800)

I am a chemical engineer who specializes in Statistical Process Control. In my 30+ year career, I have viewed and analyzed thousands of statistical charts to discover ways to improve consistency of complex manufacturing processes. One of the things I learned repeatedly was that charts can fool you if you don't drill down beneath the surface of the trends.

Back in 2006, I addressed the American Society of Mechanical Engineers at Georgia Tech, my alma mater. My presentation was titled "**Global Warming: Reasonable Doubt**." A major point I made was that any trend chart implicitly combines variation from 3 sources: the **actual process** under study, the **sampling method**, and the **measurement method**. In many charts, sources 2 and 3 may be negligibly small so they can be ignored. But when we examine climate change charts, it is likely that very large portions of the variation we see can be attributed to sampling and measurement method. This means that trying to detect changes of fractions of a degree may be a fool's errand because the noise drowns out the signal.

A close look at the famous 'Hockey Stick' chart of Michael Mann is illuminating. The eye is drawn to the dark trend line that shows a decided uptick in the late 20th century. But if you just "gray out" the trend line and look at the large gray "standard error limits" around the data, we see that the temperature in the late 20th century is almost even with the Medieval Warm Period or MWP. Adding a trend line does not nullify the uncertainty of the gray band. It merely adds a sophisticated mathematical opinion to the data.

Statistical aggregation can be highly misleading. Perhaps the most well known example of this is illustrated by taking the average of a container of balls. Half of the contents are basketballs and half are marbles. The average of the size of these two populations tells us nothing about the individuals in each population. We lose information when we take averages.

When we average temperature readings over wide geographic areas and long time spans, many sources of error can creep in. As population has grown over the past few centuries, many new cities have cropped up. These cities are only a century or even a few decades old. If many of these new cities are in warmer climates, adding them to an aggregate average skews the data to the high side. This kind of average then leads to a false conclusion. What we need is not the grand average from one time compared to the grand average from another, what we need is the average change at the same location, and then average those average changes.

Sampling and Measurement cast more than reasonable doubt on the conclusions we draw from Climate Change data. When we smear all the temperatures into one aggregate average and say the climate is warming, we must ask about sampling:

- **Geography** (polar or equatorial? Rainforest or desert? Urban or Rural? Coastal or inland? Land or Sea? Wind or Calm?)
- **Elevation** (Mountains or plains? Surface or Troposphere? Right at the surface or 6 feet above the surface?)
- **Time of Day** (are readings always taken at precisely the same time? Are adjustments made for Daylight Savings Time?)

- **Historical** (How many samples do we have now vs how many were taken in previous periods? Were all the historical samples taken at the same time of day and same locations?)
- **Adjustment** (How was the "raw data" adjusted to compensate for things like new measurement methods or urban heat island effect?)

Depending on how our samples are gathered and manipulated before aggregation, the average we get can be greatly impacted, certainly by more than tenths of a degree.

The other source of uncertainty in much of the global warming data relates to measurement method. Remember that the mercury thermometer was only invented in 1714 and computer data acquisition systems only became available a few decades ago. This means that long-term charts of global temperature often combine different measurement methods (thermometer, satellite data with proxies such as tree rings and coral growth). Some of these proxies are only available in limited geographies (tree rings in forested areas, coral in shallow seas) and the precision of the proxies has not been demonstrated to be as accurate as an actual thermometer measurement. Even more accepted measurement systems such as mercury thermometers have small amounts of variation due to flow of the glass over time, the angle at which the observer takes the reading and the number of graduations on the instrument. Satellite data can also have small amounts of variation as the satellite orbit degrades over time so it looks at slightly different locations. Each temperature sensor is only as accurate as the quality of maintenance on it, and that varies greatly.

When I was an engineer at a factory that made Polyurethane pads for polishing semiconductor wafers, I saw first-hand how hard it is to separate signal from noise. Our customers demanded very precise consistency from one pad to the next. They had to be the same thickness to thousandths of an inch. We measured these items using state of the art technology and yet we found over time that various anomalies would creep into the process. For example, a vacuum system designed to pull the pads flat to the platen on which the thickness was measured would become plugged with dust and would unevenly flatten the pad. Or the pad was not sufficiently cooled prior to measurement. Or one of the sensors might be jarred out of place. Or a calibration would be done, shifting the measurement. Remember when you're aiming for thousandths of an inch, even small perturbations like this could impact the measurement.

Our demanding customers in the semiconductor business required that we use a "Control Plan" to assure accuracy of our metrology. This included Cause and Effect Analysis, Failure Mode Effects Analysis (FMEA) and Gage R&R (Repeatability and Reproducibility). If our plant wanted to make a change to the metrology, we had to do a "qualification" where we compared old metrology and new metrology using Analysis of Variance (ANOVA) and Tukey-Cramer t- Tests to assure statistical equivalence. FMEA and Gage R&R's had to be reviewed annually to assure that the measurement method was not drifting.

If we had all this due diligence to assure measurement accuracy for making plastic pads, how much more care must be made to assure consistency of measurement of charts that cover thousands of locations and instruments. Who is policing the thousands of temperature sensors for accuracy and drift? Who assures the rigor of these measurements? Where are the Gage Studies? How do we know that a chart that spans thousands of years uses consistent methods across the entire span? These are not unreasonable questions in light of the conclusions about fractions of a degree that would drive policy.

I contend that Climate Scientists are not the appropriate parties to conclude whether or not we have warming. Scientists present their hypothesis, but it is up to trained statisticians to validate the claims by looking at the data and assessing it for anomalies like the ones I have presented. In my experience as an engineer, I have known brilliant ph D scientists who nonetheless have almost no clue when it comes to statistics. Many scientists can make compelling cases when they have a controlled experiment but cannot predict the rough and tumble of real world manufacturing processes because they are not controlled experiments.

Global warming is not a controlled experiment. We can't hold all the other natural factors constant while we study the impact of greenhouse gases. CO_2 is just one of many factors that influence climate and advanced statistics (for example, analysis of variance, partial least squares, partition analysis) are needed to estimate the relative strength of each factor. The news media never gives us these studies because they are too complex for most of us to comprehend. They also aren't dramatic. They are not click-bait.

We hear a lot about the 'certainty' of climate change. But this certainty is based on an enormously complex aggregation of millions of numbers into one number. The sheer complexity of estimating the errors due to sampling and measurement method is itself nearly incomprehensible. About the only dataset we have with a reasonable estimate of certainty is the satellite record and it is only a few decades old, a mere pinprick in geologic time. Someone needs to admit that some things are beyond our ability to measure and predict, even with the most sophisticated technology. Global warming may be one of those things.

34. The Fraud of "Follow the Science"
Accept the scientists we have chosen and ignore others not anointed by the media

A lot of pundits preach to us that we should "follow the science", particularly in the areas of climate change and Covid response. They imply and often say explicitly that "the science is settled" meaning there is no debate, there is only truth or falsehood. Who would argue with facts such as 2 + 2 = 4 or gravity attracts people and rocks to the earth's surface?

But imagine what would happen if we "back applied" this *science is settled* logic in times past. We might have said to Einstein, "No, Albert. The science of Newtonian Physics is settled. Your new-fangled theories of relativity only confuse the public. Please shut up." Instead, the scientific community looked critically at relativity and one prominent scientist, Sir Arthur Edington, helped confirm the theory with meticulous observations of gravitational lensing during a solar eclipse. While some scientists opposed Einstein, at the time there was no mass media pushing one theory or another, so science could flourish as each new theory was tested and verified.

But both in the case of climate change and Covid response, the problem is that most people are not scientists, so they do not understand the rigors of the scientific inquiry. Moreover, most of us are so busy with our everyday lives that we don't have time to read a lot of detailed, footnoted academic papers to get the information firsthand. So **what we know about science is really what the media tells us the science is**.

The media in the USA has changed its mission and tactics over the past few decades. It used to be a fairly dispassionate reporter of facts, but today it has become a participant in crusades. Most scientific research should be controversial only among rival scientists who can check and cross check to assure a rigorous adherence to the scientific method. But if we non- scientists get our information about science through the lens of the news media, we often get not a presentation of rival theories but rather an anointing of one theory to the complete exclusion of any other. The news media wants to persuade the public that climate change is an issue in urgent need of attention, and any information that compromises that goal must be omitted from widely publicized sources.

Alex Epstein outlines this issue brilliantly in his new book, *Fossil Future*. He states that between the scientists and the lay persons, **media is a layer that basically chooses preferred experts to the exclusion of alternate points of view**. For example, the preferred scientists on Climate Change are people like James Hanson of NASA and Michael E. Mann of the University of Pennsylvania. These and likeminded acolytes like Bill Nye the Science Guy and Bill McKibben of Middlebury college have seen the evidence on climate change and have concluded that it is a serious issue that could lead to catastrophe unless humanity greatly reduces its use of fossil fuels.

But other scientists, with no less distinguished credentials, have concluded something entirely different. They have concluded that yes, climate is changing and yes, humanity has caused some of the change but that no, these forces will not produce catastrophic change that will outstrip humanity's ability to adapt to the changes. Here is a partial list of prominent scientists who do not buy the alarmist position:

- Dr. Richard Lindzen (MIT)
- Dr. John Christy (Univ Alabama Huntsville)
- Dr. Roy Spencer (Univ Alabama Huntsville)
- Dr. Patrick Michaels (Univ of Virginia)

- Dr. Steven Koonin (Obama Science advisor)
- Dr. Judith Curry (Georgia Tech)
- Dr. David Legates (Univ of Delaware)
- Dr. Freeman Dyson (Princeton)
- Dr. Willie Soon (Harvard Smithsonian)
- Dr. Robert Giegengack (Univ of Pennsylvania)
- Dr. Patrick Moore, Greenpeace cofounder
- Dr. Caleb Rossiter (American University)
- Dr. Roger Pielke, Jr (phD Penn State, served at Duke, Univ of Va, and NOAA Experimental Meteorology Lab)
- Dr. Will Happer (Princeton)
- Dr. John F. Clauser (Nobel Prize in Physics 2022)

A truly balanced news media would just report that there are two schools of thought on climate change, one that it is catastrophic and the other that it is manageable. But because the media has swallowed the catastrophic interpretation, it only reports on that one side of the story and labels anyone who thinks climate change is manageable as a "denier" who simply won't believe the evidence. No one ever explains the methods the media used to select their "preferred experts." For example, why are Lindzen and Michaels not the "preferred experts"?

What "follow the science" advocates are really asking is "believe our experts and do not believe others claiming to be experts, regardless of their credentials." **They have basically injected politics into science. That does justice to neither.**

35. The Folly of Wind, Solar, and EV's
Not the renewable energy panacea, at least for the next few decades

As CO2 levels rise in the atmosphere, the usual voices from the left keep telling us we need to accelerate the conversion from fossil fuels to renewable "clean" energy sources. Over the years, several other energy sources have been proposed to partially replace fossil fuels. These include Nuclear Fusion power, alcohols such as methanol and ethanol, biofuels from switchgrass or algae, and hydrogen power using fuel cells. None of these solutions has proved to be a viable alternative to fossil fuels, at least as of the year 2024. What we appear to be seeking is the discovery of a new material called *unobtainium* that will be a magic solution to limitless pristine energy. We all want to flick on the light switch with a clean conscience that we aren't causing any environmental harm. So far, unobtanium has not yet been discovered.

Since the other alternatives have not panned out, we are stuck with a few technologies that basically "work" (although as we'll see, not very well). Today as of the year 2024, we seem to have settled on wind, solar and Electric Vehicles (EV's). While wind, solar, and EV's are vital components to an "all of the above" energy solution, it is preposterous to suggest that these three items could be the panacea we seek to replace fossil fuels any time in the next several decades, even possibly the next fifty years or more. Unless and until enormous breakthroughs occur in energy storage technology , none of these green sources can possibly compete with fossil fuels which are cheap, abundant, reliable, concentrated, and scalable. The only alternative energy source that comes close to fossil fuels is nuclear energy, and it is being impeded by environmentalists even more than fossil fuels.

Most pundits focus almost entirely on the negative side-effects of Fossil Fuels while completely ignoring their amazing benefits. On the flip side, the news media place an unapologetically positive spin on Wind and Solar. They stress their advantages ("free" and "renewable") and completely ignore their disadvantages. I aim to expose this bias and explain why wind and solar are not the cure-all they are reputed to be. I'll treat wind and solar first and then tackle EV's later. I'll begin with on practical limitations and then on environmental objections.

Practical Limitations of Wind and Solar

The world has been researching ways to harness power from wind and solar for several decades. Billions of dollars in research grants have been spent along with billions of dollars of government subsidies to entice consumers to become "early adopters". **Yet in spite of a massive multi-decade effort, wind and solar still only account for about 2 to 3% of worldwide energy consumption**. If this technology were competitive, consumers would be flocking to it in droves. Yet even with subsidies, consumers are still sticking with fossil fuels. Here is a list of practical limitations that are impeding widespread adoption of wind and solar:

- **Intermittent**: Wind and Solar do not work if the wind doesn't blow or the sun doesn't shine. As of today (April 2024), there is no large-scale way to store the energy for use during night or low wind times.
- **Capacity Factor:** Wind turbines, even when the wind is blowing, do not always generate 100% of the energy they can at peak winds. Wind turbines average a capacity factor of about 35% meaning, they are only operating at peak about 35% of the time. This means you need more than twice as many wind turbines to get a theoretical amount of power as you would think.

- **Need for Base-Load**: Because of their intermittent nature, there needs to be a "base load" of fossil fuel plants to back up wind and solar when they are not available. But these baseload fossil power stations then operate at less than peak efficiency because they have to start and stop to accommodate fluctuations in their green sources.
- **Transmission Cost**: Wind and solar farms need to be connected to existing baseload fossil fuel plants. This results in considerable cost to construct all the transmission lines and obtain right-of-ways. Even if the transmission lines end at the existing fossil fuel baseload power stations, wind and solar need their own transmission wires. Most environmentalists oppose the construction of more transmission lines.
- **Beyond Electricity**: Although we can produce electricity with both wind and solar, this would only comprise perhaps a half or less of our energy needs. Several uses beyond electricity are easily handled with versatile fossil fuels but will probably never be handled with wind and solar. These include
    - Heavy industrial heat such as iron smelting or fiberglass production where sand is melted at high temperatures
    - Air Transportation
    - Propulsion of large ocean-going ships
    - Locomotives and Trains
    - Large construction and farming equipment
    - Heavy duty large trucks
    - Plastics, fertilizers and other petrochemicals
- **China:** Many of the components used for both wind and solar come from China. This means that America would be dependent on a strategic adversary for vital energy needs.
- **Life Span:** Wind turbines were thought to have a life span of perhaps 30 years but they have turned out to be significantly shorter, requiring replacement and associated costs.

- **Minerals:** A lot of nickel, copper, cobalt and other minerals need to be mined to supply a large-scale wind and solar future. Many environmental groups oppose new mining so it is not certain that we will have enough minerals to go to a net zero situation.
- **Maintenance**: Wind Turbines need to be oiled. On any given day as you pass a wind farm, just examine how many of the turbines are actually spinning. Solar panels need to be washed frequently to avoid build up of dust and sand. This means a large water source is needed to wash the panels which are usually in desert areas with very little rainfall. Major maintenance efforts need to be expended to keep these things going.

Environmental Impacts for Wind and Solar

Wind and solar are typically depicted as "clean" energy sources, allowing us to transition to a pristine world beyond fossil fuels. But there are environmental costs that need to be considered.

- **Land Area**: Both wind and solar require very large land areas per kilowatt hour of energy produced. They lack the "concentration" value of fossil fuels which require a tiny land footprint. The extra land required for both wind and solar must be withdrawn from the stock of land that could have been used in farming, housing, or wildlife habitat.
- **Transmission Lines:** Since a lot of new transmission lines need to be constructed, all the environmental hazards associated with these new wires accrue. One potential hazard would be forest fires from electric sparking and fallen power lines. These power lines may also produce what is known as stray voltage, a hazard for livestock. In addition, many environmental groups have opposed building more transmission lines.

- **Birds:** Multiple studies published in 2013 and 2014 found that somewhere between 140,000 and 679,000 birds are killed by wind turbines annually
- **Disposal:** Wind Turbines and Solar Panels must be disposed of in landfills. This creates enormous piles of items that are made with potentially toxic minerals.
- **Minerals:** Wind Turbines and Solar Panels need a large supply of minerals including rare earths. Many tons of ore would have to be mined and processed to obtain the enormous quantities of minerals needed for Wind, Solar, and Batteries. Among these mining operations would be those for rare earth elements (REE) such as dysprosium, indium, neodymium, and tellurium, which are necessary to produce wind turbines or photovoltaic solar panels. However, mining a single ton of these REEs, according to the brief, produces up to 420,000 cubic feet of toxic gases, 2,600 cubic feet of acidic wastewater, and a ton of radioactive waste. https://heartlanddailynews.com/2022/05/vulnerable-bird-species-killed- wind-and-solar-energy/

Electric Vehicles Issues

- **Charge Time**: While it takes perhaps 3 minutes to fill up a gasoline powered vehicle, recharging an EV can take days if you're using a conventional home outlet or hours if you use a "level 2" type charging station. There are a few "superchargers" available that can charge about 200 miles in 15 minutes, but these are rare and expensive.
- **Cost:** A decent Electric vehicle will be much more expensive than a typical gasoline powered vehicle, even with government subsidies.
- **Range Degradation**: While a brand new EV may have an acceptable range in miles, the range degrades over time.

Degradation rates vary with the quality of the EV and driving methods.

- **Fire Hazard**: EV Batteries pose a significant fire hazard. In 2022, a ferry named *Felicity Ace* sank south of the Azores Islands due to EV Car batteries catching fire. As a result, some Ferry lines ban EV's on their ships.

- **Heavier Weight**: Batteries for EV's make them significantly heavier than conventional cars, increasing risk for damage in collision accidents.

- **Spare Tires**: Most EV's do not have spare tires. EVs are about 750 pounds heavier than regular cars, so the tires are specifically designed to handle that extra weight. The other reason for removing the spare is to offer more space in the trunk. The lack of a spare tire is not a big deal as long as you are driving in an urban environment. But if you have a flat in the middle of nowhere, it can be a serious issue.

- **Slave Labor in China**: Most Lithium Ion Batteries are produced in China using forced labor of the Uyghur Moslem minority

- **Minerals:** According to the International Energy Agency (IEA), an electric vehicle requires six times the mineral inputs of a comparable internal combustion engine vehicle (ICE). EV batteries are very heavy and are made with some exotic, expensive, toxic, and flammable materials. One vital component is processed graphite. Reuters reported in 2023 that China produces 61% of global natural graphite and 98% of the final processed material to make battery anodes. Once again we see the strategic position of China.

- **Recylcling:** Ninety percent of the ICE lead-acid batteries are recycled while only five percent of the EV lithium-ion batteries are. https://fee.org/articles/the-environmental-downside-of-electric-vehicles/

- **Efficiency**: Alex Epstein, author of *Fossil Future*, points out that with a gasoline powered car, the consumer gets nearly all of the energy when burning the fuel. But with an electric vehicle, the fuel must be burned to produce electricity, resulting in efficiency losses. Further losses occur in transmitting the electricity over transmission lines. EV's may actually burn more fossil fuel than gasoline powered cars.

Conclusion

While wind, solar, and EV's would make a welcome supplement to our energy resource mix, they will never replace fossil fuels. Our modern economy thrives because of the availability of cheap, abundant, reliable/on demand, concentrated energy. While EV's may be practical in a small country like Iceland with an abundance of hydro power and geothermal energy, they are not suited for a continental land mass like the USA which would have to power the EV's with fossil fuels.

Without fossil fuels America would be a third world country. We would become like many countries that burn wood and animal dung for heat and suffer from the consequent indoor pollution. Without fossil fuels, agriculture would be much less productive and we would have to live close to the farm because the produce would have no way of getting to market. Without fossil fuels, hospitals would not have on-demand power for things like incubators and ultrasound machines and infants would die. **Without fossil fuels life would be miserable**.

The assertion that we can replace fossil fuels with wind, solar, and EV's is not only absurd, it borders on fraud. Many advocates of wind and solar are getting rich as they spread their propaganda to people with short attention-spans. **We "want to believe" that there is some magic way we can replace fossil fuels with clean renewables, so we focus on the positives of wind and solar and ignore their many negatives.**

If this were the 1990's, we could say that wind and solar technology are in their infancy and we need to be patient as we work out the kinks during a suboptimal transition period. Maybe we could have even said the same thing in the 2000's. But as the 2010s and 2020s have unfolded, wind, solar, and EV's are still marginal energy sources in spite of billions of dollars in research, development, and subsidies. The consumer has spoken. Wind, solar, and EV's are a welcome supplement to our energy mix, but barring a major technological breakthrough, they will never replace cheap, abundant, reliable fossil fuels. **Let's not kid ourselves**.

36. *Unsettled,* by Steven Koonin
Book Review

As a Climate Change enthusiast, I have read many books, articles, and Internet posts on this subject. I also gave a presentation on the subject to the Mechanical Engineers group at Georgia Tech, my alma mater, in 2006. So what is new about yet another Climate Change book? Dr. Koonin, a brilliant theoretical physicist with a BS from Cal Tech and pHD from MIT, who served as an Obama Administration science advisor, provides a fresh approach. His unique angle is to not cite competing studies of Climate Skeptics but instead to accept the major mainstream Assessment Reports from organizations like the U.N.'s Intergovernmental Panel on Climate Change (IPCC) and the U.S. Government's US Global Change Research Program (USGCRP).

Koonin did what many journalists fail to do: **he carefully read the text**. Not just the "Executive Summary" or "Summary for Policy Makers", but the whole report. As he mined the reports he found some nuggets of inconsistencies between the summaries and the actual report text. His theory is that the reports have two sometimes **competing objectives**: **to inform and to persuade**. The scientists who wrote most of the report are distinguished and true to their profession. They present the data in an unbiased way: to inform. But the political types who tend to write the summaries have an objective to persuade the public that Climate Change is an urgent threat requiring drastic action. They know that dramatic statements, even if they stretch the truth, are the only way to capture public opinion. This objective to persuade is further amplified by the popular news media. They want clicks, and boring statements like "there is no evidence of a rise in frequency of hurricanes" will just not do.

Dr. Koonin presents one example after another of boring statements in the back pages of the IPCC and US Government reports that are either absent or contradicted by the Executive Summaries. Here is a sample of mundane statements made in these official, peer reviewed reports:

- There has been no significant trend in the global number of tropical cyclones nor has any trend been identified in the number of US landfalling hurricanes (buried in page 769 of the NCA 2014 assessment by USGCRP). The IPCC Fifth assessment (AR5) confirmed this finding ("low confidence").
- There is no evidence of increase in precipitation at the global scale in response to global warming. As the 2017 CSSR notes, US precipitation has risen a bit, but the fact that it varies over both years and location much more than the trend itself makes it hard to draw any solid conclusion about the relative roles of human influences and natural variability.
- There is no evidence that increased CO_2 has exacerbated trends in
    - Draughts
    - Floods
    - Forest Fires
    - Crop Yields
- Sea Level has risen at a fairly constant rate since about 1880. There has been no acceleration since the industrial revolution.
- Even with the direst of climate change predictions, the global GDP will still grow dramatically until the turn of the century, with climate change blunting that growth only by a tiny amount.
- Humans have shown that they can adapt to small changes in climate and there is no evidence that the projected changes in climate will defeat humanity's ability to adapt.

Dr. Koonin's conclusion is one I suspect is fairly widespread. Yes, the climate has warmed over the past few decades. Yes, human use of fossil fuels has contributed to this warming. But no, it is not likely to produce a catastrophe that can only be averted by major changes to our lifestyle. **Dr. Koonin says that climate change is here and it is real. But it's not a big deal**.

37. *Gun Violence*
Crime Control Instead of Gun Control

In the aftermath of another horrific mass shooting in May 2022 at an elementary school in Uvalde, Texas in which 19 children were slaughtered by a young man with serious mental issues, the politicians in Washington are nearly unanimously calling for more gun control, just as they did after other mass shootings in previous years. The theory is that if we outlaw guns we will prevent these shootings in the future. But these types of laws would only penalize innocent people and only embolden criminals bent on harm.

A far better tactic would be a **"zero tolerance" approach to those who commit a crime with a gun**. Some laws like this are on the books in some jurisdictions, but they lack vigorous enforcement. If a person commits a crime with a gun, even if no one gets hurt, that person should at minimum receive ten years probation during which he waives the right to privacy. His effects would be thoroughly searched and all guns in his possession would be confiscated. He would receive an ankle monitor, be subject to search warrants without notice, and be placed on a **national gun-offenders list**. If he is stopped by police, and they see he is on that list, they will search him and his vehicle and home to see whether he has a gun. If he does, he goes to jail. For a very long time.

The best argument against the conventional gun control laws being proposed today is that there are already many gun laws on the books that have been totally ineffective in stopping gun violence. Most of the perpetrators of mass shootings have already violated four or five gun laws. Would a sixth law be the stopper? Certainly not. People who are determined to kill others will find a gun, whether it's legal or not.

Exhibit A is Chicago. That city has the most restrictive gun laws in the nation, and yet it also has one of the highest rates of gun violence in the nation. Almost every weekend, several dozen people in Chicago will be shot. A half dozen will be killed. And many of the victims are innocent children, just like in Uvalde Texas. Yet according to the Chicago Tribune, the clear rate of gun homicides dropped to less than 50% in the year 2020. This means that **criminals are learning they have a fifty-fifty chance of getting away with murder**.

Even the criminals who are caught are often let off by prosecutors who have an agenda of ending what they see as a scourge of "mass incarceration." This tendency has been growing in many large cities beyond Chicago, including New York, Los Angeles, San Francisco, and St. Louis. In all these cities, liberal DA's are choosing not to prosecute to the fullest extent of the law because they see a higher mission in what they call "social justice." What this means is that we have to have compassion on criminals and give them a second chance. But what often happens is that they gain a second chance to murder someone. **By substituting compassion for criminals over compassion for citizens, we have prioritized the rights of violent criminals over ordinary citizens just trying to lead a quiet, peaceful life**.

In addition to lenient prosecutors, the news media has conducted a relentless crusade against police officers. In their zeal to expose police brutality, they are accentuating the few bad apples in police forces and training police to be so careful about being seen in a bad light that many officers shy away from their job of enforcing the law. They stay out of situations where their encounter may be the subject of a viral video. And they accelerate the retirement of many policemen who have just had it with all the vilification they receive on a daily basis.

We all saw the videos of violent mobs in Seattle and Minneapolis burning and taking over police precincts. In the height of the frenzy in 2020, many police departments were subjected to "defund the police" movements that gutted departments. It is not surprising that since this occurred, gun violence has soared.

Our nation has in the last few decades become a seething cauldron of violence that is boiling over into events like Uvalde. Recent societal changes that have contributed to this toxic stew include the following:

- A news media that continually stirs up racial hatred
- Entertainment that trivializes bad behavior and desensitizes us to the impact of violence
- A breakdown of discipline in schools
- A long stretch of Covid lockdowns further isolating people
- Millions of kids in fatherless households spending hours on drugs, on their phones, or playing video games that depict vivid violence
- China is flooding the USA with a device called an Auto-Sear switch, that converts a Glock Pistol into a pre capable of fully automatic fire.
- Intact two-parent families in which two careers necessitate farming out child care or exhausted parents asking children to "entertain themselves" in hours of solitude with no parental guidance
- Social media in which everyone is competing stand out and be noticed, creating millions of isolated "loners" connected only by their phones.
- China's cyber warfare is stoking anger and rage between the races.
- Sprawling homeless encampments in major cities where mentally ill or drug addicted people gather and harass people around them

- An open border over which swarm not only those seeking a better life, but along with them drug gangs like MS-13, tons of drugs, and many illegal guns.
- A widespread mentality that asserts entitlement to unearned resources
- A cancel culture that sees differences of opinion as evil or stupid because other opinions do not align with the prevailing orthodoxy
- Toleration of burning and looting if it is done for a "good cause" as we saw in the riots of 2020
- A lack of respect for law enforcement and other authorities
- The crusade to end mass-incarceration by being lenient on crimes, eliminating cash bail, depleting police resources, and second-guessing cops who placed themselves in harm's way and have to make major decisions in seconds.

By themselves, none of these negative forces is sufficient to explain school shootings or other events that used to be rare but are now commonplace including pushing people onto subway tracks, smash and grab thefts, and deaths due to drug overdoses. But over the years these forces have combined synergistically and cumulatively. They have created **a magma chamber of violent tension that erupts with increasing regularity in our culture**, reinforced by a news media who sees its mission as getting the story first and generating excitement and clicks even if the story is not quite correct factually.

Among all these negative forces, some lonely voices are trying to be heard but are drowned out in the din calling for us to "do something", as if confiscating guns is the magic solution to all these problems. But as we condone and even celebrate bad behavior, we are "training" people to commit these atrocities. As we stray from tried-and-true moralities that guided us for centuries and just make up our ethics as we go along, taking our cues from a woke media, we can't hope to solve our sick society. There is no quick fix.

Guns should only be used for sports and self-defense. But if a person uses them to commit robberies, murder, and other mayhem, that person should lose his constitutional right to keep and bear arms. We apply the same rules to other items that could potentially be used as weapons. A knife should be used in the kitchen, not to threaten or cut another human being. Matches should be used to light a controlled fire, not to commit arson. In both of these areas, we don't attempt to have "knife control" laws or "match control" laws. Instead, we vigorously punish anyone who misuses these items and commits crimes with them. Guns should be no different. The gun does not commit the crime; a criminal does. So the gun doesn't need to be controlled, instead the criminal thug needs to be controlled.

All of the forces undermining law and order have reached a deafening crescendo in recent years. There is no obvious solution except to call out the distortions in the media and attempt to be heard. But that is a very tall order and not likely to be successful any time soon. In the meantime, about all we can do is use law enforcement measures that have worked in the past.

Once our authorities make it plain that gun violence simply will not be tolerated, it will subside. Just look at the experience of New York City. When it pursued the "broken windows" policy and used "Stop and Frisk", the rate of gun violence plummeted. Notice that Gun violence dropped in New York not as a result of tough gun control laws, but because of vigorous enforcement of existing laws. Figure 6 below vividly depicts the impact of tough policing policies. When criminals know they will pay a heavy price, they will think twice about committing the next murder.

https://criminaljustice.cityofnewyork.us/wp-content/
uploads/2021/01/2020-Shootings-and- Murder-factsheet_
January-2021.pdf

Figure 6.

Murders in New York City, 1950-2020

There were 462 recorded murders in 2020, up from 319 in 2019 (45 percent increase). The last similar year was 2009, with 471 murders. While problematic, these statistics come nowhere near the levels of violence faced by the City in the 1980s and 1990s.

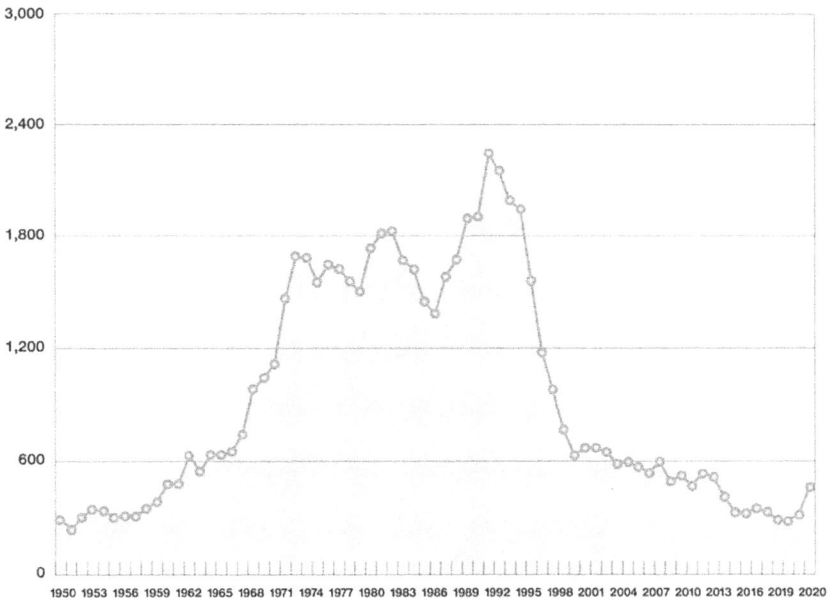

We must not create gun free zones where criminals reign unchallenged. **We must make the criminals pay dearly for the crimes they commit with a gun**. This may take some drastic measures. For example, we should create police precincts right in the middle of the most gun- prone sections of cities. When gang violence breaks out, the enforcement job is not done until the cops confiscate every weapon the criminals are using. They should be able to stop and frisk to prevent gun crime and confiscate weapons from those who are on the gun offender list.

Ronald Reagan crystalized the solution to gun violence in a pithy way: "You won't get gun control by disarming law-abiding citizens. There's only one way to get real gun control: Disarm the thugs and the criminals, lock them up and if you don't actually throw away the key, at least lose it for a long time. ... **It's a nasty truth, but those who seek to inflict harm are not fazed by gun controllers.**"

38. China
Whether we Recognize it or not, China is at war with the US

On the surface, China appears to be a peaceful, benign nation that wants to make the world a better place. It appears that China has rapidly and dramatically emerged from third world status into a leadership position in the first world. China's economy has grown dramatically and supplies the US and many other countries with inexpensive goods. Just go to the local Wal Mart and observe how many of the things you buy there were made in China. China has also extended its influence to areas like Africa and Latin America with its Belt and Road initiatives where it builds desperately needed infrastructure in poverty-stricken nations. More recently, it has also expanded its activities with some impressive projects to explore outer space, including landing on the moon. In 2019, China landed on the far side of the moon, the first nation to accomplish that feat. Although it has introduced some advanced new weapons (for example, hypersonic missiles), China has not committed large amounts of troops to participate in foreign wars in contrast to the US, which has been involved in many wars in the last several decades.

So China looks like a nation that has a lot to offer to the rest of the world, including the US. It has a rich cultural heritage going back thousands of years. Its vibrant economy supplies important items such as rare earth minerals and medical equipment to the rest of the world at low cost. Many countries, including the US, have extensive economic interconnections with China, with both sides of the trade receiving significant benefits. So what's not to like? Much, actually.

As impressive as the Chinese economic rise has been, it has presented formidable challenges to the US.

- Cheap goods are exported to the US, but in return we are not exporting goods to China, but jobs. See Chapter 31 on International Trade for details.
- China runs a brutal police state and victimizes the Moslem Uyghurs by surveilling them and confining many in reeducation camps as vividly portrayed in Geoffry Cain's book *The Perfect Police State* (see review in Chapter 16).
- China's complete control of several vitally strategic goods (rare earth minerals that power our technology as well as medical supplies and drugs) makes the US vulnerable to cutoffs of strategic provisions if a hot war were ever commenced.
- Much of the interest the US is paying on the national debt goes straight to the Chinese Communist Party (CCP). The US is thus funding China's transformation into a world superpower.
- China has belligerently claimed several islands in the South China Sea in an effort to control vital sea lanes.
- China is the number one emitter of greenhouse gases on the planet. It has shown absolutely no sense of urgency to reduce emissions. China aggressively markets wind and solar equipment to other countries but does not strongly promote these technologies within China. NPR reported in March 2023 that China is building more coal fired power plants than any other nation, the equivalent of two new coal power plants per week. This means that the more goods we buy from China, the more greenhouse gases will be emitted.

As mentioned previously, China has amassed a substantial amount of power not only over its own nation, but even over US citizens inside our borders. Basketball players have to apologize for approving of Hong Kong's efforts to withstand Chinese domination. Chinese owners exert influence on Hollywood movie productions. Chinese businesses have caused millions of US citizens to lose their jobs by flooding the U.S. market with cheap goods. China has a police presence and conducts surveillance of its citizens within the U.S. Borders. China also steals billions of dollars worth of US intellectual property with almost no repurcussions.

Several recent books look under the surface to expose a sinister Chinese agenda to displace the US and become the lone world superpower. One such work that highlights this goal is Michael Pillsbury's 2015 book *The Hundred Year Marathon (China's Secret Strategy to replace America as the Global Superpower)*

Michael Pillsbury held several staff positions at the U.S. Defense Department and the Senate before he became Director of the Center on Chinese Strategy at the Hudson Institute in Washington, D.C. He speaks fluent Mandarin and spent some time in China, but eventually the Chinese government has decided to keep him out of China. This important book outlines the Chinese strategy to replace America as the global superpower. Here is a brief summary of the major points made by the author:

- Hundred year goal. Started in 1949 with the rise of Mao and communism. Will culminate in 2049 by supplanting the US as most powerful nation on earth.

- Pillsbury noticed when he read communiques from China that the original Mandarin sometimes contained things he did not see in the official American translation. He found that American translators sometimes "leave out" belligerent rhetoric because they think it may unnecessarily ruffle feathers.

- China exudes a benign image while seething underneath in resentment of domination by the West. They give us 'soothing' messages helping reinforce our wishful thinking that economic prosperity will bring democracy and that they are 'becoming more like us.'

273

- Confucius Institutes: Chinese propaganda in European and American Universities

- Chinese military strategy: make the enemy complacent. Wait until they have weakened from within and then at the time they are weakest, strike for a sure victory. Knowledge of powerful opponent's weakest point. Lull the opponent into complacency and then strike at the unexpected time with surprising and overwhelming force.

- Don't provoke the hegemon prematurely. Soviet Union provoked US into an arms race and it lost the cold war. China will not make the same mistake. It tries to hide its military might.

- Large cyber espionage programs included downloading 20tb of data from defense department including plans for Patriot missiles. They hack into human rights NGO's to harass and intimidate critics.

- A million Chinese officials monitor the internet to censor and control it (what they call 'harmonized internet.') They sell their internet surveillance software to rogue regimes, thus expanding their influence and control.

- An environmental basket case. Burns more coal than all other countries combined. 40% of Chinese rivers unfit for drinking. Because of censorship, most don't know they should not drink the water. Cancer villages near rivers. No free press to bring these issues to light.

- Developing EMP weapons. They see a great American weakness is its dependence on advanced computers and communications.

- Theft of intellectual property and counterfeit goods may make up 10% of China's GDP.

- America was the key factor in transforming China from a 3rd world backwater in 1980 to a power with a GDP exceeding the US in just a generation. WTO and World bank crucial to China's transformation. China routinely cheats on WTO rules and plays by its own rules.

A 2010 strategic memo from China: asked what is the most important strategy for the decade, answer was 'how to manage the decline of the U.S.'

Another eye-opening book appeared in April 2024. Peter Schweizer's *Blood Money: Why the Powerful Turn a Blind Eye While China Kills Americans* exposes the Chinese strategy to wage war on a nation that doesn't even know it is being attacked. The Chinese use a strategy from the Fifth Century BC philosopher Sun Tzu who wrote, "The supreme art of war is to subdue the enemy without fighting." America's military strategy focuses on hot wars with ships, planes and tanks. But China is waging war with more indirect methods, including Fentanyl, cyber tactics, and propaganda. No invasion is necessary, but casualties including American deaths are occurring. China wants to cause America to disintegrate from within. It may at some future point resort to hot war tactics, but not until America has been so weakened as to not be able to resist conquest.

Blood Money exposes the main weapons China is deploying against the US now in 2024. Each item below is described by traditional Chinese proverbs. China is basically waging war unopposed:

- **Fentanyl (murder with a borrowed knife):** The Chinese are in control of every step of the Fentanyl supply chain. They disguise their role by operating in Mexico, who gets blamed. They control the main Mexican port that receives the Fentanyl precursors. They supply pill presses that make it easy to counterfeit pills with codes pressed into them to make them look like something else. Schweizer sums it up: "Drug warfare ... has cause untold casualties. Politicians find it convenient to focus on the blast caused by the Fentanyl missile while ignoring from where the missile was launched–Beijing."

- **Guns (watch a fire from across the river):** The Chinese supply the US with auto-sear switches that convert a normal Glock pistol into a machine weapon capable of fully automatic power. They also supply gun silencers to US criminal gangs. Interestingly, guns are illegal in China so their entire gun production enterprise is aimed at America.

- **Covid (Loot a Burning House):** Schweizer chronicles the many suspicious activities of China during the Covid crisis.
  - On September 12, 2019, the Wuhan Institute of Virology quietly removed from the internet a database of 22,000 virus samples and their sequences that had previously been open access to scientists around the world.
  - By the end of January 2020, the Chinese government blocked flights from Wuhan to the rest of China but allowed flights to leave it for the rest of the world.
  - In January, the CCP refused repeated requests from the WHO to have access to laboratory logs at the Wuhan lab.
  - In early 2020, China dramatically increased imports of critical personal protective equipment such as masks and cut off exports of these goods. It basically created a stockpile for its own use, giving it power over other nations in need.

- **Numbing and brainwashing our kids** (Hide a Dagger in a Smile). Tik-Tok, a popular application developed by Byte

Dance in China, used algorithms to get Americans hooked on short videos that fed an obsession of short attention spans and ADD.

Although the US has benefited greatly from large quantities of inexpensive goods, China has reaped even greater benefits. This trade between China and America, unlike other international trade, is really a win-lose transaction. They win. We lose.

What Can be Done?

Thus far, this book has focused on the Who, When, What, How, and Why of the Progressive dystopia we have witnessed over the last few decades. At first blush, the answer to "what can be done?" might appear to be "nothing can be done." The power centers that rule America are too entrenched to dislodge. I suspect that may have been the same conclusion many American colonists reached in 1776. Great Britain was a juggernaut that taxed and regulated them with impunity from afar. Yet, under some inspired leadership, they united and managed to throw off the tyranny of the Mother Country.

Although the situation looks bleak today, there are some things that should give us hope that we might be able to right the ship. A large swath of the American public sees the lunacy of the progressive vision. They see the crime-ridden cities and insane gender policies. They recognize the pointlessness of perpetual wars. They realize that fossil fuels are actually a blessing, not a curse that will cause our destruction.

In this section of *Lopsided*, I present some ideas on how we can at least put a speed bump in the way of the Progressive Elites before they flatten us with their overwhelming power. I begin with one topic in depth: Foreign Policy. I then move on to a laundry list of things we need to do on other major issues. Finally, in an epilogue to this book, I present the case that there may be a spiritual dimension that needs to be addressed.

39. Sensible Foreign Policy
Recognize and Deter Adversaries; Make Allies Pay their Fair Share

I am clearly not qualified to be President of the United States, but then neither are any who have held that office, with the possible exception of George Washington. Over the years I have observed a dozen presidents, and all twelve, without exception, have made mistakes, particularly in the area of foreign policy. I believe we should benefit from hindsight and make corrections for the mistakes of previous administrations. So here is how I would manage U.S. foreign policy if I were given a chance.

Before discussing tactics for relations with specific countries, I want to lay out some broad principles that should guide our relations with all countries:

- First and foremost, we should unabashedly **embrace American exceptionalism.** This nation is exceptional in so many ways that there should not even be a debate about it.
- America should almost never apologize for its leadership. We should never apologize for our treatment of African Americans or Native Americans. Dwelling on the past does not help us to prepare for the future.
- **America should never be "used" by other nations and become a "chump."**
- The primary aim for the American military should be **deterrence, not provocation**. We want to avoid being sucked into long quagmires that cost a lot and gain little for America's genuine interests.
- **All foreign aid** both military and otherwise will be **audited by Inspectors General** and all corrupt use of US aid will

279

result in disqualification for future aid dependent on the severity of the fraud.

- **Significant deployment of our military should only be used when war is declared by Congress as the Constitution demands**. Only small amounts of troops (such as a Seal Team) should be authorized without a declaration of war.
- We should recruit the most effective fighting force we can to join our military. Diversity, equity, and inclusion should not dominate recruitment. The most important qualification is whether the soldier or sailor can effectively serve to defeat our enemies.
- Our military's mission must not be compromised by prioritizing unrelated tasks such as drag queens, celebrating gay pride, and providing abortions or sex change services to soldiers. Those who want to pursue these items should be discouraged from joining the military.
- We should not telegraph to our enemies how and when we might respond to belligerent action. **Swift, sure, strategic, and unpredictable responses should be the goal**.
- **Restrictive rules of engagement should be minimal when fighting an enemy who observes no such rules**. This unfortunately means that "tidy little wars" may not be possible and civilian casualties will happen. This is why we should use deterrence as an overarching military principle. The best way to avoid civilian casualties is to avoid war.
- We must not attempt to evangelize other countries with woke principles that have nothing to do with our essential character. Radical gender and race theories should not be "preached" to other countries. **No gay pride banners should festoon American Embassies**.
- The **U.S. Navy** is vital to maintaining world peace and keeping sea lanes open for commerce. This is the one area of Defense Spending that gives a good cost/benefit balance.

- We must **use our rich energy resources and superior technology to defend American interests.**
- **International trade should be win-win transactions** and not a vehicle for hollowing out once vibrant urban centers.

With these general principles in mind, I will summarize tactics for relations with specific countries.

China

The **People's Republic of China is not a benign nation that helps America.** It is our number one threat, and it makes no bones about its ambition to displace America. Books like Michael Pillsbury's *The Hundred Year Marathon,* Peter Schweizer's *Blood Money,* and many others vividly depict China's ambition and craftiness in achieving its goal of eclipsing America by 2049. In light of this threat, we should use the following tactics to contain China's ambition:

- Wherever possible, **we should disengage with Chinese products** and try to either make them in the USA or buy from more friendly nations such as India and Mexico. We may have to pay higher prices when we buy from other countries, but we must not be vulnerable to a Chinese cutoff of critical goods in time of war.
- We should apply a sliding scale tariff to Chinese trade as described by economist Edward Conard (See chapter 31: *International Trade Deficits* for details). As our balance of trade deficit with China rises, we apply higher tariffs. They can reduce tariffs simply by buying more American goods. These tariff restrictions should be monitored for attempts to evade the tariffs by transshipping through other countries. Any countries who help China evade the tariffs will be penalized with similar tariff barriers.

- **Reciprocity should characterize our relations with China**. If it can buy U.S. Farmland near military bases in the US, then we can buy Chinese farmland near military bases. If it can establish Confucius institutes at U.S. colleges, then we can establish Jefferson institutes at Chinese colleges. If it can export guns to America, then we can export guns to China.
- **Theft of intellectual property must not be tolerated**. Swift and sure tariff penalties should be applied to deter this cheating.
- We should influence China to rein in its proxy North Korea not just by tough talk, but with action. If it fails to restrain North Korea, then we will empower Taiwan by selling more military hardware and conducting joint military exercises with American carrier groups located near Taiwan. We may also increase military exercises with other allies in the region including Japan, Korea, and the Philippines. Some voices would call this risky, reckless, and provocative. But our current policy of being hypersensitive to Beijing has not worked.
- **We should not tolerate Chinese police tactics and surveillance within the borders of the USA**. Chinese police organizations should be sent home if they violate this principle.
- Chinese cyber-attacks should be responded to with ruthless retaliation. If they stir up strife in America, we can stir up strife in China (for example, Hong Kong, Tibet).
- **China must not block Freedom of Speech within US borders**. Organizations like the NBA and movie industry should be prepared to pull out of the lucrative Chinese market if their freedom of speech within the U.S. is threatened.
- We should not be concerned about offending Chinese leaders by mentioning things like Hong Kong, Taiwan, Tibet, or Tiananmen Square. If they are offended, so be it. **We don't want to be liked; we want to be respected and feared**.
- **The more Chinese made Fentanyl that is smuggled into the US, the higher will be tariffs against Chinese exports**.

We should call out China's deliberate attack on the United States by flooding our cities with Fentanyl. We should not be fooled as China attempts to shift blame to Mexico. We should also retaliate with tariffs for Chinese exports of Auto-Sear Gun switches and gun silencers.

- We should authorize **mining for rare earth minerals in the USA despite the environmental risk**. We are vulnerable when nearly all our rare earths that power our technology come from China.

- Any **Spy Baloon** that flies over the U.S. should be immediately shot down as soon as it crosses over into U.S. airspace.

Allies (Europe, Japan, Korea, Canada)

- Seventy years is a long enough time for our once war-torn allies to have fully recovered. They should need little support from the USA. **They must pay the overwhelming bulk of costs to the NATO Alliance**. America must gradually reduce its commitment to defending these countries.

- Post WW II mandates telling Japan and Germany they are not allowed to build up their militaries must be repealed. These nations must become self-sustaining powers allied with but not dependent on the US.

- Germany, Japan, and South Korea should be given permission to develop nuclear weapons as a counter-balance to Russia and China. This principle runs counter to the prevailing wisdom that wants to limit the spread of nuclear weapons and there are risks. But the threat from nuclear powers Russia and China demands an effective deterrent.

- Foreign trade with large trading partners should not sustain very large trade surpluses with the USA (See Chapter 31:*International Trade Deficits* for logic behind this move). An automatic tariff arrangement should be in place such that the larger a trade surplus a nation sustains against the

USA, the higher the tariff. We want our trading partners to trade, and they must be willing to buy the many products we offer such as agriculture, oil, aircraft, and other products to balance their surplus. **The more US products they buy, the lower our tariff against them will be.**

Russia

- The military threat from Russia is much smaller than that from China. Although Russia has a large number of nuclear weapons, the size of its economy is very small compared both to China and the US.
- We may not like Russia rolling its tanks across its border with Ukraine, but **we are not obligated to provide assistance to a non-NATO country such as Ukraine.** We need to taper down our aid to Ukraine. We must never again pledge to help any foreign country to win a war against a strong neighbor "as long as it takes."
- Russia has a legitimate concern against NATO. After the fall of the Soviet Union, the West pledged not to expand NATO to Russia's border, and NATO reneged on that promise by admitting the Baltic States (Estonia, Latvia, Lithuania) and Poland. In Russia's eyes, this would be like Russia having an alliance with Mexico.
- **Trying to understand the Russian position does not make one a pro-Putin zealot.** Putin is an evil dictator, but people can legitimately disagree on the best course of action to check his aggression.
- **The best way to limit Russia's influence would be to develop US domestic energy resources in an all-out way.** The more oil and gas we can produce, the more we drive down energy prices, starving Russia of its main revenue stream. In addition, the more gas we sell to Europe, the less dependent they are on Russian energy.

Latin America / Immigration into US

- Any alien who attempts to enter the US between our ports of entry will be guilty of illegal immigration and will not be eligible for asylum in the US. **All applications for asylum must be initiated either in their home country or at US Ports of Entry.**
- Unless an alien has an emergency like being chased by secret police from his foreign country, aliens must wait in other countries while their applications for asylum are being processed. They can only enter the US when a court has granted them asylum.
- We should hire hundreds of new judges and other officials and place them near border ports of entry to make it possible to quickly adjudicate asylum claims, minimizing wait time for asylum seekers to get their case heard. If the court denies asylum, the person should be escorted to the border and be deported immediately. If an asylum seeker shows up with another claim after being denied asylum by the court, the new case will be very simple: what has changed since the first claim? If no new evidence is brought to bear, asylum will again be denied.
- **We should work with nations adjacent to asylum seekers to incent them to take in the asylum seekers.** For example, why can't an asylum seeker from Guatemala seek asylum in, say, Costa Rica? Why can't an asylum seeker from Honduras settle in Brazil? Why can't an asylum seeker from Afghanistan settle in, say, Tajikistan? Why is the USA the only destination suitable for asylum seekers?
- Any alien caught entering the US will be checked against records. If they have ever illegally entered the US before, they will be immediately deported with no trial. They are deemed guilty by their previous infraction.

- **All remittances sent out of the US to foreign nations by non-U.S. Citizens will be taxed,** with proceeds going toward border enforcement including wall construction.
- Anyone who enters the US without applying at our ports of entry will automatically be **ineligible for any benefits in the US**, including citizenship or welfare payments such as health care or food stamps.
- **Sanctuary Cities in the US will be abolished**. No local jurisdiction shall prevent Customs and Border Patrol from doing its job on pain of losing Federal aid dollars. But until these sanctuary cities are abolished, we should establish a conveyor line of buses to transport illegal immigrants *en masse* from border towns to sanctuary cities such as New York, Boston, Baltimore, Washington, and Chicago.
- **Our military should be deployed on our southern border and be authorized to repel any invasion from Mexican territory**. The military should attempt to use non-lethal methods such as warning shots and rubber bullets, but the military operation may result in a few fatalities, and once the message has been sent, they will stop trying to invade.

Middle East

- While the US will remain a staunch ally of Israel, it must wean Israel from automatic aid. **Israel is a prosperous country and should pay for its own military hardware**.
- Gulf states such as Saudi Arabia, the United Arab Emirates, Oman, Kuwait should generally have friendly relations with the US even though they have some unsavory dictators. **The Gulf States are the counterbalance to Iran**. We may not like them, but they are vital to limiting the power of Iran.
- Iran must not be allowed to project its power including supporting Hamas and Hezbollah. They must be treated as

a sworn enemy of the US and cannot be trusted until they are willing to renounce terrorism and achieving nuclear weapons.

- The presence of the US Military in the region must be scaled back to a few well-fortified positions in countries like Kuwait, Bahrain, and the UAE. **We must not have small outposts in places like Syria and Iraq that just become attractive targets to the bad guys**.

- **U.S. Troops must not be deployed for combat in the Middle East unless there is a dire threat to US interests** (an attack on the US homeland or an attack on Israel or on oil fields in the region).

Other Nations

- **India**: we should strengthen our ties to India as a democratic counterbalance to China. We should attempt whenever possible to buy from India instead of China. Closer ties with India may risk relations with its neighbor Pakistan. This tricky situation will require diplomatic skill.

- **Africa**: All assistance to African nations must be carefully audited by Inspectors General to assure that support we send goes to those who need the aid, not to tin-pot dictators. Fraudulent use of American Aid will result in a forfeiture of future aid. There is some risk to reducing foreign aid: ceding influence to China. But that may be a risk worth taking.

- **North Korea**: Any provocative actions of North Korea such as firing missles over allies such as Japan and South Korea will be met with equally provocative actions toward China. As China allows its proxy North Korea to harass its neighbors, the US will strengthen its ties with Taiwan, including sending them more military hardware and conducting joint military exercises with them.

- **International Organizations**: The United Nations, World Health Organization, and other international groups should gradually receive less funding from the US. For the UN, I would propose that each nation that has veto power in the Secretariat should pay an equal share. Long term, I would explore whether the UN headquarters should be moved out of the US into some third world country. I would also require that any treaties signed with any international organization be ratified by the U.S. Senate as required by the Constitution.

All of these tactics in the arena of foreign policy will be viewed by the establishment as outrageous and a threat to peace. But the Military Industrial complex has too much power in America and must be reined in. The countries we have relations with often use predatory tactics against us and can rely on us to instead live by Marquis of Queensbury rules. **America must not unilaterally cede power and influence to those who try to take advantage of our generosity. America should no longer be a chump.**

40. Practical Measures to Restore Sanity
Clawing our Way Back

The previous chapter focused on what could be done in Foreign Policy. Here I present a laundry list of practical measures we could take to slow down the deterioration of America. While it's important to understand the destructive nature of progressive activism, we need to go beyond just bemoaning and acquiescing to our fate. At first blush, it may appear that the task of reversing all this insanity is just too much. But if we are to preserve the blessings of liberty to ourselves and our posterity, we must embark on an "all fronts" fight. Unlike the progressive visionaries, we don't have a lot of time. **We must begin our effort in a "suddenly" mode**.

An overarching principle needs to guide our work: **our passion and relentlessness must match that of the far left and even perhaps surpass it.** An aggressive counter-movement will attract the slings and arrows from may scoffers on the left. They have the advantage of dominating nearly all of the avenues of communications, at least at the moment. So we may need to continue building and enhancing our own media such as Rumble, X, Epoch Times, and Daily Wire.

In our counter-revolution we must not accept the premises of the left and just tone them down. **We must not adopt their euphemisms**. We must use clear and plain language:

- Instead of "gender affirming care" we say things like "child mutilation and hormone drugging."
- Instead of "top surgery" we say "chopping the breasts off of little girls."
- Instead of "Diversity, Equity, and Inclusion", we say "anti-white and Asian bigotry."

- Instead of "Prochoice", we say "pro-abortion."
- Instead of "Abortion", we say "killing babies in the womb"
- Instead of "undocumented migants" we say "aliens who unlawfully broke in to our country"
- Instead of "potential asylum seekers" say "border invaders" (March 2024 incident)
- Instead of government "Investments" we say government "spending."
- Instead of "anti-gun control" we say "pro gun rights."
- Instead of "online content moderation" we say "online censorship."
- Instead of "voter suppression" we say "voter verification"
- Instead of "climate change" we say "climate change alarmism"

Blunt language need not be impolite. We're simply calling it what it is.

We also need more than frank rhetoric to advance the counter-revolution. We need some specific actions to mobilize opponents to the woke lunacy being peddled by the left. We need major reforms of all the centers of power who dominate America today. Government reform, though a vital piece of the task list, will not alone suffice. Advances need to be made in other power centers such as Media, Big Tech, Education, and Big Business. See the Chapter 12: *Unelected Power in America* for more details.

The power amassed by the left poses a serious threat to the America we've known and loved. It took several decades for this mess to develop, and it is unrealistic to expect there is a magic bullet that can quickly reverse course. Since more than 70% of the power in America is outside the government, simply winning a few elections will not cut it. Even if we elect an overwhelming congressional majority and a vigorous and capable president, this will not be enough to turn the tide. We need an all-fronts assault to merely slow down the deterioration of liberty.

If we vigorously pursue many of these proposals, we may begin to see a little improvement and we should stop and celebrate those events as they come. The Bud Light boycott comes to mind. But we can't let up. We must keep working, keep striving to reverse the chaos that threatens to seep out of our once vibrant and beautiful cities into suburban enclaves. Nowhere is safe until we reverse this tide of insanity.

One more thing: I have to admit that even if every single one of the solutions I propose here were implemented, we still would have a problem that we can't fix. I address this in the *Epilogue* (Chapter 41: *The Spiritual side of the Dystopia*).

Here are a few practical steps that may help mitigate the erosion of freedom:

Government:
    Federal

1. Abolish whole departments of the bureaucracy. The easiest case to make would be abolishing the Department of Education. The Tenth Amendment clearly puts Education outside the federal jurisdiction so that would be the best place to start. Flood the zone with legal action challenging the authority of federal agencies which are nor explicitly mentioned in the constitution (eg, FDA, EPA, Energy, etc). Re-invigorate enumerated powers and the tenth amendment.
2. Elect a vigorous president and Congress who will make it their top priority to fire public employees immediately, starting with those who have overseen the corruption of their departments. In particular, the Justice Department needs a thorough house cleaning:
   - FBI operations should be decentralized to more field office autonomy from Washington as it was in the past

- The hunt for "domestic terrorists" and white supremacists should be scaled back dramatically.
- The Foreign Intelligence Surveillance Act (FISA) should be extensively reformed requiring warrants when monitoring US Citizens
- Those who abused FISA should be at least fired and in some cases, prosecuted
- FBI Agents in Charge who authorized overbearing use of police state tactics such as swat teams and middle of the night door smashes in situations where the offense was minor should be disciplined and in some cases prosecuted
- Judges and federal prosecutors who engaged in lawfare should have their law licenses revoked.
- Congress should use the power of the purse to deny funds for a new FBI headquarters building until the corruption has been dealt with

3. Establish term limits for members of Congress. Many idealists come to DC with the goal of changing Washington, but instead Washington changes them. Very few have successfully resisted the power-hungry mindset that pervades the nation's capitol.

4. Establish age limits for members of Congress. No one should run for either House or Senate if they are older than 73.

5. Establish age limits for Judges. All judges should retire at or before age 75.

6. Establish time limits for serving in the Bureaucracy. No one should be employed by the U.S. Government for more than, say, ten years. There may be some practical exceptions (for example, Post Office employees, the clerks who manage sending out Social Security checks, and a few others), but there should be a compelling reason to permit a person to work for government for longer than ten years.

7. Establish a limit to the size of legislation. No one bill should be more than a page or two long. Consider forcing legislators to pass a quick multiple choice test that demonstrates their knowledge of a bill before they are allowed to vote on it.

8. Enable lawsuits against rules from bureaucrats. Overturn the Chevron principle where courts defer to government agencies. If a rule by a bureaucrat is not sufficiently grounded in the enabling legislation, it must be abolished.

9. Prohibit intelligence officials and presidential aides from publishing books or appearing in the media or being employed by Big Tech until at least 5 years after they leave office. This may mitigate the Alignment of Powers we have seen in recent years.

10. Revoke security clearances for all government officials as soon as they leave office. Require congressional approval for any exceptions to this rule.

11. Only U.S. Citizens should be included in the Census that determines representational apportionment in the states.

12. Deport foreign college students who lead protests and chant "Death To America" and other provocative actions vilifying their host nation. Other nations would do that if American students, for example, shouted "Death to Saudi Arabia."

13. Rein in entitlement programs such as Social Security and Medicare. This may entail a few modest cuts to things like Cost Of Living Adjustments.

14. Drill, baby drill. Re-establish American dominance in energy production. Build new pipelines. Expand LNG Terminal facilities.

15. Phase out mandates and subsidies for ethanol. Consider reducing required ethanol from 10% to 5%.

16. Phase out subsidies for Wind, Solar, and Electric Vehicles. Let the market drive consumer decisions.

State and Local

17. Strengthen State Governments and support them in the areas left to them including education, policing, and regulation of things like gender affirming care for minors.

18. Strengthen laws against voter fraud without placing undue obstacles to voters. Make it easy to vote but difficult to cheat. Consider reducing early voting dates. Make minimal or no use of mail in voting or ballot drop boxes.

19. Do not tolerate protests that block major infrastructure like bridges or airports. Prevent blockages by dragging protestors out of the way and make them serve jail time for these blockages.

20. Vigorously enforce laws against crimes committed with a firearm. Place offenders on National Gun Offender list and prohibit all on that list from ever possessing a gun again in their lives. Persons on the Gun Offender list waive their right against searches without warrants.

21. File lawsuits for negligence of city DA's and police officials who permit criminals with long rap sheets to roam the streets and commit more crimes like assault and murder.

22. Let State governments enforce immigration law for their own state. If the feds are lax in letting immigrants over the national border, states should enact laws that make it illegal to enter their state if a person is an illegal immigrant (almost like the opposite of sanctuary states). Some states like Oklahoma, Iowa, and Florida have begun to enact laws like these.

23. Take a page out of the George Soros playbook. Find some wealthy republican donors to sponsor conservative District Attorneys to run in big cities that are plagued by crime. These new DA's can reinstate vigorous law enforcement techniques that have worked in the past.

24. Initiate law suits in cases of unreasonable prosecution for "non crimes" such as peaceful January 6 protests. Tie up the courts to make it unacceptable for unelected bureaucrats and politicians to harass innocent citizens.

25. Initiate law suits against law enforcement agencies that use excessive force such as swat teams on peaceful citizens with no criminal record.

26. Revoke law license for attorneys and judges who engage in lawfare where persons are not prosecuted for crimes, but crimes are dreamed up to make a person subject to prosecution. A great example is Donald Trump being charged an outrageous fine for over stating the value of his holdings on a loan application.

China

27. See Chapter 38: *Sensible Foreign Policy*.

Big Tech

28. **Stay away from Google, Facebook, and Amazon if possible**. Use alternatives. For example, use Duck Duck Go instead of Google for searches. Buy things from Wal-Mart or other online services in place of Amazon. Find social media that is not overwhelmingly woke.

29. Consider abolishing Section 232 that shields big tech from lawsuits for statements posted on their sites. If they are acting like publishers, treat them like publishers. Hold them liable for slander and defamation.

30. Prohibit social media companies from interfering in elections. In particular, prohibit the use of "ZuckerBucks" that were used to tilt the 2020 election.

31. Return Search Engines to their original methods that used less biased logic in search algorithms. Customers should flood Google with challenges when they see biased results.

32. Permit lawsuits for sharing personal information without a user's consent. Foster an environment where online privacy

is as prevalent as privacy with Doctors, Lawyers, and companies like the Phone Company. Demand adherence to the Fourth Amendment's prohibition of unreasonable search and seizure.

33. Outlaw all contact between government agencies of any kind and Big Tech platforms. An FBI agent should not be able to tell Big Tech what to censor.

34. Force employees of government intelligence agencies to sign a commitment when they join government that they will not be employed in any Big Tech firm until at least five years have passed since they left government.

35. Develop a grass roots movement to deny Big Tech the right to people's private data. Force them to offer paid subscriptions that would include a guarantee that private data would not be shared without permission, despite what any "terms of service" say.

Media

36. **Remove media pundits from Presidential debates**. Structure the debates of the two major candidates with a simple system where each candidate speaks for 5 minutes, the other responds, and so on. Let the candidates determine what they will speak on. We don't need media personalities injecting their point of view.

37. **Cut the cable cord and do without Cable News entirely.** With Smart TV's and platforms like Roku, this is not as implausible as it sounds.

38. **Avoid use of businesses that don't stay in their lane.** For example, when professional sports figures preach sermons, just stop watching these sports. When Hollywood actors preach sermons at awards ceremonies, avoid their movies. When Disney produces materials with a sexual content, keep your kids from watching them.

39. **Limit your kids' access to social media and the internet**. Give them time to mature before they are exposed to the online propaganda.

40. Support Twitter's (X's) new direction toward becoming a free speech platform. Help leaders like Elon Musk when he faces withering criticism.

41. Support upstart streaming podcasts such as Joe Rogan, Rumble, Tucker on Twitter, *Daily Wire*, Dinesh D'Souza, Epoch TV, Victor Davis Hanson, and Glen Greenwald

42. Force news outlets to balance lies with truth. When they report something that later turns out to be untrue, make them post just as many retractions of the lie as they originally posted of the lie itself. For example, if they said a hundred times that police officer Sicknick was bludgeoned with a fire extinguisher a hundred times, make them post a retraction a hundred times that mentions that the autopsy reported no blunt force trauma and that he died of natural causes. Sue news outlets that intentionally spread lies. There have been some successes in this area (for example, the Covington Kids), but we need to do more.

Education

43. If you can, withdraw your kids from public education and either do home-schooling or private school.

44. **Support initiatives in your state that promote school choice so that funding follows the student**.

45. Attend local school board meetings and even run for school board. Make your voice heard and let educators know that the parents do have a role to play in education.

46. Terminate education officials and teachers who spread propaganda about gender issues to minors.

47. **Force Universities to identify costs for Diversity, Equity, and Inclusion programs and officials as a line item in**

tuition and give potential students or their parents the right to "opt out" of these programs.

48. Stop hiring graduates from the leading universities. Instead, focus on second tier universities. **Stop the group think indoctrination**.

49. **Force Universities to shoulder some of the risk of default on student loans**.

50. Reinstate the widespread use of standardized tests such as SAT's to help in college admissions.

Big Business

51. **Place clear limits on proxy voting by investment firms like Black Rock**. One simple regulation might be that no one person or firm will vote more than 1% of a company's shares unless that person owns more than 1% of the shares. Managers should not vote shares; owners should vote shares. There should be minimal proxy voting.

52. Demand that your company's pension plans avoid the use of ESG scores to determine investments.

53. Demand that your state avoid using investment firms that use ESG scores. In March 2024, Texas divested of nearly $10 Billion in investments in Black Rock. That is a good start.

54. Try to influence your company or organization to cut back or eliminate all programs that promote Diversity, Equity, and Inclusion. This can entail risk. Be advised!

55. Boycott corporations that promote "in your face" support for gender issues (like the Bud Light boycott).

Miscellaneous

56. Develop a plan to harden the US's electrical grid against a potential EMP attack. A few billion dollars would make a big difference in our ability to withstand such an attack. In particular, we need to stop buying major grid items like

transformers from China. We should invest in manufacturing some spare transformers in the USA. Even a half a dozen spares would make a big difference in attempting to recover after an EMP attack.

57. Begin a major research study on the impact of Artificial Intelligence on future employment and how we might cope with this wrenching adjustment.

58. Restore rigorous standards for selection of people in positions that influence safety such as airline pilots, ship captains, air traffic controllers, and construction workers on major projects such as tunnels and bridges. DEI must not dominate these decisions. Public safety must be a higher priority than DEI.

59. Find ways to preserve the nuclear family from tragic breakups. This is a tough challenge, but family breakup is a major root cause of many of the ills that plague modern America. There is no easy answer in this area. Innovative solutions are needed.

60. Phase out all funding for public broadcasting (PBS, NPR) and Planned Parenthood. These organizations can stand on their own. There are plenty of wealthy donors on the left who could fill the funding gap.

None of these measures by themselves are a sure-fire solution to the problem, but they are a start. **As the passengers on flight 93 said, "let's roll."**

41. Epilogue: The Spiritual Side of the Dystopian Cartoon

Up to this point in this book, my analytical approach has been from a purely secular viewpoint. As a committed Evangelical Christian, however, I think there definitely is a spiritual side to the sickness we find ourselves living through. Many reading this may shudder and say something like, "now we see your hidden agenda. You want to preach your religion. I'm tuning out."

Before you change channels, please just indulge me a little. After all, you preach *your* secular humanism religion from the rooftops in a steady stream from the internet and news media. I hear your strong almost cult-like sermons all the time. I hear them at Hollywood awards shows. I hear them from Sports channels. I see them in Disney movies. I get it. **You believe in your religion passionately. And so do I.**

So just work with me for this one chapter. Consider that wisdom that has withstood the test of thousands of years may just maybe have some validity. It may be possible that billions of Christians are not all deluded. For all you know, they might have learned something that works.

Christianity has a long track record not only in the spiritual, but in the secular world as well. Since about 1000 AD to 2000 AD, the most significant achievements in Science, Art, and Music were all inspired by the Christian faith. Sir Isaac Newton, the greatest scientist of his time, was also a devout and meticulous theologian. Astronomers Galileo and Kepler, famous painters like Leonardo da Vinci and Michaelangelo. and musicians like Bach, Haydn and Mozart were all fervent Christians. Bach signed all his manuscripts with the initials SDG: Latin for "Solely for the Glory of God." In addition, many of the first and most famous universities and hospitals were founded and nourished by Christians.

Some may accuse me of placing a positive spin on Christianity here by omitting an extended discussion of its failures. I will readily admit that Christianity has also committed some egregious atrocities, including excesses during the Crusades, the Spanish Inquisition, and the Salem Witch prosecutions in 17ᵗʰ century Massachusetts. These were horrific stains on a noble legacy. I don't want to get bogged down on a defense here except to say that most of the wicked Christian behavior occurred several centuries ago. I would encourage interested readers to consult Dinesh D'Souza's excellent book *What's So Great about Christianity* for a more thorough discussion on this topic.

Christianity has been a cornerstone of civilization in the West for many centuries. But now it is under assault as secular humanism serenades us with its siren song. We can be our own masters, it whispers. We don't need God. As government shoved the Christian religion into a closet where it must hide, potent forces have filled the spiritual vacuum left in the wake of this absence of a restraining influence. **Instead of reading their Bibles, young people are glued to their screens**. Instead of hearing about the love and grace of God, people hear about hate speech and ugly tendencies like racism and sexual perversion. Instead of hearing a message about a living hope, secular humanism feeds a steady diet of despair and doom.

Churches and other organizations are attempting to redirect people to think about noble things. Philippians 4:8 states: *Finally, brothers and sisters, whatever is true, whatever is noble, whatever is right, whatever is pure, whatever is lovely, whatever is admirable—if anything is excellent or praiseworthy—think about such things.* Yet everywhere you look countervailing voices yell into powerful megaphones, stressing all that false, gross, wrong, impure, ugly, shameful, horrible, and disgraceful. To be sure, the people in the Roman times when Philippians was written faced the same list of countervailing voices. But in Roman time, those voices were not amplified, intensified, and made ubiquitous by 24/7 saturation of a cheerleading media that keeps pouring fuel on the fire. **Philippians 4:8 whispers to us in a soft *dolce* tone while the media blares at us at triple *forte* strength**. Am I exaggerating? Just turn on the tube and make your own assessment. Is this secular prescription the remedy that will help us reach a glorious nirvana? Will dwelling on hate and strife do any good?

A prominent theme in the Christian faith is reconciliation. In his Sermon on the Mount, Jesus tells us: "Therefore, if you are offering your gift at the altar and there remember that your brother or sister has something against you, leave your gift there in front of the altar. First go and be reconciled to them; then come and offer your gift. (Matthew 5:23-24)" As God has forgiven us, so we should forgive others. This admonition contrasts sharply with secular humanism's obsession with finding reasons for one group to hate another. Instead of stoking the fires of resentment, Christians are called to build bridges between the races and classes.

Until just a few decades ago, American culture was strongly shaped by Christianity. Although it was far from perfect, Americans recognized its flaws such as racism, sexism, and sloppy stewardship of the environment, and set about correcting these defects with passionate vigor. Far from being impediments to correcting these failings, Christians were in the forefront of the corrective crusade.

Dr. Martin Luther King Jr. was a pastor with a servant heart. He applied the gospel to his situation and provided inspiring leadership that convicted whites and led them to repentance. Dr. King is most noted today as a Civil Rights leader, but I suspect Dr. King himself considered his service to Christ as an even higher calling.

Part of the blame for the erosion of the Christian faith in the twentieth and twenty-first century falls squarely on the church. **Christian believers became known as judgmental curmudgeons closely examining those around them and persistently pointing to their shortcomings.** This repelled many who got tired of hearing about their faults. The secular world then whispered its enticing message of independence from the "god myth." The Invictus poem was particularly appealing: "I am the master of my fate, I am the captain of my soul."

But have you noticed that the most irritating thing about Christians–their nitpicking judgmentalism and lack of tolerance–has become a staple of the secular humanist philosophy? In a modern equivalent of excommunication, the woke police monitor your speech for anything that smacks of being counter to its narrative. Moreover, the modern-day pharisees have all sorts of technological tools to detect your sins–and the record is permanent. **If you ever step out of line, you can be cancelled. There is no redemption.**

And so I ask, which is more oppressive? The hope, love, and grace of the Christian gospel, or the despair, hate, and punishment of the new secular Pharisees?

Without recognizing it, our modern society has succumbed to a destructive human tendency that has been around for thousands of years: **idolatry**. The Bible abounds in stories about the folly of idolatry. Many think idolatry refers to bowing down to statuettes, but it actually refers to the vain attempt to substitute artificial objects for the true God. Instead of worshiping our Creator, we create our own little gods and worship them. And since we created our gods, we wind up worshiping ourselves instead of the one true God. A typical person then becomes a "self-made man" who worships his creator. An excerpt from my personal Scripture journal on Jeremiah 10:9 illustrates this point:

Jer 10:9 *Hammered silver is brought from Tarshish and gold from Uphaz. What the craftsman and goldsmith have made is then dressed in blue and purple— all made by skilled workers.*

As I read Jeremiah and scholar Philip Graham Ryken's comment in the year 2023, I can imagine secular readers laughing this verse off. They would smile and smirk at the quaint, primitive people dressing up idol figurines and then bowing down to them. These unenlightened dolts would be fooled by the finery of the gold and purple. They would imagine that something that looked this impressive must be godlike.

But without too much of a stretch, we can apply this verse to our modern equivalent: the internet and artificial intelligence. Just like the ancient idol makers, the engineers of Silicon Valley produce very impressive images. The modern craftsmen have extraordinary skills at producing useful information. The old wooden statues can't do anything, but our more sophisticated internet can answer nearly every question. Our medical technology has greatly prolonged human life. Our scientists have studied both the very large and the very small and have compiled a vast amount of knowledge about how our universe works.

While ancient craftsmen dressed up their idols in gold and purple, today's internet craftsmen have an even more impressive array of tools. They can produce animated and very lifelike images. Our modern artists have replaced the gold and purple veneer of the ancients with algorithms and statistical models. But in the end, just as the gold and purple of the statuettes were just a thin surface coating that may have hidden the crudeness of the idol underneath, the veneer of sophistication software engineers apply to web sites and search engines only cover up the imperfections that lie underneath. Artificial intelligence is artificial and intelligent, but it is not and never will be wise. **There is no artificial wisdom. There is only divine wisdom.**

My comparison of ancient idol statuettes to our internet, science, technology, reason, and logic might sound preposterous to my contemporaries from their secular standpoint. They would say something like, no the internet and science are not gods we worship, but techniques we have mastered. **We have evolved past the need for an all-powerful God to explain things. We can just explain them ourselves. Isn't modern life fabulous?** We don't need superstitions and cults anymore. We have grown past that need.

But as pastor Joshua Knott put it, and idol is a good thing, which becomes a great thing, which becomes a god thing, which in the end becomes a nothing. Science, technology, reason, and logic are all good things. In fact they are great things. But the human propensity to elevate to the next level "a god thing" has not changed since Jeremiah's time. Artificial Intelligence and technology are not panaceas. They often disappoint us.

The Bible is a divine guidebook to help us navigate the world the Lord created. Many think they don't need the Lord's guidebook. C.S. Lewis writes in his book *Mere Christianity*

A car is made to run on gasoline, and it would not run properly on anything else. Now God designed the human machine to run on Himself. He Himself is the fuel our spirits were designed to burn or the food our spirits were designed to feed on. But many of us want to feed on something else. Something goes wrong. The machine conks. It seems to start up all right and runs a few yards, and then it breaks down. They are trying to run it on the wrong juice.

Our secular culture thinks it has "arrived" at a new level of wisdom. It has no need of advice that has moved past an expiration date. After all, the ancients didn't have computers and other technology, so they were ignorant of the new truths we have discovered in the 21st century. With our modern tools and instruments, we can fill in the gaps the ancients missed.

Yes and no. Modern technology has produced a cornucopia of benefits that have greatly enhanced human flourishing. Advances in medicine, science, and agriculture have lifted our modern life far above the assessment of the 17th century philosopher **Thomas Hobbes: life then was 'solitary, poor, nasty, brutish, and short'**. In contrast, today we are connected by the internet, abounding in food and luxuries, civilized, and live long lives. **But notice that all our modern technology has not solved the one Hobbesian adjective still alive today:** *nasty*.

Even with all that science has to offer, we still have not cracked this nut. That is because humanity is infected with sin. **No one likes that little three letter word, but there it is**. It is the one thing we can't magically fix. Only God can do that, and thanks be to God, he has done it in Jesus Christ our Lord.

A common theme in the 95 Theses of Progressive Doctrine is despair. Our society is sick, say the progressives, and the way to fix it is to follow the rules we set. The problem is that, as Bible Scholar John Kitchen puts it, "forced goodness is not goodness at all, but mere moral conformity. Moral conformity may indeed be enforced, but moral goodness requires a change of heart."

Modern America has tried the progressive rulebook for several decades. It has not changed hearts, and we now see the cumulative result. Even the vitriolic atheist Richard Dawkins recently admitted he was a "cultural Christian" because he realizes that even if one does not believe Christianity it nonetheless tends to be a much more civilizing force than other religions such as Islam. One wishes Dawkins would also compare his own religion of Secular Humanism with Christianity. He would see that several decades under humanism has given us:

- Unsafe streets and urban food deserts in our cities.
- Innocent women being "sucker punched" on the streets of New York by thugs with long rap sheets.
- A record number of people being shoved off NYC subway platforms
- Lost the respect of other nations.
- More compassion for criminals than for ordinary citizens who play by the rules
- Vilified and second-guessed law enforcement, greatly reducing the safety buffer between us and violent thugs who would do us harm.
- Attempted to mainstream perverted sexual practices.
- Sacrificed scientific logic and truth for theories with no compelling evidence.
- Become evidence deniers by answering reasoned, factual discussions with name-calling and questioning of motives.
- Opened our borders not only to valedictorians but to criminal gangs, terrorists, disease, and fentanyl that poisons our culture.
- Publicly financed heroin injection sites and crack pipe and needle distribution to addicts
- Appointed a few tech billionaires to determine what is true and false.
- Abridged freedom of speech and squelched vigorous debate.
- Replaced riveting and gripping movies with tedious woke sermons.
- Anointed a media composed of ivy league graduates to advance an agenda instead of just reporting the news and letting us decide what it means.

- Stirred up racial animosity and hate instead of building bridges between the races.
- Torn down traditions and institutions that had served us well and not replaced them with viable alternatives.
- Marginalized women who see their calling as raising families and instead obligated them to serve corporate masters.
- Removed discipline from homes and schools and have trained the new generation to be entitled malcontents.
- Substituted screens and daycare for parental love.
- Cancelled thousands of people who made an ill-considered comment that haunts them for the rest of their lives.
- Piled up trillions of dollars of debt our kids will have to pay.
- Rampant inflation and sky-high prices at the grocery store

This list vividly depicts a crumbling of the greatness that was once stamped on the American spirit. How is the Progressive Doctrine working out for us?

And so I ask you, gentle reader. Which is the better way? **The bad news of strife, condemnation, and despair? Or the good news of reconciliation, salvation, and a living hope?** Unless and until our modern world embraces the sacred wisdom of the Bible, our culture will remain nasty. Previously, I presented a few practical measures that can be taken to counteract the topsy-turvy moral climate we are mired in, but even if *all* these measures were implemented, the problem of sin would remain. **The only sure remedy to our sick culture is faith in Christ. Secular humanists don't want to hear this, but it's a truth that cannot be disproved by any of their scoffing sophistry.**

Appendix

42. Christianity 101: *Quick Notes on Scripture*
A Brief Explanation of Selected Biblical Verses

My readers may be puzzled as to why I would include an extended discussion on Christianity. The reason is simple: the rest of this book has focused on the failure of secular humanism to deliver a prosperous, civil society. But unlike cultural vandals, my aim is not simply to criticize what doesn't work, but to propose a viable alternative. I am convinced that the only solution that is guaranteed to work is faith in Jesus Christ. I say guaranteed because the Lord himself is behind his covenant of grace.

The last chapter (Epilogue) gave a long list of the results of our abandonment of the God of Abraham, Isaac, and Jacob. Here I offer a little more information on the Christian faith. My comments on a couple dozen Scripture verses (NIV translation unless otherwise specified) are intended to give just a brief glimpse of Christianity. I am not a seminary trained scholar, but I have studied Scripture closely for thirty years. See my book *Scripture Commentary Sampler* (Lettra Press, 2021) for a few more details.

While knowledge of Old Testament writings help us to understand the gospel, my selections in *this* collection emphasize the vital gospel message found in the New Testament. My theological perspective is often described as "Reformed Theology" which is consistent with the *Westminster Confession of Faith* (1647) and the *Institutes of the Christian Religion* (1559) by John Calvin. The audio files with these *Quick Notes* can be listened to in about an hour.

These scripture comments contain no specific policy prescriptions to counteract the slide America has experienced recently. Other chapters such as Chapter 39 on *Foreign policy* and Chapter 40 on *Practical measures to Restore Sanity* present secular solutions. Here I focus on just one solution: salvation in Jesus Christ, the author and perfecter of our faith (Heb 12:2).

These brief snippets of Scripture will give the careful reader just enough of the basics of Christianity to at least be cognizant of what it offers. I hope and pray it will inspire you to begin a more thorough study of the sacred text.

Postcript: Some readers may detect some dissonance between the prayer on words presented in the comment on Psalm 141:3 and some statements I have made elsewhere in this book. The prayer on words urges us to avoid "belittling words that taunt." This seems to be inconsistent with some harsh words I expressed for the LGBTQ community in Chapter 21. There I heaped scorn and ridicule on those who demand that we affirm what I and millions of others consider to be perverted practices. Such contempt should be used only very rarely. The prophets (1 Kings 18:27) and even Jesus Christ himself sometimes ridiculed and scorned the enemies of God (for example, Matt 23:25-28). I determined that derision was an appropriate response to practices I and many Christians and even non-Christians think are disgusting and depraved. In general, we should avoid such harsh and belittling talk, but there may be times when it is appropriate.

Quick Notes on Scripture

Gen 40:15 *I was forcibly carried off from the land of the Hebrews, and even here I have done nothing to deserve being put in a dungeon.*

Elder Jason Cunningham presented a message about Genesis 40 in June 2023. He made several points about what the text says, what it implies, and what it doesn't say. Genesis 40 and the entire Joseph saga (Genesis chapters 37-50) paint a vivid picture of God's exquisite providential plan. It contains a "micro story" (the repeated unjust treatment of Joseph followed by seemingly endless, mundane, routine things that happen to Joseph) and a "macro story" (the final glorious outworking of God's plan to save many in the land of Egypt). We, like Joseph, are living in the micro story. The months of incarceration for something he didn't do just drag on and on, with no seeming purpose or progress. Meanwhile in the macro story, God is training Joseph to be the viceroy of Egypt who will manage the food crisis after years of famine. But Joseph is unaware of this larger macro story. He (and we) can only rise each day and do the tedious tasks we are given with reliability, integrity, and grace. This is exactly what we see Joseph doing. We see this in the way he faithfully carries out his tasks so that he has the complete trust of his boss (Gen 39:22, 23) and in the way he treats the new prisoners (the cupbearer and baker) with compassion and genuine caring (40:7: "why do you look so sad today."). In verse 15 we see another nugget of Joseph's integrity as he asks the cupbearer to remember him when he is restored to his former job. Joseph wants to be released from prison, but notice the way he describes his unjust treatment in verse 15. He does not identify the perpetrators of the injustices he has suffered. He does not say something like, "my despicable brothers sold me to slavery." He does not say "Watch out for that horrid woman Mrs. Potiphar. She will lie and falsely accuse you of crimes you did not commit." No, he just states the facts dispassionately and has faith that that justice will someday be carried out by his faithful God. Toward the end of Chapter 40, we read that the cupbearer forgot Joseph and in 41:1 that another two years had to drag by before Joseph would get is big chance. We the enlightened readers who know the end of the story are aware that God is training Joseph for his big moment and it can't be rushed. We are not only enlightened as to Joseph's story, we also have the whole New Testament to help us to see how our micro stories connect to the Lord's glorious plans. And yet as we suffer injustice and carry out our tedious assignments, we often forget the larger macro story. We should be inspired by Joseph's example to carry out our assigned tasks with integrity as we demonstrate to the needy world around us the wonder of God's providence and grace. We should pray for the Holy Spirit to remind us of our place in God's larger purpose.

2 Chr 7:14 *if my people, who are called by my name, will humble themselves and pray and seek my face and turn from their wicked ways, then will I hear from heaven and will forgive their sin and will heal their land.*
As we observe our nation in 2023, we might lament that we do not humble ourselves, pray and seek his face. And we certainly aren't turning from our wicked ways. If you want to confirm this, just look at the news. But just as the Lord assured Solomon that he would hear from heaven and forgive their sin and heal their land, so through his holy Word he assures us today that he will hear from heaven, forgive our sin, and heal our land, if we would but humble ourselves and pray and seek him and turn from our wicked ways. And as bleak and hopeless as America may appear today, it was perhaps even more bleak in 1863, when Abraham Lincoln proclaimed a National Fast day with these words:

Excerpt from Abraham Lincoln's proclamation of a National Fast Day, March 30, 1863:

> Whereas, the Senate of the United States, devoutly recognizing the Supreme Authority and just Government of Almighty God, in all the affairs of men and of nations, has by a resolution, requested the President to designate and set apart a day

for National prayer and humiliation. And whereas it is the duty of nations as well as of men, to own their dependence upon the overruling power of God, to confess their sins and transgressions, in humble sorrow, yet with assured hope that genuine repentance will lead to mercy and pardon; and to recognize the sublime truth, announced in the Holy Scriptures and proven by all history, that those nations only are blessed whose God is the Lord.

We have been the recipients of the choicest bounties of Heaven. We have been preserved, these many years, in peace and prosperity. We have grown in numbers, wealth and power, as no other nation has ever grown. But we have forgotten God. We have forgotten the gracious hand which preserved us in peace, and multiplied and enriched and strengthened us; and we have vainly imagined, in the deceitfulness of our hearts, that all these blessings were produced by some superior wisdom and virtue of our own [Deut 8:17-18]. Intoxicated with unbroken success, we have become too self-sufficient to feel the necessity of redeeming and preserving grace, too proud to pray to the God that made us. It behooves us, then, to humble ourselves before the offended Power, to confess our national sins, and to pray for clemency and forgiveness.

President Lincoln's words reach out to us today in 21st Century America. Immediately after the Civil War, a Great Awakening of the Christian faith occurred under the leadership of Dwight L. Moody and others. This great renewal of faith probably included a lot of prayer and repentance, and the war-torn land was healed. A strong case can be made that it was the Lord who healed our land. After division and a bloody civil war in the 1860's America rose to become a global superpower. Our nation is nearly as divided today as we were back then. May he heal our land again as we humble ourselves and seek him and turn from our wicked ways..

Ps 141:3: *Set a guard over my mouth, O LORD; keep watch over the door of my lips.* <u>Morning Prayer on Words</u> (author unknown) found in my Mother's effects after her death:

O Divine Father, source of my reflection, Strength of my life, origin of my hope; I pause to ponder the words that surround my day, my use and misuse of them, their power to lift or to destroy, to build or to maim. Forgive me, merciful Lord, the folly of things said which would be better left unsaid:

> Heated words that accuse,
> Jealous words that hate,
> Unwarranted words that blame
> Belittling words that taunt,
> Mean words that sour,
> Dishonest words that deny,
> Timid words that disgrace,
> Thoughtless words that sear,
> Hasty words that harm.

Allow instead:

> Kind words that cheer,
> Uplifting words that inspire,
> Tender words that comfort,
> Wise words that guide,
> Affirming words that build,
> Forgiving words that heal,
> Encouraging words that challenge,
> Thoughtful words that redirect,
> Appropriate words that explain,
> Prayerful words that intercede.

May my words flow less from the heat of the moment than from a heart disciplined by Thy will and tempered by Thy Word. Through Him who is the Word of Life.　　　　Amen

Prov 19:11: *A man's wisdom gives him patience; it is to his glory to overlook an offense.*
In our 21st century world, many people are offended by what is spoken in their presence. In fact, some have developed a kind of science to avoid offending someone. This science speaks of "trigger warnings" and "microaggressions." The very word "micro-aggressions" conveys that these offenses are quite petty; its as if you need either a microscope or special expertise to detect them. The assumption by secular purveyors of this topic is that anything that offends someone else must be avoided at all costs. But this proverb gives another perspective. If everyone is afraid of offending someone else, frank and controversial topics will be avoided and the truth will be shrouded in cryptic and indirect language. While we must be sensitive to the feelings of others, we also should not be hypersensitive when we are insulted. We need to "just let it go." Imagine how much more tranquil and harmonious our world would be if everyone took this proverb to heart!

Mt 7:3-5: *"Why do you look at the speck of sawdust in your brother's eye and pay no attention to the plank in your own eye? How can you say to your brother, 'Let me take the speck out of your eye,' when all the time there is a plank in your own eye? You hypocrite, first take the plank out of your own eye, and then you will see clearly to remove the speck from your brother's eye.* In our interpersonal encounters, we sometimes are confronted with VDP's (Very Draining People). It is soooo much easier for us to see faults in other people than in ourselves. But whenever we observe some obnoxious behavior in others, we should ask, "do I sometimes say and do similar things?" If we are honest, we would have to admit that, yes, we sometimes do almost exactly the same things.

We too can be VDP's. So before our sanctimonious hackles are raised, Christ recommends that we remove the plank from our eyes so we can see more clearly to advise our fellows of their faults. VDP's can actually be good teachers. As we are irritated with others, may we strive to avoid the blunders of VDP's and instead develop our skills to build others up. And how can we do that? We should ask the Lord to "see if there is any offensive way in me and lead me to the way everlasting" (Ps 139:23-24). The more we submit to the Lord's leading, the more pleasing our ways will be both to Him and to others. Who knows? With the plank removed from our own eyes, we might even be able to see not the speck in their eye, but the nobility of their spirits. After all, they were made in God's image just like we were.

Mt 18:21-22 *Then Peter came to Jesus and asked, "Lord, how many times shall I forgive my brother or sister who sins against me? Up to seven times?" Jesus answered, "I tell you, not seven times, but seventy-seven times* Bible Scholar Michael Green says that in proposing to forgive someone seven times, Peter thought he was offering the moon. But Jesus stuns Peter by telling him not just seven times, but seventy times seven times. This does not mean we are making marks on a tote board, counting the times we forgive, but that we do it so frequently that we lose count. Christ wants us to let the Spirit work through us so that we forgive so automatically that we don't even notice it. As we become more accustomed to forgiving wrongs done to us, we discover the joy that comes with forgiveness. We realize that carrying a burden of resentment often hurts us more than the object of our resentment. The term "resentment" carries the connotation of "re-sensing" the malicious act that caused our frustration in the first place. We are just playing a tape in our heads over and over and we find that our annoyance just grows and grows. Christ here recommends the opposite approach. Instead of continually dwelling on the wrong that was done to us, we are to continually forgive wrongs done to us. And, amazingly, it give us more peace and contentment. But it's not only for our own good that we learn to forgive others as a matter of course. As we do this more and more, we come to appreciate the grace of our Lord more and more. After all, he forgives us not just seventy times seven times, but millions of times. Just think of all the times you disappointed Christ and how many times he gave you a second or third or twentieth chance. Christ calls us to that kind of grace. Just imagine what life would be like if everyone took Christ's advice here.

Commentator Chuck Swindoll sums it up: "Forgiveness is not an elective in the curriculum of the Christian life. It's a required course. In fact, it's part of Christianity 101. Every believer must learn it. Though the concepts are simple, the exams are hard to pass. But what a relief when we pass them!"

The next time we forgive someone twice and congratulate ourselves, may we remember that twice is not enough. We need to cultivate the spirit of grace by letting the Spirit live through us instead of our taking the reins with the flesh. Let us hand over control of our actions to the Spirit in the rough and tumble of our lives. May our instinct to forgive become automatic as the Spirit takes over.

Lk 15:29: *But he answered his father, 'Look! All these years I've been slaving for you and never disobeyed your orders. Yet you never gave me even a young goat so I could celebrate with my friends.'* The elder son's reaction is an arresting portrait of the ugly sin of envy [cf discussion of Ps 106:16, Mal 3:14, Job 5:2]. When we think about this human emotion, we should recoil in revulsion not only at its failure to give thanks for blessings already received*, but on the illogical assumption upon which it rests: I am hurt when something good happens to someone else (Gen 26:14, Mt 20:12, Eccl 4:4). Simple envy has caused untold bitterness and strife over the centuries and still does today. Envy is not just wicked, ungrateful, and illogical, it is corrosive—but not to the object of our envy, only to the envier (cf discussion on 1 Sam 18:7-8). Proverbs 14:30 puts it well: "A heart at peace gives life to the body, but envy rots the bones." May we all be quick to recognize and quell envy in our own lives so that it does not rot our bones.

"As a moth gnaws a garment, so doth envy consume a man."
John Chrysostom (Archbishop of Constantinople, AD 347-407)

John 20:16a: *Jesus said to her, "Mary."*
Bible scholar Bruce Milne vividly describes this incident: "Then comes the moment of recognition, and it is beautifully told. One word which remade her world and transformed her life forever after, and the word was her own name! The first word out of the mouth of the resurrected Christ was Mary's name. This is a memorable confirmation of the personal nature of our Lord's dealings with his people." A few verses later, we read that "Mary Magdalene went to the disciples with the news: 'I have seen the Lord!' And she told them that he had said these things to her" (John 20:18). Mary Magdalene was a vital actor on the stage of the Lord's redemption of his people, as were other women as well. In Matthew's gospel (28:5-6) we read that the angel at the tomb gave instructions to Mary Magdalene and the other Mary: *Come and see, go and tell.* These two women thus became the very first witnesses to the resurrection. They could plausibly be described as "apostles" which means "sent ones." God and his angel entrusted these women with the announcement of this vital event. Elsewhere in the New Testament we read of many other women who supported the apostolic band.

- In John 11 we see Martha hearing directly from Jesus' mouth that he is the resurrection and the life.
- In Matthew 26:13, after the woman poured perfume on Jesus's feet, he proclaims that "wherever this gospel is preached throughout the world, what she has done will also be told in memory of her. And true to his promise, her story is told

in memory of her as we read the scriptures two thousand years later.

- In Luke 8:3 we learn that Joanna and Susannah were supporting them out of their own means.
- The Apostle Paul selects Phoebe to bear the vital letter to the Romans (16:1-2).
- In Acts 16, we learn of Lydia who hosted a church in her home.
- In Acts 18:26 we read of the couple Priscilla and her husband Aquilla who helped instruct Apollos in the fine points of the gospel. Notice that Priscilla's name precedes that of her husband Aquilla five of the seven times the couple is mentioned.

In the Old Testament, we read of Esther who boldly acted on behalf of her people to save them from the genocidal plot of the royal advisor Haman. In 1 Samuel 25, we hear about Abigail, who saved the future king David from a sin he would have greatly regretted if not for Abigail's intercession. And Rachel was Joseph's mother. Her care for Joseph was instrumental in molding him into a mighty man of God.

We must remember that ancient cultures often marginalized women, yet even against the backdrop of this demeaning treatment, Scripture records their pivotal actions in furthering the gospel. Though the roles of women in Scripture are a bit less prominent than men, they nonetheless serve the Lord with dignity and grace. They exhibit the servant heart that the Lord fuels by his example in Jesus Christ and the promptings of the Holy Spirit.

In our modern churches, we all benefit from the diligent work of our women who continue to bring people to Christ. They often just "get things done" without much fanfare. The church is truly blessed to have women who model the love of Christ and serve as examples to a world that desperately needs salvation.

Acts 17:11: *Now the Bereans were of more noble character than the Thessalonians, for they received the message with great eagerness and examined the Scriptures every day to see if what Paul said was true.*

Luke reveals an important tip for us as we make our life's journey in our fallen world: we need to cultivate a Berean attitude in our quest to know the Lord better. As the modern news media tells us what they think we need to know, we need to remember that what we need is not Fox News or CNN but TLW: The Lord's Word. We need to look forward to hearing God's word eagerly and enthusiastically at Church and from our own Bible study whether in groups or at home in our quiet time.

As we study the Word, however, we run the risk of raising comments on the Word to nearly the same level as the Word itself. Luke cautions us against this approach. The Bereans kept going back to the source even when listening to the eminent apostle Paul. Our pastors and Sunday School teachers don't even come close to the Apostle Paul, so as they expound the word to us, we should have our bibles in front of us, seeing whether the message we are receiving matches with what we see in our Bibles. Each Scripture verse is like a precious jewel that reveals important truths to us. As each verse is examined from different angles, it sparkles and radiates meaning we might have missed the last time we read it. Bible Scholars can help us to capture significance from the verse by relating it to other Scripture and applying it to our lives. But expositors, if they are not careful, might encrust a verse with dross and ore, making it more difficult for us to see the divine truth. We want to mine the Word for all it is worth, but we should avoid things that may sound good but instead diminish the luster of the Word.

There should be a congruence between what the expositor is saying and the Scripture verses being described. May we use our God-given brains to continually check the accuracy of any descriptions we are given. We need to keep going back to the original: the Scripture itself.

Rom 5:6,9: *You see, at just the right time, when we were still powerless, Christ died for the ungodly.* **9:** *Since we have now been justified by his blood, how much more shall we be saved from God's wrath through him!* This verse brings to mind a message delivered by Pastor John Wood of Cedar Springs Presbyterian Church in the 1990's. The sermon was titled *How Much More*, and its moving message sticks with me today. Pastor Wood told an arresting account about a young pastor he met at a conference. Mr. Wood asked him to tell his story. The man as a child lived in an abusive and poverty-stricken home. He had to sleep on sheets that were soaked with urine because he repeatedly wet his bed and his punishment for that offense was to have to sleep on those sheets night after night. One night, the abusive father killed the mother and the son was whisked away to an orphanage, where the conditions were not much better. After several years, news came of a family who was considering adopting this boy. The venue for their introduction was to be a bowling alley. At the bowling alley, the young man kept praying to the Lord, "Please let me bowl just one strike, so I can impress these people." But he kept bowling gutter ball after gutter ball. He had given up hope of adoption. But the couple accepted him[1], gave him new clothes[2], adopted him[3], and gave him their name[4].

Pastor Wood used this powerful metaphor to describe our vain attempts to please the Lord by our efforts and to realize that his grace is his free gift. Even when we bowl gutter balls in our attempts to impress the Lord, he is reaching out to us in love, just as the father did to the Prodigal in Luke 15. Remember verse 6: the Lord saves us when we are powerless to save ourselves.

[1]Ezek 43:27   [2]Isa 61:10   [3] Rom 8:16   [4]Acts 11:26, 1 Pet 4:16

Rom 7:24-25a *What a wretched man I am! Who will rescue me from this body that is subject to death? Thanks be to God, who delivers me through Jesus Christ our Lord!*

The Apostle confesses his continual struggle against the flesh in Chapter 7. He has to wrestle vigorously against a robust opponent. In 7:15, he admits that "I do not understand what I do. For what I want to do I do not do, but what I hate I do." Many a believer can probably say the same thing. We know what the Lord wants. We know what is right. Yet we continue to do wrong. We, like Paul, might conclude "What a wretched man I am!" (7:25).

Eugene Peterson's vivid paraphrase from *The Message* brings home the Apostle's frustration:

> *I've tried everything and nothing helps. I'm at the end of my rope. Is there no one who can do anything for me? Isn't that the real question? The answer, thank God, is that Jesus Christ can and does. He acted to set things right in this life of contradictions where I want to serve God with all my heart and mind, but am pulled by the influence of sin to do something totally different.*

Just as Paul seems to reach the end of his rope, he makes the majestic proclamation of 8:1: *There is now therefore no condemnation for those who are in Christ Jesus.* *We* are weak but He is strong. *We* may seem to be losing our struggle, but *Christ* has won the victory for us.

Romans 7 and 8 paint a vivid contrast between the flesh and the Spirit. Chapter 7 is all about the flesh. But Chapter 8 is all about the Spirit. We, like Paul, can turn from despair to exultation as we comprehend the greatness of the Spirit. In this life, we know that the flesh is a formidable adversary. But in the life to come the flesh will be vanquished as our "split personality" is replaced by the glorious outworking of the Spirit. In this life, we go three steps forward two steps back. But the Holy Spirit is transforming us in ever-increasing glory (2 Cor 3:18) that will culminate in our spending eternity with our Lord who knows our faults yet forgives them because of Christ's sacrifice. So like Paul, we do not lose heart (2 Cor 4:16). It may seem like we are "at the end of our rope", but the other end of that rope is held by the strong arm of Christ who will never let us go. There is no condemnation. Instead there is salvation. May we never forget that glorious truth.

Rom 11:33-36: *Oh, the depth of the riches of the wisdom and knowledge of God! How unsearchable his judgments, and his paths beyond tracing out! "Who has known the mind of the Lord? Or who has been his counselor?" "Who has ever given to God, that God should repay him?" For from him and through him and to him are all things. To him be the glory forever! Amen*

The apostle bursts out in doxology as he reflects on the inexpressible mercy and grace of God. Commentator John Stott puts it this way: "Paul's horizons are vast. He takes in time and eternity, history and eschatology, justification, sanctification, and glorification. Now he stops, out of breath. Analysis and arguments must give way to adoration." As we read this doxology in the 21st Century, we realize that the rhetorical questions it hurls out still demand the same answer: No one! No one has ever known the mind of God. Theologians have attempted this project, but none has succeeded. No one has ever been God's counselor, although in our fallen nature we sometimes think we can "advise" God on a course of action. No one has ever given anything to God, yet again in our fallen nature, we sometimes inanely think that we are "owed" something from our sovereign creator. All we are owed is condemnation, yet wonder of wonders, Paul has declared in 8:1 that there is no condemnation for those who are in Christ Jesus our Lord.

This doxology cures us of our tendency to marginalize our sovereign Lord. In our modern society, the self-anointed intelligentsia declares that we have transcended our need for God. Some think he has been moved so close to the margin as to be shoved completely out of our lives. But his sovereignty remains. No matter how hard we try to replace our worship of him with worship of self, he is still there, still ruling and reigning over his creation, whether we think he is or not. As we hear all the propaganda about self-actualization and self-love, may we keep coming back to this profound doxology. May it move and stir us to reflect on his majestic glory and grace.

May our hearts sing his praise each and every day as we realize just how crucial he is, not only to our little lives on earth, but to the eternal life to which he is leading us. We need not know the mind of God. He has revealed enough for us to grasp the salvation he offers to undeserving people like us. What a wonder that he stoops to save and seat us with him in the heavenly realms (Eph 2:6)!

1 Cor 13:6-7 *Love does not delight in evil but rejoices with the truth. It always protects, always trusts, always hopes, always perseveres.*
Pastor John Batusic's summary of 1 Cor 13
This chapter has 15 action words. We're not talking about how we feel, but what we do. The Corinthians love the dramatic, but that is nothing compared with Love. You can take a dozen mission journeys, but without love, it adds up to zero. Love is patient: we put up with faults of others. Love is kind: especially helpful when the lines are long and tempers are short. Love never seeks to be the center of attention. Love keeps no record of wrongs, completely deleted from our computer. Self says: 'I will do whatever I like and if you don't like it, tough'. Love says: 'I will do whatever matters to others, and if I don't like it, tough'. Love bears all things: hate is strong, but love has already won the victory at the cross. We can't simply turn love on. Only the gospel can do that.

Pastor John Batusic, April 22, 2018

2 Cor 12:7-9: *To keep me from becoming conceited because of these surpassingly great revelations, there was given me a thorn in my flesh, a* *messenger of Satan, to torment me. Three times I pleaded with the Lord to take it away from me. But he said to me, "My grace is sufficient for you, for my power is made perfect in weakness."*

These verses, which succinctly describe the paradox of strength in weakness, are among the most famous from the Apostle's pen. Both the Old and New Testaments abound in verses that reinforce this concept. The stronger we try to be apart from God, the weaker we become [Jn 15:5], while the more we submit to his grace, the more able we are to tap the inexhaustible dynamo of strength he lavishes upon us. The paradox is counter-intuitive, but human intuition falls flat before the wisdom of God (cf discussions on Isa 55:8-9, 1 Cor 3:19). May we never forget that God is the source of all we have (James 1:17), including our wealth, our talents, and our intellect [Dt 8:17-18].

These verses also instruct us in how we communicate with God when tough circumstances confront us. In our fallen human nature, we just want the Lord to magically take away unpleasant situations so we can get on with our own agendas without "distractions." But as we mature in our Christian walk, we realize that the Lord normally does not give us quick fixes.

Commentator David Garland states that when Paul prayed that the thorn be removed, the answer from the Lord was basically "request denied." This does not mean Paul did not get an answer. But the answer he got was that the thorn was trying to teach him something. In his commentary on John's gospel, Chuck Swindoll put it this way: "Whereas we pray for God to change *circumstances*, He prefers to change *us*." He must rely on the Lord to grant him the stamina to bend but not break. We in our 21st Century American lives can learn from Paul's dilemma.

When tough circumstances occur in our lives, we should not be asking for a magic solution from the Lord, but instead should ask him for his strength to endure and ask what he is trying to teach us in the trial. In the short term, this seemingly rough treatment from the Lord makes us more uncomfortable. But in the long run, it teaches us to tap the strength he and he alone can provide. As Paul states in 12:10 "when I am weak, then I am strong."

Gal 5:22-23: *But the fruit of the Spirit is love, joy, peace, patience, kindness, goodness, faithfulness, gentleness and self-control. Against such things there is no law.*

Early in my Christian walk I was trying to internalize certain key scripture passages by memorizing them. I would be saying them over and over in my mind as I went about my business (eg, walking from a parking lot into a store). One day as I entered a discount department store, I was trying to memorize the Fruit of the Spirit verses (Gal 5:22-23). When I came to the checkout stand, there was a long line and several people in front of me had items for which the clerk could not find the price. I waited perhaps five minutes and by the time it was my turn I was steaming with impatience. Then as I exited the store, I slapped my forehead and realized I had totally violated the very verse I was trying to memorize. I believe the Lord wanted to teach me a lesson, because the very next day, I went to the same store, memorizing the same verse. As I came to the checkout stand, the clerk ran out of tape on her cash register and took some time changing it. She was very apologetic as she fumbled with the paper and I just patiently waited and said, 'No problem, take your time.' She gratefully gushed 'most people get really upset when I have this problem. Thanks so much for your patience.' I realized that the previous day, I was walking by the flesh, but the next day, I let the Spirit live through me.

Life often gives no warning on stressful situations. For example, someone doesn't say 'Now brace yourself. I am going to say something really obnoxious to you, so be prepared with a Christian answer.' The abuse just comes tumbling out and we as Christians can only respond appropriately by letting the Spirit live through us. Easy to say. But we (at least I) often still fail.

Eph 2:8-10: *For it is by grace you have been saved, through faith–and this not from yourselves, it is the gift of God– not by works, so that no one can boast. For we are God's workmanship, created in Christ Jesus to do good works, which God prepared in advance for us to do.*

Chapter 2 verses 1-10 strike the keynote of Ephesians and of the gospel. These verses present the core of the gospel eloquently and succinctly. The chapter opens by describing our fallen nature. We must grasp this unpleasant diagnosis of what we are without Christ if we are to accept his gift of grace. Eugene Peterson's lively paraphrase of verses 1-3 from *The Message* sets the tone:

> It wasn't so long ago that you were mired in that old stagnant life of sin. You let the world, which doesn't know the first thing about living, tell you how to live. You filled your lungs with polluted unbelief, and then exhaled disobedience. We all did it, all of us doing what we felt like doing, when we felt like doing it, all of us in the same boat.

Once we realize that we have no hope without him, we hear the good news of the gospel in two triumphant words: ***But God***. He is rich in mercy and saves us in spite of our flaws and rebellion against him. Verse 6 then soars to celestial heights as we see that not only are we saved, we are exalted to sit with him in the heavenly realms. This mind-boggling destiny awaits us if we would just surrender ourselves to his grace.

Verses 8-10 then emphasize the radical nature of grace. It is a gift. It is not something we earn. We cannot boast. Christians cannot look down on the secular world as if we have achieved some special status on our own. No, our response to his amazing gift can only be incredulity that he would save a wretch like me. All we earned was his disappointment. Yet he saved us and raised us to the heavenly realms.

After he grants us his grace, he empowers us to do good works. Notice we do not do the good works to earn salvation. In grateful response to salvation, we do the good works he created us to do. Our lives become a testimony to matchless love of our perfect Savior. We do good works not to blow our own horn of self-congratulation and virtue signaling, but to bring glory to Him who is the source of all our goodness. Our good works spring not from ourselves, but from his gracious Holy Spirit that pumps power into our feeble efforts.

Other religions of the world (notably Judaism and Islam) say *do*. Christianity says *done*. Salvation is entirely a work of God, so no one can boast that he has achieved what only God can give. To use another Christian aphorism, "grace is the root and works are the fruit. We do not do good deeds to work ourselves into God's favor; he grants his favor and we do good works in gratitude for the rich inheritance he bestows.

The apostle here crystalizes the good news. May we embrace the Father's rich mercy, the Son's perfect life and gracious atonement for us, and the Spirit's sanctification of our souls as we look forward to the day when these verses culminate in glory.

Phil 2:13-16: *for it is God who works in you to will and to act according to his good purpose. Do everything without complaining or arguing, so that you may become blameless and pure, children of God without fault in a crooked and depraved generation, in which you shine like stars in the universe as you hold out the word of life*
'Do all things without complaining or arguing' has been a tough verse for me over the years. I don't have to work to complain or argue, it just comes naturally. While I have improved in this area recently, it still keeps me humble. Like the grumbling Israelites, I more easily

can enumerate my grievances than I can count my blessings (Num 10:10, 20:5). I think the key here is the verse which immediately precedes 2:14. Easy to say, but not easy to live out.

Observers in the secular world would look at verse 14 as proof of my hypocrisy. They might say something like, "you Christians have some fine-sounding ideals, but you flagrantly violate those ideals and not just occasionally, but often." I respond: "Guilty as charged." I often fail to live out the life Christ calls me to. But I thank him that his grace keeps lifting me up as I stumble and fall. I thank him that though I disappoint him time after time, he forgives me time after time and gives me another chance.

In October 2023, Pastor Ben Phillips of CMPC preached on this passage in a message titled "Let's Work Through This Together." He explained that we often know intellectually that holy behavior and refraining from complaining and arguing is what we should do. We say "yes and amen" but fail to apply the verses to our own conduct. During the week we might fall into this nasty habit and say "now what we just say last Sunday?" Our intentions say one thing but our actions say another. But sanctification by the Holy Spirit is not a "one and done" task, but a continuous process that lasts for years. We need to remember that according to verse 13, God himself is at work within us to apply the Word and bring glory to Him and to His Son. We need to shift our focus from self-preservation to exaltation of our Lord and Savior.

May I take these verses to heart the next time I feel the gremlins of resentment rising in my bowels. May I recall his great goodness instead of complaining about things that ultimately really do not matter.

Phil 2:25 *But I think it is necessary to send back to you Epaphroditus, my brother, co-worker and fellow soldier, who is also your messenger, whom you sent to take care of my needs.*

In October 2023, Pastor Dee. Hammond delivered a message titled "A Company of Heroes" on this passage. Here the apostle pauses to praise two of his personal heroes: Timothy and Epaphroditus. Pastor Dee began with a story of a little boy asking a question: "Grandpa, were you a hero in World War II?" The man answered, "no I wasn't a hero, but I served with some heroes." Though the grandfather said he wasn't a hero, he exhibited the chief characteristic of genuine heroes: a servant heart. Both Timothy and Epaphroditus have this key feature of a hero. Timothy is a true hero, certified by the apostle Paul with the simple statement of verse 20 (I have no one else like him) followed by several more verses outlining Timothy's concern for others. Here Timothy personifies the type of person you like to be around. Later, Paul would also describe the opposite of a "Timothy" in 2 Tim 3:2-5. Eugene Peterson's lively paraphrase in *The Message* vividly portrays the type of people we want to avoid:

> As the end approaches, people are going to be self-absorbed, money-hungry, self-promoting, stuck-up, profane, contemptuous of parents, crude, coarse, dog-eat-dog, unbending, slanderers, impulsively wild, savage, cynical, treacherous, ruthless, bloated windbags, addicted to lust, and allergic to God. They'll make a show of religion, but behind the scenes they're animals. Stay clear of these people.

Pastor Dee states that with this type of person, we are counting the seconds till their departure and our relief. This type of person just sucks the life out of you. This type of person wants to be the center of attention. They are "know-it-alls" who know nothing about serving others.

But when someone like Timothy shows up, we have the opposite reaction. We like them. We want them to linger. Pastor Dee than asks which type are you? Are you a Timothy or an anti-Timothy? Next, Pastor Dee introduces Epaphroditus, who is "cut from the same cloth" as Timothy. Both of these men bleed Jesus. Dee imagines the Philippian believers gathered in their house church. The leader asks "who can go to take our gift to Paul?" Epaphroditus raises his hand and says "Here am I. Send me." (Isa 6:8). He then undertakes the hundreds of miles of treacherous road to Rome, and nearly dies en-route. When he arrives, we can see from verse 25 that Paul is delighted to see him, not just because he brought the gift, but because Epaphroditus is a brother, co-worker and fellow soldier.

Holy Scripture gives us admonitions but it also provides examples like Timothy and Epaphroditus to show what it looks like to have a servant heart. The heroes of this passage had two things in common: they had servant attitudes but, like us, were sinners saved by grace. Pastor Dee closed this message by describing the ultimate hero who died for the villains: Jesus Christ. His sacrifice is summed up in 2 Cor 5:21: *God made him who had no sin to be sin for us, so that in him we might become the righteousness of God.* The Father sent him on a much more dangerous mission than the one Epaphroditus went on. May we remember God's principle that the way down is up and the way up is down. May we pray as William Borden prayed: "Lord , make me willing to be willing."

Heb 11:1 *Now faith is being sure of what we hope for and certain of what we do not see.*

Pastor John Wood of Cedar Springs Church in Knoxville Tennessee once preached on Heb 11:1, eloquently showing how faith is usually the beginning point to knowledge. He illustrated this with a hypothetical example of a young man standing outside a college Physics classroom. He buttonholes the professor and says "Prove to me that force equals mass times acceleration!

Prove to me that gravitational forces are inversely proportional to the square of the distance! Prove to me that quarks exist (I can't see them with a microscope)! If you cannot prove these to me here and now, forget it—I'm not coming into your classroom."

The professor would rightly brush aside this brash young man. He may offer him some advice that would go something like this. "Physics is a complicated subject. Before you can question it, you must learn the basics. You have to suspend your disbelief for a time and accept some of the things I teach on faith. After you have learned the basics, you will be progressively equipped to challenge my teaching. But you don't have the knowledge to do so here in this hallway."

Many outside the Christian faith are like this young student. They insist on proofs before they are willing to even consider whether the Bible might be telling the truth. Like Physics, the Bible is complex. It is an intricate book which has been studied by scholars and theologians over the centuries and still contains surprises and new insights. Surely it is worthy of at least a cursory examination before it is to be declared irrelevant.

James 4:17: *Anyone, then, who knows the good he ought to do and doesn't do it, sins.*
James knocks us all down a peg elsewhere in his letter (eg, 1:22, 2:10) but especially here. A smug Christian walk is an oxymoron, yet there are some who believe they can play it safe and simply avoid bad things to please God (Mt 25:25). But the upward call (Phil 3:14) is more demanding than that. We must not just avoid the bad, but positively seize the good. We must pounce on every opportunity to do good. We are all "busted" on James 4:17.

1 Pet 1:3-4 *Blessed be the God and Father of our Lord Jesus Christ! According to his great mercy, he has caused us to be born again to a living hope through the resurrection of Jesus Christ from the dead, to an* *inheritance that is imperishable, undefiled, and unfading, kept in heaven for you* [ESV]

In Chapter 3 of John's gospel, a pharisee named Nicodemus visits Jesus by night. Jesus tells him that he must be born again and here the apostle Peter develops this key concept of Christianity.

He begins with adoration, praise, and wonder at the mercy God lavishes upon us in causing us to be born again to a living hope. The believer lives entirely in the flesh before the spirit gives him or her the second birth. In Ephesians 2 and Romans 7, Paul describes life in the flesh before the second birth. But just as Romans 8 abruptly shifts from flesh to Spirit, so here Peter proclaims that the believer undergoes a radical transformation from the hopelessness of the flesh to the living hope of the Spirit. The process of being born again varies from believer to believer. For some, it is a gradual process that may take months. But for others, it is nearly instantaneous. One day, a person is imprisoned in the flesh and, bingo, the next day he or she suddenly realizes with joy that a rich inheritance awaits his or her claim in heaven. As Paul puts it in 2 Corinthians 5:17: *Therefore if anyone is in Christ, he is a new creation; the old has gone, the new has come!*

Peter uses three alliterative Greek words to illustrate this inheritance: *aphthartos, amiantos, amarantos,* rendered imperishable, undefiled, and unfading in the ESV translation. Notice that all three of these adjectives express an opposite. Flesh is perishable, defiled, and fading. But after our second birth, we receive benefits that do not perish, are not defiled, and do not fade.

Because of Jesus' resurrection from the dead, his disciples receive a glorious resurrection to this new living hope. And, as scholar Charles Swindoll points out, we won't arrive at heaven and hear some celestial receptionist ask, "Now what is your name again?" No, the Lord has called us by name to this living hope that is kept in the vault of his heavenly realms. After being born again, the believer can bank on the Lord's salvation and eternal pleasures in his presence (Ps 16:11). We can do nothing to cause our second birth; only the Lord can bring that about. But thanks be to God, he, the only one who can, does it. In fact, in verse 2, the apostle tells us that this call and salvation come about through the united work of Father, Son, and Holy Spirit. May we comprehend the exhilarating living hope he has given us through our second birth! May our new lives in the Spirit bring honor and glory to our Lord and Savior!

Rev 3:20: *Here I am! I stand at the door and knock. If anyone hears my voice and opens the door, I will come in and eat with him, and he with me.* Notice the Lord Jesus does not just barge in and break down the door. Although he already owns the house and our hearts, he nevertheless knocks and waits for us to open the door. Can you imagine what it would be like to actually hear your doorbell and open the door, and there is Christ? If you recognized him, would you beg him to enter and sup with you as he did with the disciples on the road to Emmaus after his resurrection? Although the Emmaus disciples did not recognize him, they sensed that he was something special. In Luke 24:28-29, we read, "As they approached the village to which they were going, Jesus continued on as if he were going farther. But they urged him strongly, "Stay with us, for it is nearly evening; the day is almost over." So he went in to stay with them."

It may seem to be a little far-fetched to imagine Christ standing on the front porch of your home. But he is standing on the front porch of your heart. He is knocking and desiring fellowship with his people. And he is inviting us to the wedding supper of the lamb later in revelation.

May we be as overjoyed as Rhoda was when she found Peter knocking on the door after he escaped from prison (Acts 12:13-14). As we view him through the peep-hole of our doors, we should joyfully swing the door wide and ask him come in and take his place in our hearts and lives. May we experience the joy of fellowship with our Savior as our honored guest. Although we are unworthy, he invites us to dine with him. May we embrace his gracious invitation!

Rev 21:6: *He said to me: "It is done. I am the Alpha and the Omega, the Beginning and the End. To him who is thirsty I will give to drink without cost from the spring of the water of life."*

Our story began in Genesis with the Lord God creating a world which he deemed to be be very good (Gen 1:31). But then Adam and Eve messed up the creation by disobeying the one restriction they were given. They chose to eat from the Tree of the Knowledge of Good and Evil, thus usurping the Lord's role. Instead of consulting God, they formed their own theories. They were locked out of the Garden of Eden (Gen 3:24) and lost the fellowship they formerly had with the Lord.

But God had not given up on humanity. He had a glorious plan that He worked through many twists and turns to this glorious conclusion. We might wonder why his plan had to be so circuitous but as we stand on the threshold here, we need to subdue our natural inclination at second-guessing and instead allow our finite minds to marvel at this stupendous moment.

Analysis needs to give way to adoration and wonder.

The Apostle John has presented a breathtaking and riveting description of the consummation of the Lord's strategy to make all things new. The apostle begins Revelation with a quick synopsis of the church age with his letters to the seven churches. He then takes us into the throne room, where we witness Christ boldly taking the scroll from the Father's hand as the twenty-four elders cast their crowns before him. As we read the revelation, we realize that at present we are spectators but that in the end of times we will be participants in the Lord\'s solution to the problem of sin. We could only be made fit to stand in the Lord's presence through the interposition of the Son's perfect life between us and God's righteous judgment. One might have thought that the resurrection would have been the last step in redemption. But the Lord in his infinite grace began the church age to give millions of believers the chance to partake of the salvation he freely offered. Non believers mocked Christians about the "delay" of his second coming. But 2 Peter 3:9 states his reason: *The Lord is not slow in keeping his promise, as some understand slowness. Instead he is patient with you, not wanting anyone to perish, but everyone to come to repentance.* Every believer today should be infinitely thankful for the Lord's infinite patience and grace to save the likes of us.

As we stand back and look at the Lord's plan from his divine perspective, we see it had three main steps, each punctuated with an expression of completion.

1. Creation
2. Salvation
3. Consummation

In Genesis, the Lord completed the first step: *Thus the heavens and the earth were completed in all their vast array. By the seventh day God had finished the work he had been doing; so on the seventh day he rested from all his work.* (Gen 2:1-2). He achieved salvation for his people on the cross as Jesus proclaimed, *It is finished* (John 19:30). And now here in revelation, we catch a glimpse of how the final glorious step will work out.

We are currently in the Church Age, the time between steps two and three. We have been saved by Christ's atonement on the cross, but the final step is yet to come. The apostle John pulls the curtain aside and gives us a peek at the future. Long before the modern inventions of movies and videos, the apostle, under divine inspiration, masterfully weaves mere words into a picture that is so vivid that we might imagine we are actually seeing it. And hearing it. And feeling it. And tasting it. We see the New Jerusalem where sin and death have been vanquished. The streets are paved with gold and the Lord's light bathes every corner and crevice in dazzling luminescence. All who stand here are worthy to stand here because they have been washed in the blood of the lamb and sanctified by the Holy Spirit.

In the final chapter of revelation, John declares that *they will reign forever and ever* (22:5). Who is John referring to? Who is *they?* Christian believers, *we* are they! We will participate in this astonishing culmination of God's magnificent strategy and his permanent fix. The Lord did not just give us a drug to desensitize us to the bad effects of sin. He gave us new life to a living hope and removed our sin by pulling it out by the roots. His Son atoned for us and His Spirit then transformed us.

He invites those who are thirsty refreshing drafts of the water of life. We had been dragging our bodies through a desert wilderness and our souls had become parched. But now we are can slake our thirst on living water, free of charge because Christ has picked up the tab. We will never thirst again.

The promise Jesus made to be with us to the end of time is finally fulfilled. This process, though often painful and convoluted is now finally "done." Really done. Amazingly done. The Lord has made all things new. He can now truly say, "Behold. It was very good." Praise the Lord!

Christian Quotations

People are often unreasonable, irrational, and self-centered. Forgive them anyway.

If you are kind, people may accuse you of selfish, ulterior motives. Be kind anyway.

If you are successful, you will win some unfaithful friends and some genuine enemies. Succeed anyway

If you are honest and sincere people may deceive you. Be honest and sincere anyway.

What you spend years creating, others could destroy overnight. Create anyway.

If you find serenity and happiness, some may be jealous. Be happy anyway.

The good you do today, will often be forgotten. Do good anyway.

Give the best you have, and it will never be enough. Give your best anyway.

In the final analysis, it is between you and God. It was never between you and them anyway.

Mother Teresa of Calcutta *(1910-1997) Catholic Nun*

"There are two kinds of people: those who say to God, 'Thy will be done,' and those to whom God says, 'All right, then, have it your way.'"

C. S. Lewis (1898-1963) British Author

"Let us weigh the gain and the loss, in wagering that God is. Consider these alternatives: if you win, you win all; if you lose, you lose nothing. Do not hesitate, then, to wager that He is."

Blaise Pascal (1623-1662)   French Mathematician and Scientist

> Lord, make me an instrument of Thy peace;
> Where there is hatred, let me sow love;
> Where there is injury, let me sow pardon;
> Where there is doubt, let me sow faith;
> Where there is despair, let me sow hope;
> Where there is darkness, let me sow light;

And where there is sadness, let me sow joy.
O Divine Master,
grant that I may not so much seek to be consoled as to console;
To be understood, as to understand;
To be loved, as to love;
For it is in giving that we receive,
It is in pardoning that we are pardoned,
And it is in dying that we are born to Eternal Life.   Amen
Prayer of Francis of Assisi (1182-1226) Italian Catholic Friar

"You have made us for yourself, and our heart is restless until it finds its rest in you."
Augustine of Hippo (354-430)   North African Theologian

"Oh most merciful Redeemer, Friend, and Brother, may I know thee more clearly, love thee more dearly, follow thee more nearly, day by day."
Richard of Chichester (1197-1253) English Bishop

Hymn: *Crown Him with Many Crowns* (1847)

Text: Matthew Bridges, 1800-1894, and Godfrey Thring,
1823-1903 Music: George J. Elvey, 1816-1893

Crown him with many crowns,	[Rev 19:12]
The Lamb upon his throne,	[Rev 7:17a]
Hark! how the heavenly anthem drowns all music but its own.	[Job 38:7, Ps 148:2]
Awake, my soul, and sing	[Ps 57:8]
Of him who died for thee,	[1 Pet 3:18a]
And hail him as thy matchless King through all eternity.	[1 Tim 1:17]
Crown him the Lord of life,	[John 1:4]
Who triumphed o'er the grave,	[Acts 2:31, 1 Cor 15:54]
And rose victorious in the strife	[1 Cor 15:55]
For those he came to save.	[Lk 19:10]
His glories now we sing,	[Isa 12:5]
Who died, and rose on high,	[1 Th 4:14]
Who died, eternal life to bring, and lives that death may die.	[1 Th 5:10, Rev 20:14]
Crown him the Lord of peace,	[Eph 2:14]
Whose power a scepter sways	[Heb 1:8]
From pole to pole, that wars may cease,	[Isa 2:4b]
And all be prayer and praise.	[Ps 66:20]
His reign shall know no end,	[Rev 11:15]
And round his pierced feet	[Rev 1:7]
Fair flowers of paradise extend their fragrance ever sweet.	[Isa 51:3, 2 Cor 2:14]
Crown him the Lord of love;	[Ps 36:5]
Behold his hands and side,	[John 20:27]
Those wounds, yet visible above,	[Isa 53:5]

341

in beauty glorified.	[Phil 3:21]
All hail, Redeemer, hail!	[Isa 54:5b]
For thou hast died for me;	[Rom 5:8]
Thy praise and glory shall not fail throughout eternity.	[Dan 4:34b]
Crown Him the Lord of years,	[Rev 15:3]
the Potentate of time,	[Ps 90:2]
Creator of the rolling spheres,	[Isa 40:26, Amos 9:6]
ineffably sublime.	[Rom 11:33, 36]
All hail, Redeemer, hail!	[Job 19:25]
For Thou has died for me;	[2 Cor 5:15]
Thy praise and glory shall not fail throughout eternity.	[Ps 145:1, Dan 7:14b]

Choral Anthem: *Yet Not I but through Christ in Me* (2021)
Jonny Robinson; Michael Farren; Rich Thompson

Note: Copyright Laws prohibit my quoting more than eight lines of this excellent song. The rest of the lyrics are available online. Please search the internet for several inspiring performances of this superb song.

With every breath I long to follow Jesus	[Mt 16:24]
For He has said that He will bring me home	[John 14:2]
And day by day I know He will renew me	[2 Cor 3:18, 4:16]
Until I stand with joy before the throne	[Jude 1:24]
To this I hold, my hope is only Jesus	[Eph 1:12]
All the glory evermore to Him	[Eph 3:21]
When the race is complete, still my lips shall repeat	[2 Tim 4:7]
Yet not I, but through Christ in me	[2 Cor 1:20]

www.ingramcontent.com/pod-product-compliance
Lightning Source LLC
Chambersburg PA
CBHW022043020426
42335CB00012B/525